DESKTOP PUBLISHING

STAGE II & III

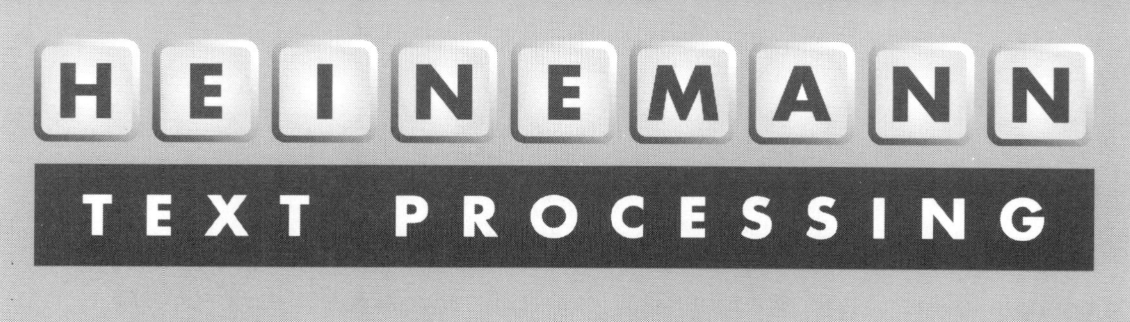

DESKTOP PUBLISHING

STAGE II AND III

SHARON SPENCER

Heinemann Educational Publishers,

Halley Court, Jordan Hill, Oxford OX2 8EJ

a division of Reed Educational & Professional Publishing Ltd

Heinemann is a registered trademark of Reed Educational & Professional Publishing Limited

OXFORD MELBOURNE AUCKLAND JOHANNESBURG BLANTYRE GABORONE IBADAN PORTSMOUTH NH (USA) CHICAGO

First published 1998

2002 2001 2000 99 98

10 9 8 7 6 5 4 3 2 1

A catalogue record for this book is available from the British Library on request.

ISBN 0 435 45393 9

Designed by Jackie Hill

Typeset by TechType, Abingdon, Oxon

Printed and bound in Great Britain by The Bath Press, Bath

Contents

Acknowledgements

I would like to thank all those who helped in the preparation of this book, particularly Rosalyn Bass and Natasha Goddard at Heinemann Educational for their advice and encouragement. I would also like to thank my family – Ian, Lucy and Joseph for their help, support and patience while writing this book.

About this book

This book is designed for anyone who wishes to take a simple step-by-step approach to learning desktop publishing, from the basic skills on how to set up a page to how to produce professional, accurate work.

The book is suitable for use in the classroom, in an open-learning workshop or as a private study aid. It will also be useful in the workplace for those who need to produce professional looking documents but have not been formally trained in this specialist area. It is suitable for use with all desktop publishing software, but you should ensure you have access to a software manual for the application you are using.

The book is divided into three sections.

■ 1 Introduction to Desktop Publishing

This section introduces you to the basics of desktop publishing. You will learn how to set up a basic page layout, import text and graphics and apply different text styles.

At the end of this section you will be ready to take the CLAIT (Desktop Publishing Application) assessment, and two consolidation pieces are included for practice.

■ 2 Intermediate Desktop Publishing

Section 2A teaches you how to work with larger blocks of text and produce documents that have a more professional look.

Section 2B deals with amending documents that have already been created. This is quite a different skill to creating your own documents.

At the end of Section 2 you will be ready to take the RSA Stage II DTP examination.

■ 3 Advanced Desktop Publishing

Section 3A gives you the opportunity to design your own page layouts within a specified design brief. You will also learn advanced copyfitting techniques, to help make your document look more professional.

Section 3B teaches you how to prepare colour documents ready for printing. You will also work on non-standard page sizes so that you can confidently produce business cards, leaflets and other documents.

At the end of Section 3 you will be ready to take the RSA Stage III DTP examination.

Importing text and graphics

Throughout the exercises in this book you will be required to import specific text and graphics files. All the files which must be imported to complete the exercises can be found on the disk that accompanies this book. There is a 'Read Me' file on this disk which lists the files and their corresponding page numbers.

Terms used in desktop publishing software

There are a number of terms connected with desktop publishing that you may not be familiar with. Sometimes the terms will differ between software so that the terms you come across in this book may not be the same as those used in your desktop publishing software. A glossary of terms can be found at the back of the book.

Format of the book

Worked examples of all the exercises and consolidation practice are included at the back of each section so that you can check your own work (Section 1 – pages 22–28, Section 2 – pages 77–93 and Section 3 – pages 134–145). The printed worked examples in this book are reduced to A6 size and displayed two to a page.

Section 1

Introduction to Desktop Publishing

Before you start this section make sure that you can:

- open the desktop publishing software
- create a new document
- open an existing file
- print a document
- save a document
- exit the desktop publishing system.

In this section you will learn how to:

- set up a page layout
- set up column guides
- set up heading guides
- import text and images
- change the size and appearance of type
- insert lines and boxes.

This section provides the basic theory necessary for using desktop publishing software. You should make sure you learn everything in this section thoroughly as it provides the basis on which advanced skills are built.

All the text and graphic files that need to be imported to complete this section can be found on the disk that accompanies this book.

Using the desktop publishing tools

There are a number of tools that are used in desktop publishing to enable you to manipulate graphics and text easily. Depending on the software you are using, you may have a tool box on screen or toolbars at the top or bottom of the screen.

Below are a few of the tools that you will need to use. When you are drawing boxes or ellipses remember to start the item at the top left-hand corner and then drag across and down. If you have not had much experience of drawing items, take a little time now to practice drawing boxes, ellipses and lines before you move on.

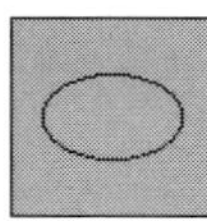

Ellipse tool

Use this to draw ellipses or circles. If you wish to draw a true circle, then hold down the **SHIFT** key as you draw.

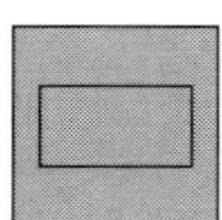

Box drawing tool

Use this to draw rectangles or squares. If you wish to draw a true square, then hold down the **SHIFT** key as you draw.

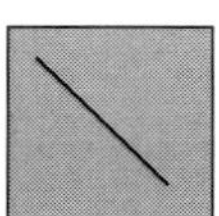

Line drawing tool

Use this to draw lines. If you wish the lines to be perfectly straight (multiples of 45°), then hold down the **SHIFT** key as you draw.

Pointer/arrow tool

In some software you will need to use this to select your graphics and text boxes. In other software you may find that this is on automatically – ie you don't need to select it. When you are moving or resizing items this may change appearance – for example, to a four-headed or two-headed arrow.

Text tool

Use this to insert a text box and to enter or amend text.

Other tools you may find on your software include:

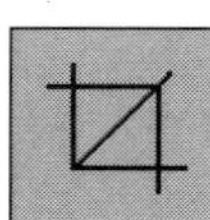

Graphic cropping tool

Use this to crop (cut) your graphics.

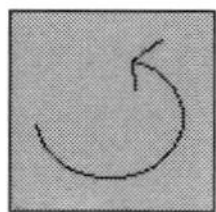

Rotation tool

Use this to rotate items. You can do this freehand or by typing in a value in a value box. Rotating items can change the way the text or images appear on screen. For example, a piece of text could be rotated so that it appears vertically on the page while the remainder of the text is still displayed horizontally.

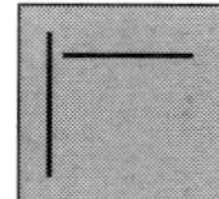

Straight line tool

Use this to draw straight horizontal or vertical lines (multiples of 90°) without having to hold down the **SHIFT** key. (Not all software has this facility.)

Creating a page

When you start a new document to work on, there are a number of decisions to make regarding the page layout. These include:

- the size of the page
- the orientation
- the size of the margins
- the number of columns
- the size of the space between columns.

Size and orientation

The most widely used size of paper in the workplace is A4. This measures 297mm x 210mm and is the default size used in most desktop publishing software.

A4 paper can be displayed in two ways, portrait and landscape (see Figure 1.1 and Figure 1.2):

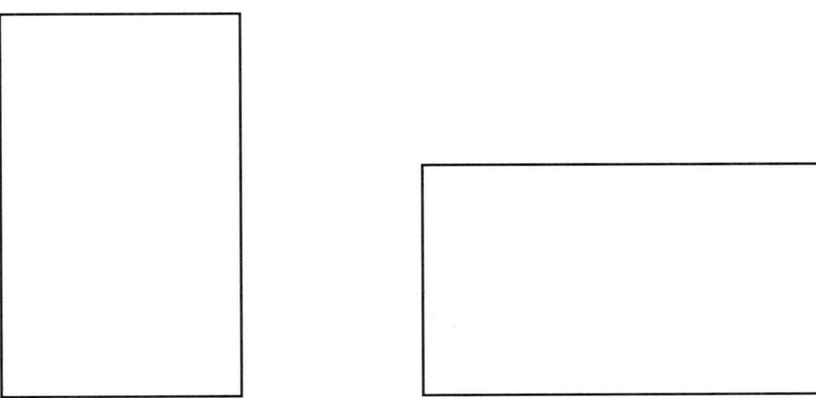

Figure 1.1 A4 portrait

The page is displayed with the shorter edge at the top.

Figure 1.2 A4 landscape

The page is displayed with the longer edge at the top.

Rulers

Once you have opened a new page, you should see a number of rulers on screen. These should be at the top and left-hand side of the page. They will help you line up items on the page with a high degree of accuracy.

Margin guides

When using desktop publishing software you will notice that the blank page has a number of coloured lines. These are the margin guides. Unlike word-processing software the lines are only guides and you can place text or graphics outside of these lines.

If you do decide to place text or images outside of the margin boundaries you should check on the print preview facility that the printer is able to print close to the edge of the paper.

Column guides

There should be an automatic column guide facility on the software that will place column guides for you. Look at Figure 1.3.

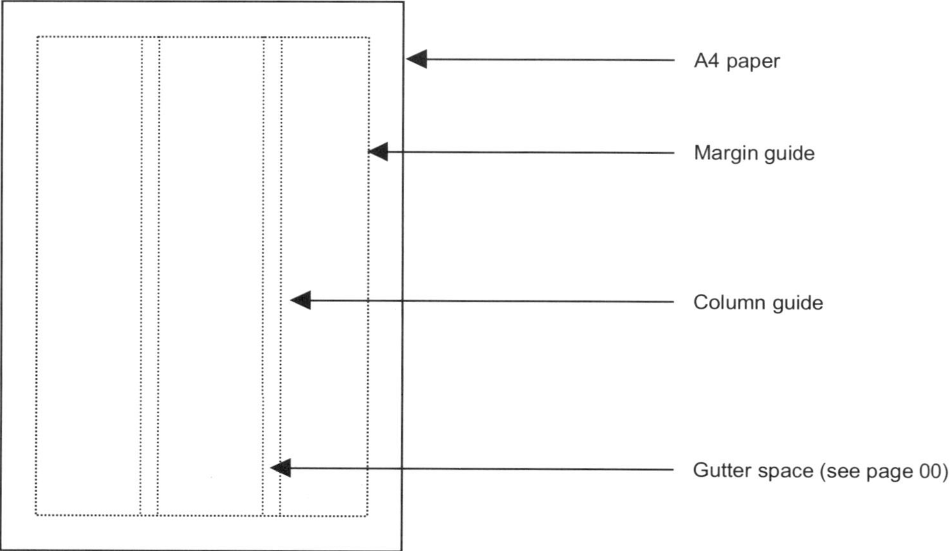

Figure 1.3 Column guides

When you set a column guide, two lines with a space between them will appear on screen. A two-column page will need one set of column guides. A three-column page, as in Figure 1.3, will need two sets of column guides. A page without any columns is known as a one-column page. The space between two columns is known as a gutter. We will look at gutters in more detail in Section 2.

Setting a space for a heading

If you wish to have a heading that spans across the width of the page, you will need to set a space across the top of the publication in which a heading can be inserted later. The problem with this is that most software packages will only allow the column guides to run from top margin to bottom margin. In order to overcome this problem we have to be a little inventive.

If you are using a software program that inserts text boxes, then insert a text box that stretches from left margin to right margin. If not, then draw a guideline at the top of the page where you will be inserting the heading. Look at Figure 1.4:

This example has a text box inserted across the top of the page (but under the margin guide) in which a heading can be keyed.

This example has a horizontal guide pulled down from the top ruler and placed, to indicate where the heading will be keyed in.

Figure 1.4 Page-wide heading

Exercise 1

You are going to start by setting up five page layouts of A4 size with portrait orientation. Load the desktop publishing application.

Exercise 1.1

Set up a page layout for your document. You will need a page-wide space for a heading and two columns.

Save your work as: **ICING1**.

Exercise 1.2

Set up a page layout for your document. You will need a page-wide space for a heading and three columns.

Save your work as: **TRAIN1**.

Exercise 1.3

Set up a page layout for your document. You will need a page-wide space for a heading and two columns.

Save your work as: **COM1**.

Exercise 1.4

Set up a page layout for your document. You will need a page-wide space for a heading and three columns.

Save your work as: **19501**.

Exercise 1.5

Set up a page layout for your document. You will need a page-wide space for a heading and two columns.

Save your work as: **TUDOR1**.

Importing text files

It is usual practice in the workplace for text files to be created in word-processing software and then **imported** into the desktop publishing software. Depending on the software you are using you may have to create some text boxes on the page before you are able to import text.

Text boxes are usually drawn on the page in the same way as you draw a graphic box. You should start at the top of the column in which you wish to place the text and then drag across the column and down. If you are working with a block of text that will fill more than one column, you will need to create two separate boxes, one for each column. Depending on the software you are using, you may need to **link** the boxes so that the text flows naturally from the first box into the second box and so on. If this is the case, find out how to do so on your software now. If you need to draw text boxes make sure you leave the gutters clear.

Once you have drawn any necessary text boxes, you are ready to import the text. Most programs have an **insert text**, **import text** or **place text** command that will do this quickly and easily. Find out where this is located now.

Inserting text into columns

Text should flow into the columns filling each column as it goes across the page (see Figure 1.5). If you have drawn text boxes and then linked them this should happen automatically. If your software does not have text boxes then you will have to do this manually as follows:

- drag the text box 'handle' from the top to the bottom of column one
- 'pick up' the text by clicking on the handle at the bottom of column one (this usually looks different to a normal handle if there is text remaining to be placed)
- click at the top of the second column
- drag the text across and down to fill column two and so on.

Alternatively, if your desktop publishing software has it, you can use the autoflow facility. If you use this facility the text will automatically flow from column to column until there is no more text left to be placed.

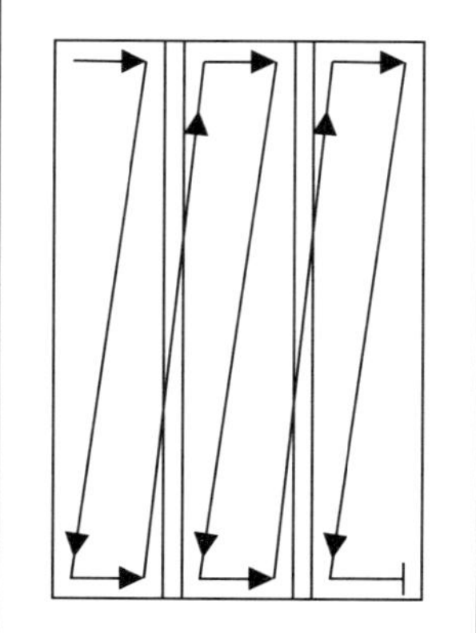

Figure 1.5 Flow of text from column to column

When you place the text, start underneath the heading box and fill the first column. Then go to the second column and repeat. The text should look like Figure 1.6:

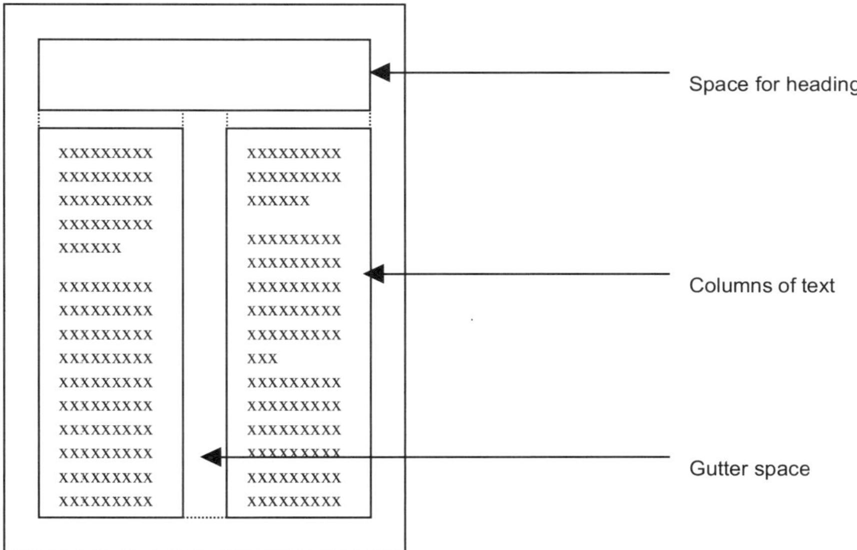

Figure 1.6 Text in columns

Importing images

If you wish to have images in your document you will also need to import (insert) these. You may have a selection of images in your clipart files that are attached to the software. Alternatively, you may be given scanned images that need to be imported into the document.

If you have been given a layout to follow, make sure you place the image exactly as shown. Depending on the software you are using, you may have to create image boxes before you can import images. Use the image box tool to draw a suitable box in the correct place. If you do not have to draw an image box, then just import your image into the document and move it using the four-headed arrow tool.

The software command for importing image files is usually in the same place as importing text. Find out how to import images into your document now.

When you place the image file, it may not be the correct size for your document. You may have to resize the image in order to fit it into a column. To do this, select the image handles with the arrow tool, and then stretch it either diagonally or horizontally to make it smaller, or larger.

Exercise 2

Now you are going to practice importing text and graphics. If the desktop publishing application is not loaded, load it now.

Exercise 2.1

Open the document: **ICING1.**

Import the previously prepared text file: **ICING** and place it in the two columns.

Import the previously prepared graphic file: **CKBLN** and place it at the top of the first column above all text. If you have already placed the text in the columns you may need to move it to make room for the graphic. To achieve this you can do one of the following.

- Move the text box down to make space for the graphic.
- Set text wrap around the graphic so that the text moves automatically (see page 37 for more information).

Save your work as: **ICING2**.

Exercise 2.2

Open the document: **TRAIN1**.

Import the previously prepared text file: **TRAINING** and place it in the three columns.

Import the previously prepared graphic file: **TEACHER** and place it at the bottom of the first column below all text.

Save your work as: **TRAIN2**.

Exercise 2.3

Open the document: **COM1**.

Import the previously prepared text file: **TECH** and place it in the two columns.

Import the previously prepared graphic file: **GLOBE** and place it at the bottom of the second column below all text.

Save your work as: **COM2**.

Exercise 2.4

Open the document: **19501**.

Import the previously prepared text file: **FIFTIES** and place it in the three columns.

Import the previously prepared graphic file: **JUKEBOX** and place it at the top of the third column above all text.

Save your work as: **19502**.

Exercise 2.5

Open the document: **TUDOR1**.

Import the previously prepared text file: **TUDOR** and place it in the two columns.

Import the previously prepared graphic file: **SHIP** and place it at the top of the second column above all text.

Save your work as: **TUDOR2**.

Changing the appearance of the text

Once you have imported the text into your document, you can then alter its appearance in the following ways:

- alignment
- text size
- font or style
- text enhancements such as bold or italic.

Text alignment

There are six main ways to align text:

- justify
- left align
- right align
- centre
- force justify
- first-line indent

In order to change the text alignment you must highlight the text and then either click on the correct alignment icon, or go to the format menu and change the alignment.

Look at the examples below:

The text in this box has been justified. It stretches from margin to margin and gives a neat effect. This alignment is often used in reports, magazines and newspapers. However, it is not the best alignment for long lines of text – for example, the full width of an A4 page – as it can be difficult for the eye to follow.

Figure 1.7 Justified text

The text in this box has been left aligned. This is usually the default setting on the software. The lines end naturally and are easy to read. Do not press return at the end of each line as the text automatically wraps from line to line.

Figure 1.8 Left-aligned text

The text is right aligned.
Note that the lines end in the same place on the right hand side and extend to the left.
If a document was typed in this style it would be difficult to read.

Figure 1.9 Right-aligned text

This text is centred within the box. In order to make text centred in the middle of
a page you must ensure your text box runs from margin to margin.

Figure 1.10 Centred text

This piece of text has been force justified. It will justify a line with as little as one word, which makes it very difficult to read. Force justification can sometimes be useful if you are trying to fit a piece of text into a limited space. Ordinary justification, however, will probably be sufficient for your examination work.

Figure 1.11 Force justified text

In desktop publishing it is usual not to have spaces between paragraphs. In order to make the distinction between one paragraph and another the first line can be indented, as shown here.

Look at some newspapers and magazines to see other examples. When setting the indent, choose a small value – around 5mm is sufficient.

Figure 1.12 First-line indent

Text sizes

You may wish to make each of the three different parts of the text: heading, subheading and body text a different size in order to give emphasis to your headings:

- headings (or headline) – these are placed at the top of the document
- subheadings – these are headings within the main text
- body text – this is the main text of the publication.

The text sizes for the different types of text should be sufficiently different to show up on the printed version of your publication. For example, if you used 9, 10 and 11 point sizes, the difference between the three are so slight it would be difficult to tell the difference between heading, subheading and body text. A good combination for the three is shown in Figure 1.13.

Heading – 18 or 16

Subheading – 16 or 14

Body text – 12 or 10

Figure 1.13 Different point sizes

In Figure 1.13, the heading was typed in 18, the subhead in 16 and the body text in 12. You can easily see the difference between the three sizes.

Try to ensure that you have at least two point sizes between each type of text. To change the text that you have placed in your publication, highlight and then click on the type size value box.

Fonts

There are two types of font – serif and sans serif. You will need to know the difference between these fonts (also known as typefaces).

Serif fonts have small strokes at the top and/or bottom of some letters that help guide the reader's eye across the page. Most of this book has been typeset using a serif font. One of the most common serif fonts is Times New Roman.

Sans-serif fonts are 'without' serifs – strokes at the bottoms of certain letters. These fonts are best used for headings and points of emphasis, as large blocks of sans-serif text can be difficult to read. A common sans-serif font is Arial.

This is a serif font – look at the strokes at the bottom of the letters **1**, **m** and **k**.

This is a san-serif font – there are no strokes at the bottom of any letters.

Figure 1.14 Serif and sans-serif fonts

There are many different fonts, both serif and sans serif. It is important that you know which is which. Look at the fonts that are available on your computer. Which are serif and which are sans serif? A selection of fonts is given in Figure 1.15.

This is Impact – it is a sans-serif font.
This is Bookman Old Style – it is a serif font.
This is Comic Sans MS - it is a sans-serif font.
This is Courier New – it is a serif font.
This is Garamond – it is a serif font.
This is Tahoma – it is a sans-serif font.
This is Verdana – it is a sans-serif font.

Figure 1.15 Serif and sans-serif fonts

Although it is tempting to use a variety of fonts in your document it is better to keep to one or two and use different sizes and enhancements to emphasise the different parts of the text. Ornate fonts, particularly those in a script style *(for example, this font, which is called OrnamentalFreestyle Script)* can be extremely difficult to read if presented in large blocks of text.

Proportional fonts

The fonts that you use will probably be proportional fonts. This means that each letter will take up only the amount of space that it requires. For example, the letter **l** will take up less space on a line than the letter **m**.

Monospaced fonts

There are some fonts, such as Courier, that are monospaced. This means that each letter takes up the same amount of space on a line regardless of its size. These fonts imitate the typewriter, where letters always take up the same amount of space on a line. The monospaced font does not look as professional as other fonts.

Text emphasis

You may wish to emphasise your text in some way, particularly headings and subheadings. Using the **bold** and/or *italic* enhancements can be very effective. It can change the appearance of a font quite considerably. Look at Figure 1.16.

This is bold text – it looks very dark and the letters are slightly thicker.

This is italic text – it slants to the right. Both of these examples have been typed in the same font.

Figure 1.16 Bold and italic text

Drawing lines and boxes

Another way to emphasise parts of your documents is to use lines and/or boxes.

The important thing to remember is that the box or line must not touch anything around it. Look at Figure 1.17.

The box has been placed around the graphic to ensure the lines do not touch on any side

Figure 1.17 Box surrounding a graphic

Remember to drag the box from the top left-hand corner and pull it across and down.

When you are drawing lines, pull the line-drawing tool from left to right. If you wish to draw a perfectly straight line, then hold down the **SHIFT** key whilst you do so. Lines come in a variety of weights and use point sizes, just like text. You can choose the weight of line to suit your document.

Although there are many different line designs, such as dotted, dashed etc, it is much neater to use a plain line.

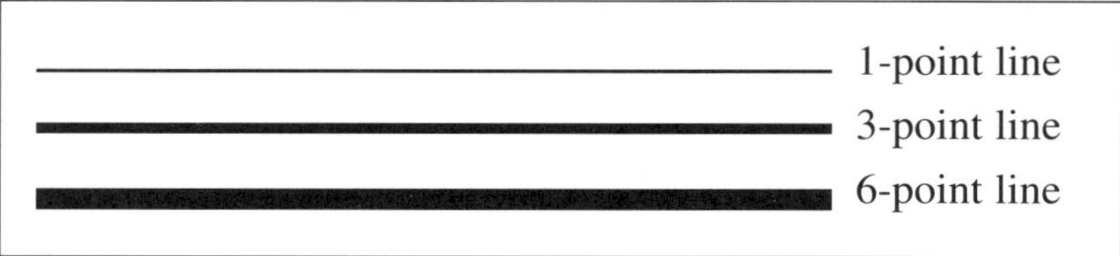

Figure 1.18 Line weight

Display text effectively

It is very likely that you will have to input a small amount of text, and display it. For example, you may need to insert a heading, centre it and set the correct text alignment and type size. In an assessment or exam it is very important to follow the instructions *exactly*. If you do not, then you are unlikely to pass. At work too, you must follow instructions. Your document may form part of a much larger work and will need to follow the same style.

Exercise 3

In the following exercises you will be changing the appearance of the text you have previously imported into your documents and importing and displaying a small amount of text. You will be using three text styles:

- heading – a large font size – 18–24 pt will be suitable
- subheading – a medium font size – 14–18 pt
- body text – a smaller font size – 10–12 pt.

1

Exercise 3.1

Open the document: **ICING2**.

In the headline space, using a serif font and a heading type size, key in a heading **ICING ON THE CAKE**.

Centre the heading, ensuring that it is on one line and clearly centred across the two columns.

For the rest of the text, use a sans-serif font and fully-justified alignment. Use the body text type size.

Save your work as: **ICING3** and print one copy.

Exercise 3.2

Open the document: **TRAIN2**.

In the headline space, using a sans-serif font and the heading type size, key in a heading **MANOR HOUSE TRAINING CENTRE**.

Centre the heading, ensuring that it is on one line and clearly centred across the three columns.

Ensure that the body text is in the body text type size, a serif font and left aligned (with a ragged right-hand margin).

Ensure that the subheadings are in the subheading type size and a sans-serif font.

Draw a box around the image. Ensure that the box does not touch the image or the surrounding text.

Save your work as: **TRAIN3** and print one copy.

Exercise 3.3

Open the document: **COM2**.

In the prepared space, using a serif font and the heading type size, key in a heading **COMMUNICATION TODAY**.

Centre the heading, ensuring that it is on one line and clearly centred across the two columns.

For the rest of the text, use a serif font and fully-justified alignment. Use the body text type size.

Save your work as: **COM3** and print one copy.

Exercise 3.4

Open the document: **19502**.

In the prepared space, using a sans-serif font and the heading type size, key in a heading **The 1950s**.

Centre the heading, ensuring that it is on one line and clearly centred across the three columns.

Ensure that the body text is in the body text type size, a sans-serif font and left aligned.

Ensure that the subheadings are in the subheading type size and a sans-serif font.

Draw a line from margin to margin, between the heading and the text. Ensure that it does not touch any text.

Save your work as: **19503** and print one copy.

Exercise 3.5

Open the document: **TUDOR2**.

In the prepared space, using a serif font and the heading type size, key in a heading **LIFE IN TUDOR TIMES**.

Centre the heading, ensuring that it is on one line and clearly centred across the two columns.

Ensure that the body text is in the body text type size, a sans-serif font and left aligned.

Ensure that the subheadings are in the subheading type size and a serif font.

Save your work as: **TUDOR3** and print one copy.

Changing your document

Once you have applied all the text styles and enhancements, you may feel that you would like to alter one or two styles in order to make your document look neater. You can do any of the following:

- alter the size of one or more of the type styles, eg heading, subheading and body text
- change the font, eg from serif to sans serif
- change the alignment, eg from left align to fully justified
- add emphasis to a part of the text
- alter the size of the image.

If you decide to alter the text in any way, then you will need to highlight the part of the text you wish to change before you do anything else. Once the relevant area of text has been highlighted then you can change the font, size or emphasis.

You may decide to resize and/or reposition the image. This might mean one or more of the following:

- moving the image from one column to another
- moving the image from one position in a column to another
- stretching the image to make it larger
- reducing the image to make it smaller.

Remember to make sure that you do not lose or cover any text when you are altering images.

Exercise 4

Exercise 4.1

Open the document: **ICING3**.

Reduce the size of the image and move it to the bottom of the second column below all text.

Change the subheadings to a serif font and subheading type size.

Change the body text size so that it fills the two columns.

Draw a box around the graphic image.

Save your work as: **ICING4** and print one copy.

Exercise 4.2

Open the document: **TRAIN3**.

Increase the size of the image and move it to the top of the second column above all text.

Change the subheadings to a serif font.

Change the body text size so that it fills the three columns and is fully justified.

Save your work as: **TRAIN4** and print one copy.

Exercise 4.3

Open the document: **COM3**.

Move the image to the top of the second column above all text.

Change the body text type style to sans serif and the body text size so that it fills the two columns.

Ensure the subheadings are displayed in a serif font and the subheading type size.

Draw a line between the heading and the text, stretching from margin to margin.

Save your work as: **COM4** and print one copy.

Exercise 4.4

Open the document: **19503**.

Increase the size of the image and move it to the top of the first column above all text.

Change the heading to a serif font.

Change the body text size so that it fills the three columns. Change the alignment to fully justified.

Save your work as: **19504** and print one copy.

Exercise 4.5

Open the document: **TUDOR3**.

Increase the size of the image and move it to the bottom of the first column below all text.

Change the subheadings to a sans-serif font.

Change the body text size so that it fills the two columns. Ensure the text is fully justified.

Draw a box around the graphic image.

Save your work as: **TUDOR4** and print one copy.

You have now completed all the work necessary for you to be able to do the RSA CLAIT Desktop Publishing assessment. Try the following two mock assignments to prepare you for the desktop publishing application in CLAIT.

Consolidation 1

You will need:

- desktop publishing application
- previously prepared text file: **TRAVEL**
- previously prepared graphic file: **TOWER**
- a serif type face (font)
- a sans-serif type face (font)
- three type sizes, one for each of the following:
  - heading (large)
  - subheading (medium)
  - body text (small).

Note: The text and graphic files for this consolidation can be found on the disk that accompanies the book.

1 Load the desktop publishing application.

2 Set up a page layout for your document. You will need a page-wide space for a heading and two columns.

3 Import the previously prepared text file: **TRAVEL** and place it in the two columns.

4 Import the previously prepared graphic file: **TOWER** and place it at the top of the first column above all text. Ensure no text is obscured by the image or lost off the page.

5 In the prepared space, using a serif font and the heading type size, key in a heading **PARIS**.

6 Centre the heading, ensuring that it is on one line and clearly centred across the two columns.

7 Ensure that the rest of the text is in the body text type size, a sans-serif font and fully justified.

8 Save your work as: **PARIS1** and print one copy.

9 Reduce the size of the image and move it to the bottom of the second column below all text. Ensure no text is obscured by the image or lost off the page.

10 Change the subheadings to a serif font and subheading type size.

11 Change the body text type size so that it fills the two columns.

12 Draw a box around the graphic image ensuring that it does not touch the image or the surrounding text.

13 Save your work as: **PARIS2** and print one copy.

14 Exit from the desktop publishing application.

Exam Practice 1

You will need:

- desktop publishing application
- previously prepared text file: **NAPOLEON**
- previously prepared graphic file **NB**
- a serif type face (font)
- a sans-serif type face (font)
- three type sizes, one for each of the following:
  - heading (large)
  - subheading (medium)
  - body Text (small)

Note: The text and graphic files for this consolidation can be found on the disk which accompanies the book.

Assessment Objectives	
5.1.1	Load the desktop publishing application.
5.1.2	Set up a page layout for your document. You will need a page-wide space for a heading and two columns.
5.1.3	Import the previously prepared text file: **NAPOLEON** and place it in the two columns.
5.1.4	Import the previously prepared graphic file: **NB** and place it at the bottom of the second column below all text. Ensure no text is obscured by the image or lost off the page.
5.2.1, 5.2.4, 5.2.5	In the prepared space, using a sans-serif font and the heading type size, key in a heading: **NAPOLEON BONAPARTE**.
5.2.2	Centre the heading, ensuring that it is on one line and clearly centred across the two columns.
5.2.3, 5.2.4, 5.2.5	Ensure that the body text is in the body text type size, a serif font and fully justified.
5.4.1, 5.4.2	Save your work as: **NAP1** and print one copy.
5.3.2	Reduce the size of the image and move it to the top of the first column below all text. Ensure no text is obscured by the image or lost off the page.
5.3.1, 5.2.4, 5.2.5	Change the subheadings to a sans-serif font and subheading type size.
5.3.1	Change the body text size so that it fills the two columns.
5.2.6	Draw a line between the heading and the text stretching from margin to margin ensuring the line does not touch any text or graphic images.
5.4.1, 5.4.2	Save your work as: **NAP2** and print one copy.
5.4.3	Exit from the desktop publishing application.

CLAIT Checklist

Did you remember to …	Assessment Objective	CLAIT Consolidation 1	CLAIT Exam Practice 1
set up two columns and leave a space for the heading?	5.1.2		
import the text and graphic files and place where specified?	5.1.3 5.1.4		
check that no text was lost or obscured when you placed the graphic images?	5.1.3 5.1.4		
key in the heading, using the correct font and size with 100% accuracy?	5.2.1 5.2.4 5.2.5		
centre the heading making sure that it fitted across the page?	5.2.2		
correctly apply the body text and subheading styles, fonts and alignments?	5.2.3 5.2.4 5.2.5		
save your work and print as specified?	5.4.1 5.4.2		
reduce and move the image as specified without losing or obscuring any text?	5.3.2		
change the text sizes, fonts and styles as specified?	5.3.1 5.2.4 5.2.5		

Did you remember to …	Assessment Objective	CLAIT Consolidation 1	CLAIT Exam Practice 1
draw the line and/or box as specified without touching any text?	5.2.6		
save and print a second copy of your work?	5.4.1 5.4.2		

Exercise 3.1

ICING ON THE CAKE

Cake decoration has become a popular hobby in recent years. Weddings, anniversaries, birthdays, Christmas and christenings all require a beautifully decorated cake. We can offer a cake decorating service or will be pleased to advise you on the best preparations to use for decorating your own.

Basically, there are four main types of icing; fondant, royal, buttercream and glace. Each has its own use, but fondant or royal are probably the most popular for formal cakes. Buttercream and glace icings are often used for small cakes such as fairy cakes or for covering sponge cakes. Buttercream icing is made with butter and icing sugar and has a soft, creamy texture. Glace icing is a soft icing made from icing sugar and water, or glycerine. Various food colourings and flavourings can be added to these.

Royal Icing

This is hard icing used for Christmas and wedding cakes. It is important that the ingredients for royal icing are used in the correct proportions so that the icing is neither too hard or too brittle.

Applying royal icing can be a time-consuming activity. The icing should be built up in layers allowing each layer to dry thoroughly before applying the next. However, once the cake is completely dry it can be decorated with a wide range of piping, sugar flowers and other decorations.

The secret of a good royal icing is its smoothness. In order to achieve this, many professional decorators use a substance called albumen powder instead of fresh egg white. The powder is dissolved in water before mixing with the icing sugar.

Buttercream Icing

Buttercream icing can be used as a filling for cakes as well as an icing. This has a lovely creamy texture, but is obviously high in fat and calories. A good icing must be made with real butter, margarine does not have the correct taste.

Glace Icing

Glace icing is made with water and icing sugar, sometimes with gelatine added to give a smooth, shiny appearance. This icing remains soft and is often used for fairy cakes and other sponge cakes.

Fondant Icing

You can buy ready-made fondant icing in a number of colours and so it is good for making novelty cakes for birthdays and other special occasions. It is easy to use and can be modelled into many different shapes.

Exercise 3.2

CLAIT - Exercise 2
First print

MANOR HOUSE TRAINING CENTRE

Why not take up a course at our training centre? These can be fun as well as giving you a chance to improve your skills and qualifications. They are an excellent way of making new friends.

We offer a wide range of courses to suit all interests. Whether you enjoy keeping fit or speaking a foreign language we will be able to offer you a suitable class.

The Facilities

Our facilities are excellent. We have state of the art kitchens, a new sports centre and have just invested in two new information technology rooms. Why not try our cybercafe?

The two information technology rooms each contain over fifty multi-media computers. There is a wide range of software available from word processing to computer aided design. Our self-study materials are excellent and with our qualified and experienced staff on hand to assist, you will quickly learn new computer skills.

In our Cybercafe, we have a number of computers that are linked to the Internet. For a small fee you can surf the net whilst enjoying a coffee. This service is open to students and non-students.

For those interested in languages we have a marvellous language laboratory. Here you can learn almost any language. Using tapes and videos you can work at your own pace. It is possible to book the facilities on an hourly basis. Ideal if you cannot manage to attend classes on a regular basis.

Our brand new sports centre caters for every type of sport. It boasts ten squash courts, four all weather tennis courts and an Olympic-sized swimming pool. Of course, there is a fully equipped gymnasium and trainers are always available to oversee your fitness programme.

Once you have finished your exercising you can relax in the sports centre bar or café. Both offer a wide range of healthy but tasty low-fat meals. There is also a large function room with bar which can be hired for parties and other events.

We also offer a wide range of art and craft courses from handweaving to still-life painting. If there is a craft that you would like to try, come along and try one of our one-day taster courses. These allow you to have a trial session before enrolling on a course.

Business Courses

For those of you who are looking to increase your career opportunities our business learning centre is bound to offer a course to suit you. Management training, personnel skills, and accountancy are just some of the many courses we can offer. We are also able to offer on-site training for your workforce. Our management consultants would be pleased to discuss your individual requirements.

Call us today to find out how we can help you achieve your potential.

Exercise 3.3

CLAIT - Exercise 3
First Print

COMMUNICATION TODAY

Over the past ten years there has been a revolution in communications. No longer are we reliant on letter writing and telephoning as the major forms of communication. We can now link up to our friends, family and work colleagues anywhere in the world from the comfort of our own home.

Computers

Using a computer, modem and telephone line we can connect to other computers with the same facilities anywhere in the world. Exchanging information could not be easier. E-mail is one of the fastest and most economical forms of communication available.

Video conferencing is also becoming very popular. Using the same equipment, but with the addition of video software, people can link up and take part in conferences without having to leave the office. Businesses are keen to take advantage of this facility as it is much more economic, in both money and time, than sending employees abroad to conferences.

Even without video conferencing software, an inexpensive microphone will allow you to talk to your friends and family over the modem. Although we can achieve this by picking up the telephone, this method is far cheaper. This can be of great benefit if your friends and family live overseas.

As well as communicating directly with others, you can link up to the Internet. Here you can find information on almost any subject. You can research your assignments, keep up with the latest news and find out what is going on around the globe. Virtual shopping is also becoming very popular with several of the major supermarkets already piloting a full shopping and delivery service in several regions.

On a lighter note, you can also link up and play your favourite computer game with others over the modem. You must remember though, that as you are enjoying your game, you are also running up a large telephone bill.

Mobile Telephones and Pagers

As well as computer and modem systems, there is also a range of mobile telephones and pages. These items ensure that we can send and receive messages anytime and anywhere.

What will we see ten years from now? Anything seems possible.

Exercise 3.4

CLAIT - Exercise 4
First print

The 1950s

The 1950s saw the beginnings of consumer culture, brought about after years of rationing and making do. The people of post-war Europe and America wished to look to the future, not the past and designers reflected this in their modern yet practical designs.

The Kitchen

People had more money to spend and they wanted to spend it on new, modern equipment and luxury items. A great deal of this new-found wealth was spent on improving and up-dating their homes, in particular the kitchen. Many new appliances were introduced, such as electric can openers and food mixers, and these proved very popular.

In America new designs for fridges and cookers came in a range of colours to match the kitchen walls - a concept which has been revived in fashionable kitchens of today.

Interior Design and Furniture

After the long war years where furniture was designed in the 'utility' style, people were ready for bright, modern designs.

Plastic, the new material of the 1950s, was widely used in the manufacture of furniture, especially towards the end of the decade. As furniture was made out of new materials, it could be colourful and interesting.

The colourful theme was extended to interior decoration. For the first time, bright colours were used in any room. Matching colours was not important, it was the use of colour that counted.

Leisure Time

A range of new appliances was also introduced for leisure time. Tape recorders, camera and television sets became much more accessible. In 1950, 3 million Americans owned a television set. This figure had increased to 50 million by the end of the decade.

Today

50s items have been popular with collectors for at least 10 years. It is still possible to find an original item at car boot sales or jumble sales, but this is becoming increasingly rare. In some cities, shops entirely devoted to 50s memorabilia have opened and have had an excellent response from the public.

Exercise 3.5

LIFE IN TUDOR TIMES

The Tudor age began in August 1485, the date of the Battle of Bosworth. Henry Tudor, the victor of this last battle of the War of the Roses, was crowned King Henry VII in October of that year.

The Tudors ruled over England, Wales and part of Ireland. The Stuarts ruled Scotland at that time. The monarchy was poor after the long years of war. The king raised rents and imposed large fines and taxes in an effort to increase the wealth of the monarchy.

Trade

England became a major trading centre during Tudor times. Ports such as Bristol and Liverpool grew quickly and were used for importing and exporting. English exports included iron, sugar, salt, coal and wood.

The cloth industry was also thriving and centres were set up in towns such as Halifax and Manchester.

Fashion

Queen Elizabeth I was a great collector of fine clothes. It is reported that at the end of her life she owned approximately 250 gowns. A silk gown could cost as much as £80.

Wealthy people wore linen, silk and fine wool cloth, whereas the working classes wore coarse wool and cotton. A law was passed in 1571 which made everyone over the age of 7 wear a woollen cap on Sundays.

Ruffs, which were worn around the neck, were at one point so large that wearers had to eat with a long-handled spoon.

Food & Drink

The Tudor diet was generally good although the main part of each meal was meat

or fish. By law, fish, rather than meat, had to be eaten on Fridays and during Lent.

Dairy food, such as butter and eggs was regarded as food for the poor. Vegetables were less popular until the end of the sixteenth century.

Most cattle and pigs were killed in the autumn as farmers could not feed them during the winter months. The meat was preserved in barrels of salt to keep it edible during this period.

As water was not clean enough to drink, the working classes drank ale, cider or buttermilk, wine was reserved for the rich.

Exercise 4.1

ICING ON THE CAKE

Cake decoration has become a popular hobby in recent years. Weddings, anniversaries, birthdays, Christmas and christenings all require a beautifully decorated cake. We can offer a cake decorating service or will be pleased to advise you on the best preparations to use for decorating your own.

Basically, there are four main types of icing; fondant, royal, buttercream and glace. Each has its own use, but fondant or royal are probably the most popular for formal cakes. Buttercream and glace icings are often used for small cakes such as fairy cakes or for covering sponge cakes. Buttercream icing is made with butter and icing sugar and has a soft, creamy texture. Glace icing is a soft icing made from icing sugar and water, or glycerine. Various food colourings and flavourings can be added to these.

Royal Icing

This is hard icing used for Christmas and wedding cakes. It is important that the ingredients for royal icing are used in the correct proportions so that the icing is neither too hard or too brittle.

Applying royal icing can be a time-consuming activity. The icing should be built up in layers allowing each layer to dry thoroughly before applying the next. However, once the cake is completely dry it can be decorated with a wide range of piping, sugar flowers and other decorations.

The secret of a good royal icing is its smoothness. In order to achieve this, many professional decorators use a substance called albumen powder instead of fresh egg white. The powder is dissolved in water before mixing with the icing sugar.

Buttercream Icing

Buttercream icing can be used as a filling for cakes as well as an icing. This has a lovely creamy texture, but is obviously high in fat and calories. A good icing must be made with real butter, margarine does not have the correct taste.

Glace Icing

Glace icing is made with water and icing sugar, sometimes with gelatine added to give a smooth, shiny appearance. This icing remains soft and is often used for fairy cakes and other sponge cakes.

Fondant Icing

You can buy ready -made fondant icing in a number of colours and so it is good for making novelty cakes for birthdays and other special occasions. It is easy to use and can be modelled into many different shapes.

Exercise 4.2

CLAIT - Exercise 2
Second print

MANOR HOUSE TRAINING CENTRE

Why not take up a course at our training centre? These can be fun as well as giving your chance to improve your skills and qualifications. They are an excellent way of making new friends.

We offer a wide range of courses to suit all interests. Whether you enjoy keeping fit or speaking a foreign language we will be able to offer you a suitable class.

The Facilities

Our facilities are excellent. We have state of the art kitchens, a new sports centre and have just invested in two new information technology rooms. Why not try our cybercafe?

The two information technology rooms each contain over fifty multimedia computers. There is a wide range of software available from word processing to computer aided design. Our self-study materials are excellent and with our qualified and experienced staff on hand to assist, you will quickly learn new computer skills.

In our Cybercafe, we have a number of computers that are linked to the Internet. For a small fee you can surf the net whilst enjoying a coffee. This service is open to students and non-students.

For those interested in languages we have a marvellous language laboratory. Here you can learn almost any language. Using tapes and videos you can work at your own pace. It is possible to book the facilities on an hourly basis. Ideal if you cannot manage to attend classes on a regular basis.

Our brand new sports centre caters for every type of sport. It boasts ten squash courts, four all weather tennis courts and an Olympic-sized swimming pool. Of course, there is a fully equipped gymnasium and trainers are always available to oversee your fitness programme.

Once you have finished your exercising you can relax in the sports centre bar or café. Both offer a wide range of healthy but tasty low-fat meals. There is also a large function room with bar which can be hired for parties and other events.

We also offer a wide range of art and craft courses from handweaving to still-life painting. If there is a craft that you would like to try, come along and try one of our one-day taster courses. These allow you to have a trial session before enrolling on a course.

Business Courses

For those of you who are looking to increase your career opportunities our business learning centre is bound to offer a course to suit you. Management training, personnel skills, and accountancy are just some of the many courses we can offer. We are also able to offer on-site training for your workforce. Our management consultants would be pleased to discuss your individual requirements.

Call us today to find out how we can help you achieve your potential.

Exercise 4.3

CLAIT - Exercise 3
Second Print

COMMUNICATION TODAY

Over the past ten years there has been a revolution in communications. No longer are we reliant on letter writing and telephoning as the major forms of communication. We can now link up to our friends, family and work colleagues anywhere in the world from the comfort of our own home.

Computers

Using a computer, modem and telephone line we can connect to other computers with the same facilities anywhere in the world. Exchanging information could not be easier. E-mail is one of the fastest and most economical forms of communication available.

Video conferencing is also becoming very popular. Using the same equipment, but with the addition of video software, people can link up and take part in conferences without having to leave the office. Businesses are keen to take advantage of this facility as it is much more economic, in both money and time, than sending employees abroad to conferences.

Even without video conferencing software, an inexpensive microphone will allow you to talk to your friends and family over the modem. Although we can achieve this by picking up the telephone, this method is far cheaper. This can be of great benefit if your friends and family live overseas.

As well as communicating directly with others, you can link up to the Internet. Here you can find information on almost any subject. You can research your assignments, keep up with the latest news and find out what is going on around the globe. Virtual shopping is also becoming very popular with several of the major supermarkets already piloting a full shopping and delivery service in several regions.

On a lighter note, you can also link up and play your favourite computer game with others over the modem. You must remember though, that as you are enjoying your game, you are also running up a large telephone bill.

Mobile Telephones and Pagers

As well as computer and modem systems, there is also a range of mobile telephones and pages. These items ensure that we can send and receive messages anytime and anywhere.

What will we see ten years from now? Anything seems possible.

Exercise 4.4

CLAIT - Exercise 4
Second print

The 1950s

The 1950s saw the beginnings of consumer culture, brought about after years of rationing and making do. The people of post-war Europe and America wished to look to the future, not the past and designers reflected this in their modern yet practical designs.

The Kitchen

People had more money to spend and they wanted to spend it on new, modern equipment and luxury items. A great deal of this new-found wealth was spent on improving and up-dating their homes, in particular the kitchen. Many new appliances were introduced, such as electric can openers and food mixers, and these proved very popular.

In America new designs for fridges and cookers came in a range of colours to match the kitchen walls - a concept which has been revived in fashionable kitchens of today.

Interior Design and Furniture

After the long war years where furniture was designed in the 'utility' style, people were ready for bright, modern designs. Plastic, the new material of the 1950s, was widely used in the manufacture of furniture, especially towards the end of the decade. As furniture was made out of new materials, it could be colourful and interesting.

The colourful theme was extended to interior decoration. For the first time, bright colours were used in any room. Matching colours was not important, it was the use of colour that counted.

Leisure Time

A range of new appliances was also introduced for leisure time. Tape recorders, camera and television sets became much more accessible. In 1950, 3 million Americans owned a television set. This figure had increased to 50 million by the end of the decade.

Today

50s items have been popular with collectors for at least 10 years. It is still possible to find an original item at car boot sales or jumble sales, but this is becoming increasingly rare. In some cities, shops entirely devoted to 50s memorabilia have opened and have had an excellent response from the public.

Exercise 4.5

LIFE IN TUDOR TIMES

The Tudor age began in August 1485, the date of the Battle of Bosworth. Henry Tudor, the victor of this last battle of the War of the Roses, was crowned King Henry VII in October of that year.

The Tudors ruled over England, Wales and part of Ireland. The Stuarts ruled Scotland at that time. The monarchy was poor after the long years of war. The king raised rents and imposed large fines and taxes in an effort to increase the wealth of the monarchy.

Trade

England became a major trading centre during Tudor times. Ports such as Bristol and Liverpool grew quickly and were used for importing and exporting. English exports included iron, sugar, salt, coal and wood.

The cloth industry was also thriving and centres were set up in towns such as Halifax and Manchester.

Fashion

Queen Elizabeth I was a great collector of fine clothes. It is reported that at the end of her life she owned approximately 250 gowns. A silk gown could cost as much as £80.

Wealthy people wore linen, silk and fine wool cloth, whereas the working classes wore coarse wool and cotton. A law was passed in 1571 which made everyone over the age of 7 wear a woollen cap on Sundays.

Ruffs, which were worn around the neck, were at one point so large that wearers had to eat with a long-handled spoon.

Food & Drink

The Tudor diet was generally good although the main part of each meal was meat or fish. By law, fish, rather than meat, had to be eaten on Fridays and during Lent.

Dairy food, such as butter and eggs was regarded as food for the poor. Vegetables were less popular until the end of the sixteenth century.

Most cattle and pigs were killed in the autumn as farmers could not feed them during the winter months. The meat was preserved in barrels of salt to keep it edible during this period.

As water was not clean enough to drink, the working classes drank ale, cider or buttermilk, wine was reserved for the rich.

Consolidation 1: PARIS1

PARIS

Paris is, of course, the capital of France. It has also been regarded as the capital of style, fashion and culture. What is so special about Paris? Like London and other major cities, Paris is always busy and life never stops. It has a wealth of museums, theatres and art galleries. There is always something to do in the city.

Shopping

Shopping is one of the major attractions of Paris. There are chic boutiques full of expensive clothes, jewellers and, of course, all the major fashion houses have showrooms in Paris.

Even if you cannot afford to buy, go window shopping and see what is on offer.

Museums and Art Galleries

There are a number of excellent museums and art galleries in Paris. However a trip would not be complete without a visit to the Louvre to see the Mona Lisa. Go early, as there are queues of tourists every day.

Food and Drink

The French love their food and rightly so. They always use the best ingredients and everything is freshly prepared. Regardless of your budget, you will always be able to eat well. Filled baguettes from small delicatessens will be as lovingly prepared as gourmet meals in luxury hotels.

Paris has a vast number of restaurants covering every type of food you can think of.

Tourist Attractions

Probably one of the best ways to soak up the Parisian atmosphere is to just wander around. A boat trip along the Seine is highly recommended.

Visiting the Eiffel Tower is a must. The views from the top of the tower are magnificent.

If you wish to go further afield then there is the Palace of Versailles which is approximately 45 minutes from Paris. This wonderful palace and gardens will take at least a day to visit and is well worth the effort.

A different type of day out is a trip to Disneyland Paris. Easily accessible from the centre, it is also well worth a visit, although you may find a day is not long enough.

How To Get There and Where to Stay

Your travel agent will be able to advise you on the many different packages available. Alternatively, you can arrange the trip yourself. Your local coach or train station will be able to help you book your travel requirements. The train takes just over 3 hours from London.

There are many hotels and guest houses in Paris. You should be able to find something to suit your budget. The French Tourist Information Service will be able to help you find accommodation.

Consolidation 1: PARIS2

PARIS

Paris is, of course, the capital of France. It has also been regarded as the capital of style, fashion and culture. What is so special about Paris? Like London and other major cities, Paris is always busy and life never stops. It has a wealth of museums, theatres and art galleries. There is always something to do in the city.

Shopping

Shopping is one of the major attractions of Paris. There are chic boutiques full of expensive clothes, jewellers and of course, all the major fashion houses has a showroom in Paris.

Even if you cannot afford to buy, go window shopping and see what is on offer.

Museums and Art Galleries

There are a number of excellent museums and art galleries in Paris. However a trip would not be complete without a visit to the Louvre to see the Mona Lisa. Go early, as there are queues of tourists every day.

Food and Drink

The French love their food and rightly so. They always use the best ingredients and everything is freshly prepared. Regardless of your budget, you will always be able to eat well. Filled baguettes from small delicatessens will be as lovingly prepared as gourmet meals in luxury hotels.

Paris has a vast number of restaurants covering every type of food you can think of.

Tourist Attractions

Probably one of the best ways to soak up the Parisian atmosphere is to just wander around. A boat trip along the Seine is highly recommended.

Visiting the Eiffel Tower is a must. The views from the top of the Tower are magnificent.

If you wish to go further afield then there is the Palace of Versailles which is approximately 45 minutes from Paris. This wonderful palace and gardens will take at least a day to visit and is well worth the effort.

A different type of day out is a trip to Disneyland Paris. Easily accessible from the centre, it is also well worth a visit, although you may find a day is not long enough.

How To Get There and Where To Stay

Your travel agent will be able to advise you on the many different packages available. Alternatively, you can arrange the trip yourself. Your local coach or train station will be able to help you book your travel requirements. The train takes just over two hours from London.

There are many hotels and guest houses in Paris. You should be able to find something to suit your budget. The French Tourist Information Service will be able to help you find accommodation.

Exam Practice 1: NAP1

NAPOLEON BONAPARTE

In 1789 the French Revolution began and the king and queen were executed. Napoleon Bonaparte (1769 – 1821), a Corsican by birth, showed himself to be a skilful and ambitious leader. In 1799 he took control of the French government and in 1804, in the presence of Pope Pius VII, crowned himself Emperor of France.

The General

In 1802 a peace treaty was signed between Britain and France. However, by the next year, Napoleon was planning to invade Britain. This proved too difficult as he could not defeat the British Navy, which was led by Lord Nelson. Napoleon's dream of conquering Britain was finally dashed when his navy was defeated by Nelson at Cape Trafalgar in 1805.

Napoleon then turned his attention to Austria and Prussia, defeating their armies in a series of battles. His attempts to overcome Russia ended in disaster. He captured Moscow in 1812, but his army, that was starving, was forced to retreat. Half a million soldiers were lost by the French Army.

In the meantime, the French Army had gained control of Spain by 1807. The British Army was sent to Spain to assist the Spanish. This army was led by Sir Arthur Wellesley, who eventually became the Duke of Wellington. In what is known as the Pennisular War, Napoleon's army was defeated at Vittoria in 1813.

During 1814, the allied armies entered France and captured Paris. Napoleon had no choice but to surrender. He was exiled to the Mediterranean island of Elba. A year later he escaped.

The Battle of Waterloo, in 1815, was Napoleon's final battle. The British infantry held back the French cavalry, and was later joined by the Prussian Army. Napoleon was re-captured and held prisoner at an island called St Helena. He remained there until his death in 1821.

The Emperor

In 1804, Napoleon crowned himself Emperor of France. At Notre Dame cathedral, he took the crown from Pope Pius VII and placed it on his own head, to show he had personally gained the right to wear it.

He was a popular leader and gained the respect of the French army.

During his time as Emperor he drew up a new code of law. Many of these laws remain in force today.

Napoleon abdicated as Emperor in 1814, after the defeat in Paris, in favour of his son. The allied armies refused to accept this and he was forced to abdicate unconditionally.

Exam Practice 1: NAP2

NAPOLEON BONAPARTE

In 1789 the French Revolution began and the king and queen were executed. Napoleon Bonaparte (1769 – 1821), a Corsican by birth, showed himself to be a skilful and ambitious leader. In 1799 he took control of the French government and in 1804, in the presence of Pope Pius VII, crowned himself Emperor of France.

The General

In 1802 a peace treaty was signed between Britain and France. However, by the next year, Napoleon was planning to invade Britain. This proved too difficult as he could not defeat the British Navy, which was led by Lord Nelson. Napoleon's dream of conquering Britain was finally dashed when his navy was defeated by Nelson at Cape Trafalgar in 1805.

Napoleon then turned his attention to Austria and Prussia, defeating their armies in a series of battles. His attempts to overcome Russia ended in disaster. He captured Moscow in 1812, but his army, that was starving, was forced to retreat. Half a million soldiers were lost by the French Army.

In the meantime, the French Army had gained control of Spain by 1807. The British Army was sent to Spain to assist the Spanish. This army was led by Sir Arthur Wellesley, who eventually became the Duke of Wellington. In what is known as the Pennisular War, Napoleon's army was defeated at Vittoria in 1813.

During 1814, the allied armies entered France and captured Paris. Napoleon had no choice but to surrender. He was exiled to the Mediterranean island of Elba. A year later he escaped.

The Battle of Waterloo, in 1815, was Napoleon's final battle. The British infantry held back the French cavalry, and was later joined by the Prussian Army. Napoleon was re-captured and held prisoner at an island called St Helena. He remained there until his death in 1821.

The Emperor

In 1804, Napoleon crowned himself Emperor of France. At Notre Dame cathedral, he took the crown from Pope Pius VII and placed it on his own head, to show he had personally gained the right to wear it.

He was a popular leader and gained the respect of the French army.

During his time as Emperor he drew up a new code of law. Many of these laws remain in force today.

Napoleon abdicated as Emperor in 1814, after the defeat in Paris, in favour of his son. The allied armies refused to accept this and he was forced to abdicate unconditionally.

Intermediate Desktop Publishing

Before you start this section make sure you can:

- open the desktop publishing software
- create a new document
- open an existing file
- save and print documents
- set up page layouts
- set up column guides
- import text and images
- change text appearance
- insert lines and boxes.

In this section you will learn how to:

- set up a master page
- set up and apply style sheets
- insert headers and footers
- wrap text around images
- resize images in proportion
- copyfit your work
- use correction signs
- use bullets
- multi-layer text and images.

Section 2A

This section helps you to deal with larger blocks of text and introduces ways of making your work look more professional.

Section 2B

You will learn how to amend an existing document in this section by changing style sheets and using proofreading skills and the spell check.

The first section of this book showed you how to set up a page layout and import one short text file and one graphic image. In this section we will be dealing with larger blocks of text and two or more graphic images.

Working with large blocks of text can be quite time-consuming, especially when changing point sizes or type styles. There are a number of tools available on desktop publishing software that can help you work with large blocks of text quickly and easily.

Master pages (templates, working on background)

Each type of software appears to have its own name for master pages. In this book, reference to master pages will cover all the above terms.

What are master pages?

Master pages are blank pages that can be used as a template for documents. They are used for setting items on the page which you would like repeated throughout a document. For example, if you were setting out a magazine, you might want to have a page number, the title of the magazine and the logo on every page. Instead of having to place these items on each page, you can set them on the master pages. You can have two different master pages, one for right-hand pages and one for left-hand pages.

There are several important points to remember when working on master pages.

- You must remember to move back to the 'real' pages when importing text or graphics otherwise the same text or graphic will print on every page.
- If you wish to amend anything on the master pages (or background) you will have to return to the master page. You can not amend these items from your 'real' pages.
- If you are working on a multi-page document, don't forget that the master pages work in the following order: page 1 and all subsequent odd-numbered pages are on the the right hand side and page 2 and all subsequent even-numbered pages are on the left hand side.

Saving the master page

Once you have set up the blank master page you should save it so that you can work on it a number of times. For example, if you were setting up a newsletter and on each page you wanted to have the company logo, the page number and the date, then you would import the text/images, set these on the master page and then save it. You would then reload the master page and work on the newsletter. When you want to save your newsletter you must do so under a *different* name. In the workplace you may be able to save your master pages as a template file. If you do this, then when you open the file, you will be given a choice of opening the template or a copy. You should open a copy and work on it, then save it using a different name.

Look at Figure 2.1.

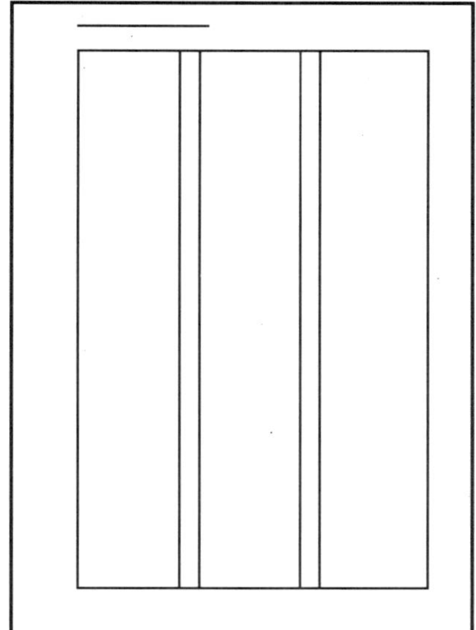

File one saved as a blank master page

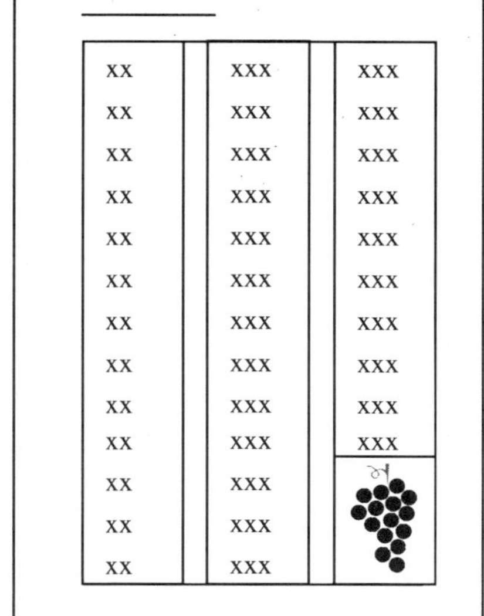

File two saved with text and images under a different name

Figure 2.1 First two files

Working on two or more pages

Depending on your software you may set up the number of pages that you require at the same time as defining the page size and margins, or you may just add second and subsequent pages as you work on your document.

It is much easier if you set up two pages at the beginning. This is because, when you are inserting the text, it will flow onto both pages, making the manipulation of text smoother. We will be dealing with this later.

■ Facing pages

When you are designing a document you can set up as many blank pages as you need before you actually place anything on them.

If you think about a book or magazine, you will note that the inside margin of the pages has to take into account the binding. This means that the inside margin is generally wider than the outside margin. These are called 'facing pages'. Look at Figure 2.2.

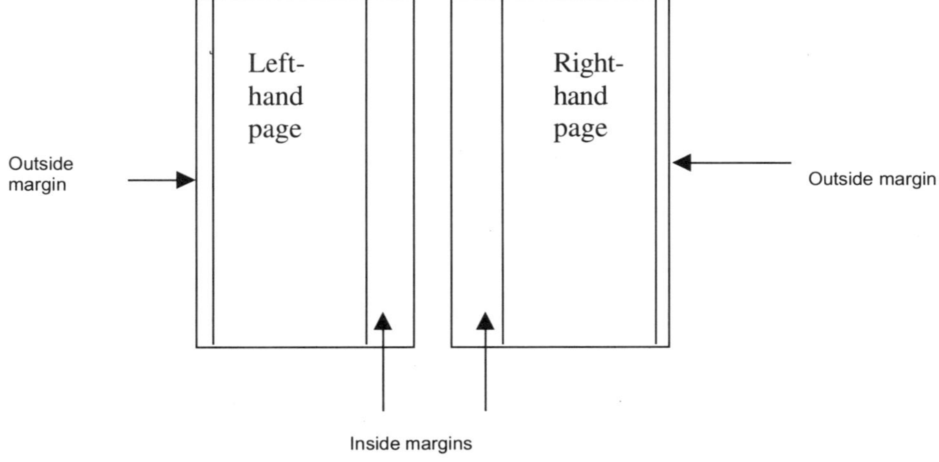

Figure 2.2 Facing pages

When setting multiple pages you will see that the left-hand pages are always even-numbered pages and the right-hand pages are always odd-numbered pages. This means that if we were to set up a three-page document, you would see the pages on screen in the order shown in Figure 2.3.

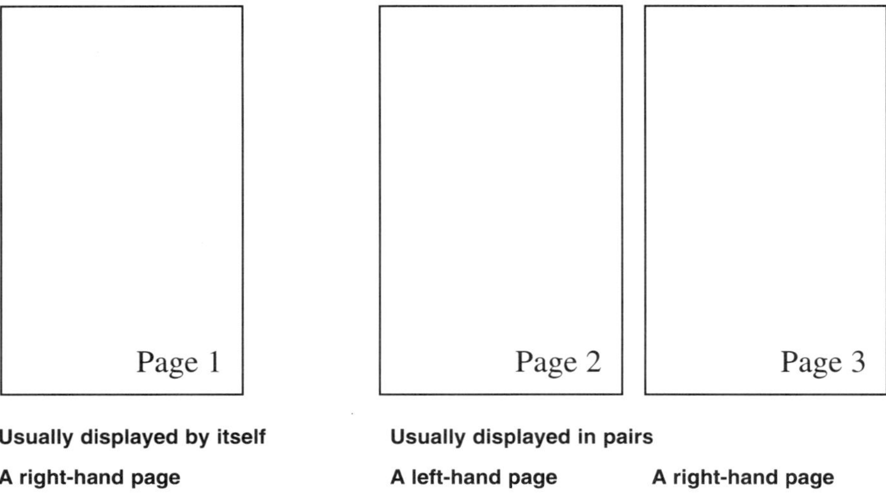

Usually displayed by itself — **A right-hand page**

Usually displayed in pairs — **A left-hand page** / **A right-hand page**

Figure 2.3 Three-page document

Some software programs give you the option of having facing pages or single pages. The margin options on the page setup option will change accordingly. For example, if you are using facing pages then the options are top, bottom, inside and outside margins – for single pages you will have top, bottom, left and right options.

Setting accurate margins

When you set up your page you will have to specify the margins required. It is important that you do this *before* you do anything else, particularly inserting text and/or graphics. If you are given specific margin measurements it is important that you keep to them. In an examination you could incur errors if you do not. If you are given specific margins in the workplace, this could be because your document is going to fit into a larger publication and needs to be consistent, or it may be because of the printing process.

Adjusting gutter space

You have already set columns in your document and you know that the gutter space is the space between the column guides. Most software programs will allow you to state the size of space required. Again, it is important that if you are given specific measurements for the gutter space you keep your work within them.

Preparing style sheets

Style sheets or text styles are very useful when dealing with multi-page documents. You can set all your styles for the text and name them so that when you are editing it is easy to assign the correct style for each part of the document. For example, if you wanted to have all your main headings in bold, closed capitals and underlined, you could set this up and call the style **main heading**. Each time you came across a main heading all you would need to do is highlight the words and then click on the correct style name. The text should then appear in your chosen style.

It can be useful to set the style sheet when preparing your master pages. Then, as soon as you have imported the text, you can easily assign the correct styles.

Depending on the software you are using, you may be able to enter a style sheet menu and set all your styles at once. Some software programs, such as PageMaker, have sophisticated style-sheet menus that link each style. You will be able to see this because it will say something like, **style based on** and then give a name of the style that you have already set.

2

For example, if you set the main heading in bold at size 36 in Times New Roman, it would automatically make the sub-heading bold, Times New Roman and say, size 24. If this is the case, then you must ensure that each time you set a new style it is not based on any other style (sometimes this is called **no style**). Although this is a useful tool if you are designing a publication, you should not use this in an examination. This is because the examination paper will often ask you to set a heading in a serif font and a subheading in a sans-serif font, to test your knowledge of fonts. Therefore if the style sheet automatically links styles you will be using the wrong type of font. To overcome this problem you may need to change to no style manually before you set a new type style.

It is also a good idea to clear all existing type styles on your style sheet before setting any new ones. This is so that you do not accidentally apply the wrong style.

In Section 1 you dealt with three styles:

- heading or headline
- subheadings
- body text – the paragraphs of text in your document.

You used a large font size for the headline, a medium for the subheading and a smaller font for the body text.

In this section you are going to be given a specific point size and font type. Make sure that you use the exact size given. If this does not appear on your software, you can type in the correct size in the point size value box. Remember the differences between serif and sans-serif fonts and use the correct type. If you find it hard to see the difference, learn one of each type, for example Times New Roman as a serif font and Arial as a sans-serif font and then keep to them.

You can also set any text enhancements such as bold and/or italic in the style sheet. These enhancements are generally used for headings and subheadings. It is easier if you do this so that you do not forget to apply it. However, if you are not using a style sheet or cannot specify the text enhancement, then you must ensure that only the specified text appears in bold or italic. If you forget to turn the enhancement off it will extend to the text which follows.

Hyphenation

If you are using justified text, your software program will add hyphens to your words in order to make the lines fit neatly. If you wish to turn this off or control the number of hyphens that are contained on each page you can usually do this within the style sheet. If you switch off hyphenation it will not remove the hyphen from words that are already hyphenated in the text, eg first-class, part-time.

Setting up headers and footers

Footers are placed at the bottom of a document, outside of the normal margins. Headers are placed at the top of a document, again outside of the normal margins. They are useful for placing page numbers, the date, initials, the copyright symbol etc.

It is advisable to set headers and footers on the master page(s). However, you must remember to set the header and/or footer on each page as some software programs will not place them automatically on both the left- and right-hand pages. This is because if you were designing a magazine or book you might wish to align the left-hand header and/or footer at the left margin and the right-hand header and/or footer at the right margin. You might also wish to have different text in your headers and footers. You can use the copy and paste facility to do this rather than keying in new headers and footers for each page. See Figure 2.4.

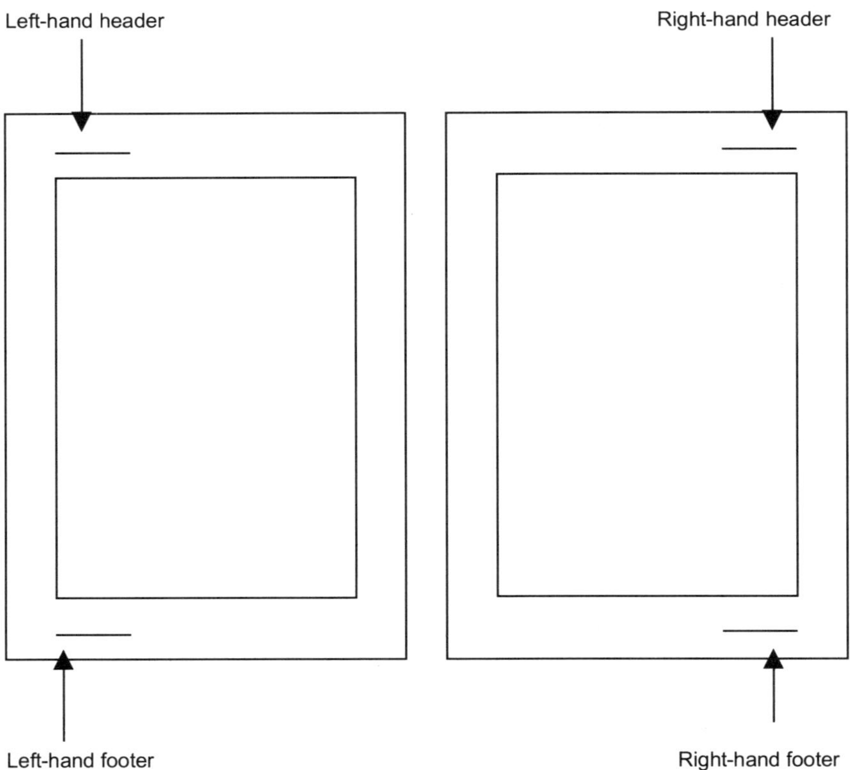

Figure 2.4 Headers and footers

The header and/or footer should always print *outside* of the margins. Ensure you leave a clear space between the bottom of the text and the footer. Sometimes you may find that the footer does not align correctly. This may be because the body text is touching the footer text wrap. If this happens then move the footer text box down a little so that it is completely clear of the body text.

The text style you use does not matter unless it has been specified, although it looks more professional to display headers and footers in the body text style or in a slightly smaller font.

The header and/or footer may be in more than one part. For example, you may be given an instruction which states that the header and/or footer should be as given below:

Your initials here (left aligned)	Page No (centred)	Date (right aligned)

Depending on the software you are using you may have to set tabs in order to place each item correctly. For the above example, you could set a left tab to anchor the information to the left margin; a centre tab for the page number and a right align tab for the date.

Other software programs have a simple insert headers and footers facility which will allow you to place the various elements easily. Find out how to insert headers and footers on your software now.

2

Page numbering

Page numbers can be inserted into the header and/or footer quite easily. Your software will usually automatically number your pages once you have inserted the correct command.

If you are setting the page numbering on master pages, you may find that the number appears as a # sign. In some software programs such as PageMaker it may appear as LM (on left-handed master pages) and RM (on right-handed master pages). The number itself will appear on the printed pages.

You may be asked to start page numbering at a number other than 1. You should be able to amend your software command to do this. Find out how to amend the page-numbering facility now.

Exercise 1

In the following exercises you must save the files as master pages. The headings that are imported with the rest of the text should stay in the first column unless otherwise specified. It is important that you read the layout instructions carefully to ensure that the heading is in the correct place. In the workplace you can add a line space after headings, but you should make sure you are consistent throughout the document. In these exercises some of the worked examples have line spaces after the headings.

Exercise 1.1

Set up a two-page document. The paper size should be A4 and the orientation should be landscape.

Specify three equal columns with a 5mm gutter and set left, right, top and bottom margins of 20mm.

Set up a style sheet with the following styles:

Name	Font	Size	Alignment
Headline	Sans serif, bold	24	Centred
Subheading	Sans serif, italic	18	Left
Body text	Serif	12	Justified

Set a header and footer as follows, using the body text typestyle:

Header	Working from Home (Left aligned)		
Footer	Task1 (Left aligned	Page No Centred	Your name Right aligned)

Page numbering should start from page 8.

Save as: **DES1**.

Exercise 1.2

Set up a two-page document. The paper size should be A4 and the orientation should be portrait.

Specify two equal columns with 8mm gutter and left, right, top and bottom margins of 25mm.

Set up a style sheet with the following styles:

Name	**Font**	**Size**	**Alignment**
Headline	Sans serif	22	Left
Subheading	Sans serif, italic	16	Centred
Body text	Sans serif	10	Left

Set a header and footer as follows, using the body text typestyle:

Header	Task2 (Right aligned)	
Footer	Page No (Left aligned	Your name Centred)

Page numbering should start from page 4.

Save as: **BANKS1**.

Exercise 1.3

Set up a two-page document. The paper size should be A4 and the orientation should be landscape.

Specify three equal columns with 6mm gutter and left, right, top and bottom margins of 20mm.

Set up a style sheet with the following styles:

Name	**Font**	**Size**	**Alignment**
Headline	Serif, bold	22	Centred
Subheading	Sans serif	18	Centred
Body text	Serif	14	Justified

Set a header and footer as follows, using the body text typestyle:

Header	Page No (Left aligned)	
Footer	Your name (Left aligned	Task3 Right aligned)

Page numbering should start from page 3.

Save as: **AUC1**.

Exercise 1.4

Set up a two-page document. The paper size should be A4 and the orientation should be landscape.

Specify two equal columns with 7mm gutter, left and right margins of 25mm and top and bottom margins of 20mm.

Set up a style sheet with the following styles:

Name	**Font**	**Size**	**Alignment**
Headline	Serif, bold	20	Centred
Subheading	Sans serif	18	Right
Body text	Serif	10	Left

Set a header and footer as follows, using the body text typestyle:

Header	Shopping (Right aligned)	
Footer	Your name (Left aligned	Page No Centred)

Page numbering should start from page 6.

Save as: **SHOP1**.

Text wrap

To stop the text from going over the image you will need to set text wrap. This is an invisible barrier that separates images and text and stops one from being superimposed on the other. How it is set depends on the software you are using. Some software packages have sophisticated options that allow you to set the amount of barrier and its alignment. Check what is available on your software now.

If your software asks you to set the amount of barrier, between 2 and 4mm will be sufficient. There must be some clear space between the text and the images. Look at Figure 2.5.

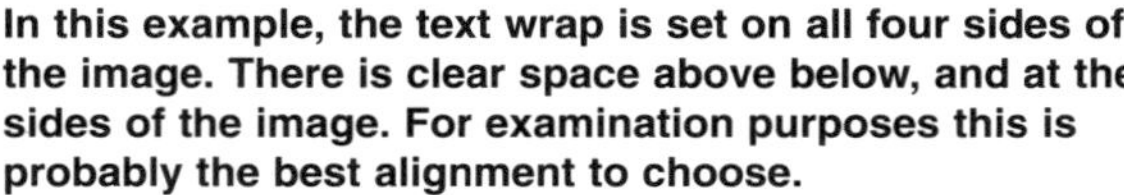

In this example, the text wrap is set on all four sides of the image. There is clear space above below, and at the sides of the image. For examination purposes this is probably the best alignment to choose.

This example shows the text wrap set only at the top and bottom of the image, allowing the text to flow on each side. This can look effective when designing newsletters etc.

Figure 2.5 Text wrap

If you have applied text wrap and you notice that the next column has now got a large space, then it may be that the text wrap has extended into the adjacent columns. In order to rectify this, pull in the text wrap so that the text flows back into place. This can also happen with headings, headers and footers. If you have placed a graphic at the top or bottom of a column, then sometimes the text wrap may 'hit' the heading, header or footer out of place. Again, in order to rectify this, just pull in the text wrap a little.

If you are given specific instructions on where to place the images you must ensure you follow them carefully. You may be given a diagram of the page layout, called a design brief to help you.

Apply text styles

Once you have imported the text into the your document, you can then apply the text styles that you set up in the style sheet.

How to apply the text styles

As previously mentioned, you may wish to highlight your text and then click on the appropriate style as given in your style sheet. You must ensure that *all* the text has been altered. You may find that when the text changes, for example from a 12 point font to a 10 point font, that the text realigns itself on the page. If this is the case you may miss some text, particularly if you are working in whole page view.

Document editor

It is far safer to use the document editor facility if you have one. This may also be called story editor. In the document editor you can work through the document article by article (or story by story), applying the text styles as you go. You do not have to rely on highlighting sections and then waiting for the text to realign itself.

■ Checking your work

It is important that you check your text styles once you have applied them. If it is possible, it can be easier to print out your work and check that the styles are as specified. If this is not possible then ensure that the page view is at a size where the text can be read easily and check each heading, subheading and paragraph.

2

Exercise 2

You are now ready to try some more exercises. These will help you practice importing text and images and applying your style sheet to the text.

Exercise 2.1

Open the document: **DES1**.

Import the text file: **OFFICE**. Apply the three typestyles to the appropriate text.

Import the two graphic files: **DESK** (Image 1) and **COMP** (Image 2). Place Image 1 at the top of the first column on
page 1 below the headline. Place Image 2 at the bottom of the second column on page 2. Figure 2.6 shows the correct placement.

Save your document as: **DES2** and print one copy.

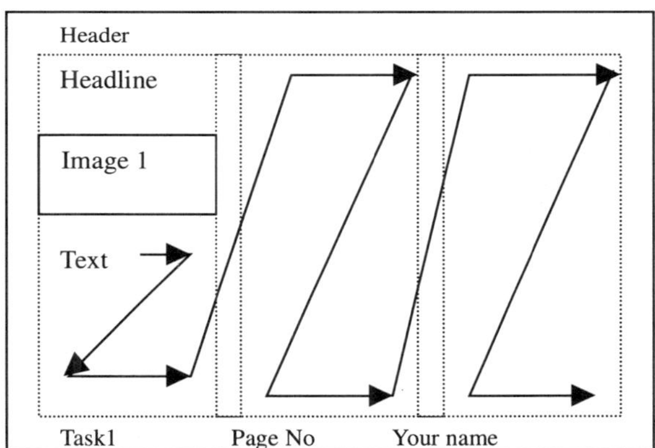

Page 8

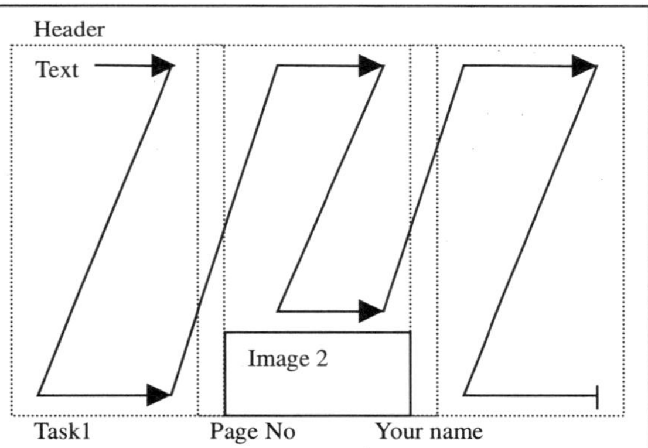

Page 9

Figure 2.6 Layout for Exercise 2.1

Exercise 2.2

Open the document: **BANKS1**.

Import the text file: **BANK**. Apply the three text styles as appropriate.

Import the two graphic files: **MONEY** (Image 1) and **CASH** (Image 2). Place Image 1 in the middle of the second column on page 1. Place Image 2 at the top of the first column on page 2. Figure 2.7 shows the correct placement.

Save your document as: **BANKS2** and print one copy.

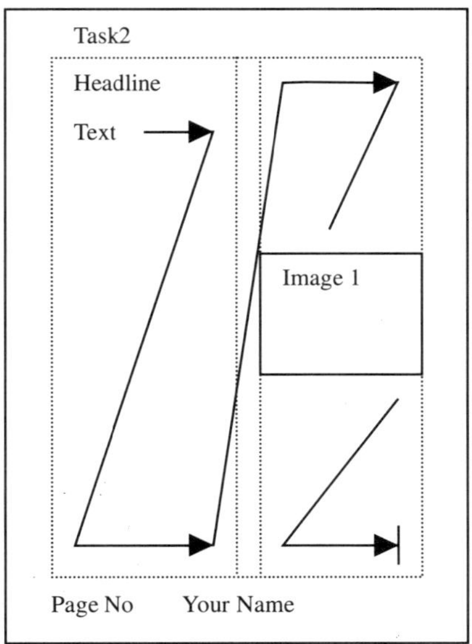

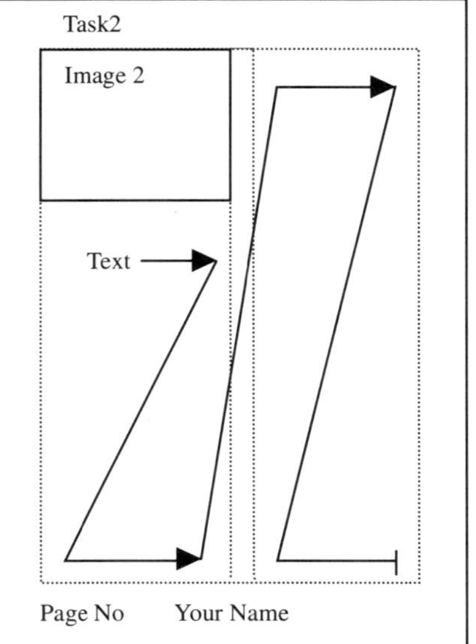

Page 4 **Page 5**

Figure 2.7 Layout for Exercise 2.2

Exercise 2.3

Open the document: **AUC1**.

Import the text file: **SALE**. Apply the three text styles as appropriate.

Import the two graphic files: **MAN** (Image 1) and **BIDS** (Image 2). Place Image 1 at the top of the third column on page 1. Place Image 2 at the bottom of the first column on page 2. Figure 2.8 shows the correct placement.

Save your document as: **AUC2** and print one copy.

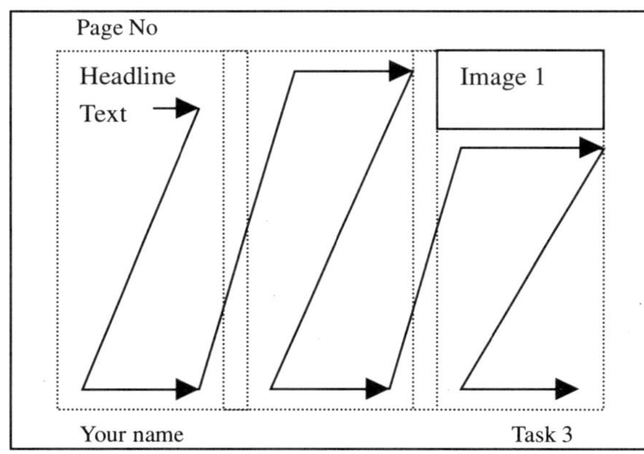

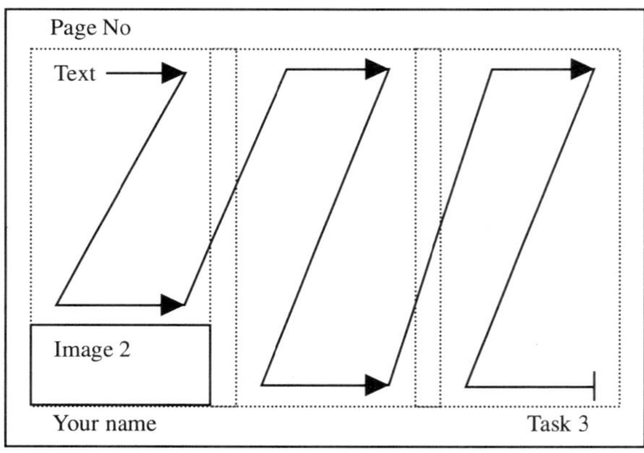

Page 3 Page 4

Figure 2.8 Layout for Exercise 2.3

Exercise 2.4

Open the document: **SHOP1.**

Import the text file: **LOYALTY**. Apply the three text styles as appropriate.

Import the two graphic files: **BASKET** (Image 1) and **FRUIT** (Image 2). Place Image 1 at the bottom of the first column on page 1. Place Image 2 at the top of the second column on page 2. Figure 2.9 shows the correct placement.

Save your document as: **SHOP2** and print one copy.

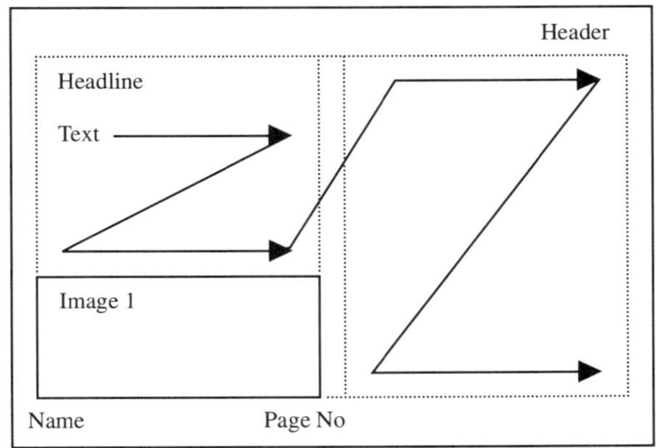

Page 6

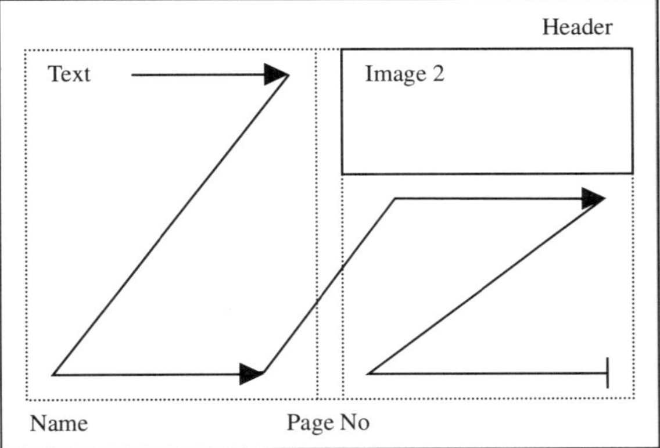

Page 7

Figure 2.9 Layout for Exercise 2.4

Resizing images

Once you have imported your images, you may need to resize one. This could be to extend an image across two or three columns or to decrease its size from three columns to two. The image should remain in proportion when you have finished.

■ Resizing images in proportion

In order that the image does not look too distorted you should resize it in proportion. On most software packages this means you have to hold down the **SHIFT** key while you are resizing the image.

It can be very difficult to resize an image in proportion, as in order to keep the dimensions correct the image may take up too much space. Generally, if you ensure that the image is increased (or decreased) in both length and height, in equal sizes, without any noticeable distortion, this will be acceptable. Look at Figure 2.10.

This is the original image and you can see that the proportions are correct.

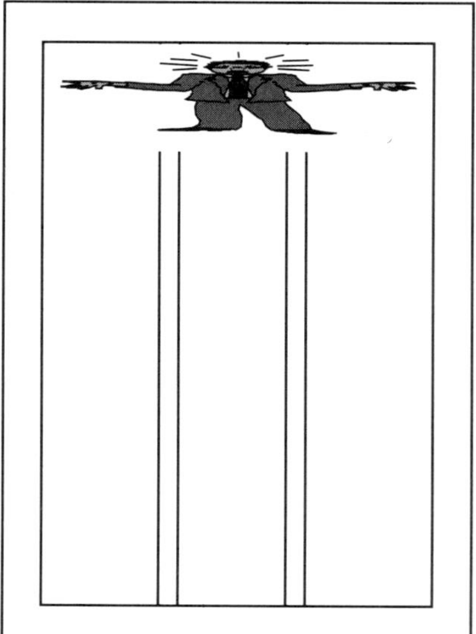

The width of the image has been increased and the length decreased. The image is not in proportion and looks distorted.

Figure 2.10 Resizing images

Copyfit tools

The skills you learn for this section will make your work look much more professional.

Headings and related text

You should ensure that a heading and at least two lines of text are in the same column. Look at the Figure 2.11.

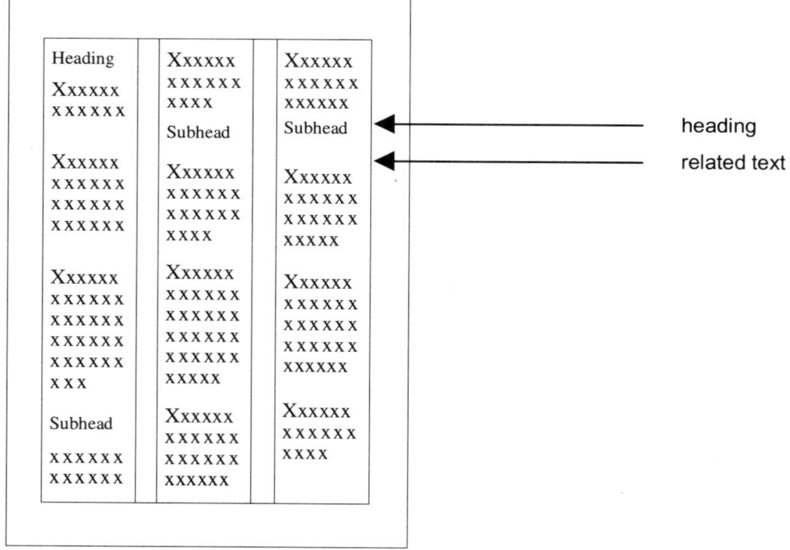

Figure 2.11 Headings and related text grouped together

In order to achieve this you can do one of the following:

- Switch on the 'keep with' facility within your style sheet, if you have one. This will automatically keep your headings and text together. On some software packages you can specify how many lines of text must stay with a heading. If you have this facility, it is by far the most accurate.
- Manually adjust the size of the images, if there are any, so that the text flows in a different position – this is not a particularly technical method and is therefore unreliable.
- Roll up the text so that it ends in the correct position, then physically put it into the correct column – again this can be unreliable.

2

Widows and orphans

One line (or word) that appears either at the top or bottom of a column or page is classed as a widow or orphan. Look at Figure 2.12.

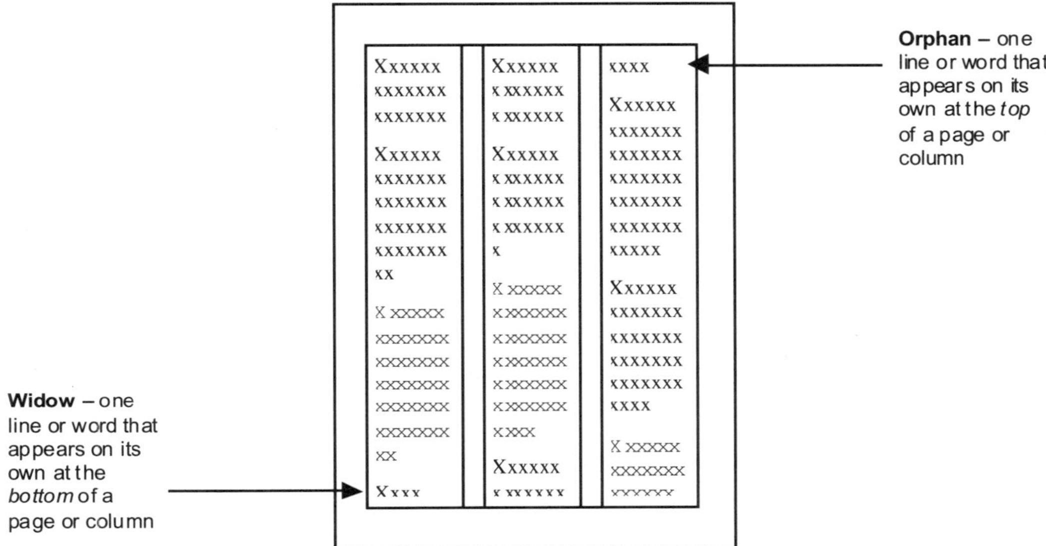

Figure 2.12 Widows and orphans

You can control these in the following ways:

- When you are setting your text styles you may be able to use a widows and orphans facility (if your software has one). As with the headings and related text problem this is by far the most accurate method.
- You can roll up or pull down the text so that it reflows.
- You can adjust the size of any images so that the text reflows.

Superimposing text/graphics on other text or images

We have already discussed the use of text wrap to ensure that the text and images are not superimposed. However, when you are adjusting text and images to copyfit, it is easy to move the text and/or image out of line. Before you print your work, you must check very carefully that the text and images are not touching. If necessary, zoom to a reasonably large size so that the borders of the image can be clearly seen.

Paragraph spacing

The paragraph spacing of your text should be consistent throughout the document. Traditionally, when a clear space is not left between paragraphs, the first line of each paragraph is indented to make the distinction.

If your imported text has clear spaces between each paragraph this is perfectly acceptable; there is no need to go through the document, altering each paragraph. However, what you must ensure is that the space is equal. If, for example, you have several paragraphs with a clear space between and several without, your work will look untidy. Check your work carefully on screen before printing. as again, when you are manipulating your text and images, it is easy to put in extra spaces or take them out.

Exercise 3

Now try the following exercises. These are designed to help you practice copyfitting your work. You must ensure the following:

- headings and related text are grouped together
- one line or less of text is grouped with the rest of the related text
- text/graphics are adjusted so that they are not superimposed on other text or images
- paragraph spacing is consistent.

Exercise 3.1

Open the document: **DES2**.

Resize, in proportion, Image 2 on the second page to extend across the first and second columns as in Figure 2.13.

Save your document as: **DES3** and print one copy.

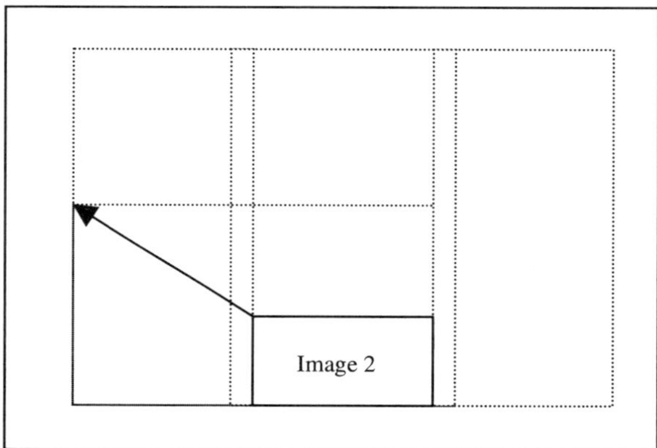

Page 9 – Image resized in proportion

Figure 2.13 Layout for Exercise 3.1

Exercise 3.2

Open the document: **BANKS2**.

Resize, in proportion, Image 2 on the second page to stretch across both columns as in Figure 2.14.

Save your document as: **BANKS3** and print one copy.

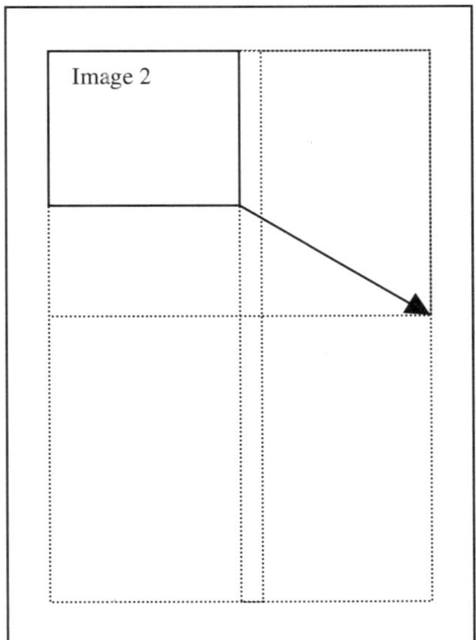

Page 5 – Image resized in proportion.

Figure 2.14 Layout for Exercise 3.2

Exercise 3.3

Open the document: **AUC2**.

Resize, in proportion, Image 1 on the first page to extend across the second and third columns as in Figure 2.15.

Save your document as: **AUC3** and print one copy.

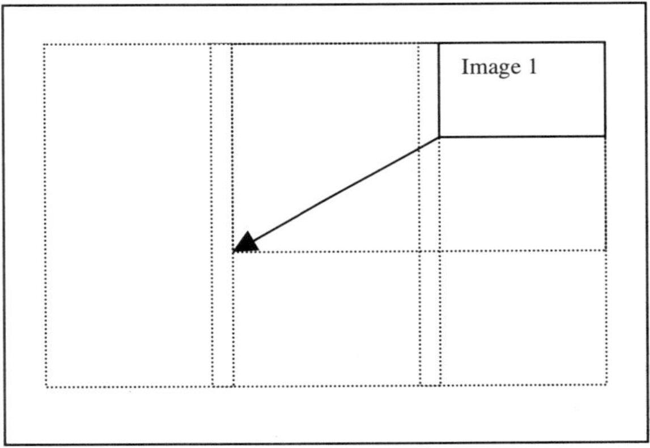

Page 3 – Image 1 resized in proportion

Figure 2.15 Layout for Exercise 3.3

Exercise 3.4

Open the document: **SHOP2**.

Resize, in proportion, Image 1 on the first page to extend across the two columns as in Figure 2.16.

Save your document as: **SHOP3** and print one copy.

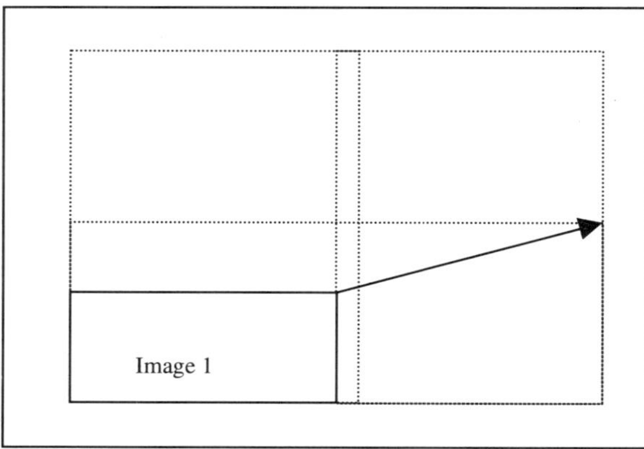

Page 6 – Image resized in proportion

Figure 2.16 Layout for Exercise 3.4

Amending an existing publication

You may find that there are times when you have to amend a document that has been created by someone else. You will need to know about correction signs and be able to make amendments to the text following these.

Amending style sheets

If you are working on a previously prepared document and need to change the type styles, there is a great temptation to use the highlighting method, particularly if you are feeling rushed for time. However, although this may seem the easy option, it is not as reliable as changing the style sheet.

Most software programs have an option to amend the style sheet rather than create a new one. Find out how to amend the style sheet on your software now.

Don't forget you can change the following within a style sheet:

- type size
- font
- alignment
- enhancements such as bold or italic
- first-line indent
- hyphenation.

Using correction signs

Each proof correction should be marked both in the text and in the margin. This will help ensure that you do not miss any. When you are amending documents, it may be helpful to cross off each correction sign on the paper copy once you have made the correction.

Given opposite is a list of common correction signs. Make sure that you know what each means.

Instruction	Mark in text	Mark in margin
Insert new copy	It is hoped that you will attend ...	and a guest
Correct version:	It is hoped that you and a guest will attend ...	
Delete (remove)	I ~~very much~~ hope to see you on ...	
Correct version:	I hope to see you on ...	
Insert space	Please leave aspace.	/
Correct version:	Please leave a space.	
Start new paragraph	...end of sentence. This starts a new paragraph. *OR* ...end of sentence. This starts a new paragraph.	
Correct version:	...end of sentence. This starts a new paragraph. *OR* ...end of sentence. This starts a new paragraph.	
Close up	...c lose up the space.	
Correct version:	...close up the space.	
Stet	Correct ~~Incorrect~~ word...	
Correct version:	Correct word...	
Set in caps	use a capital letter...	
Correct version:	Use a capital letter...	
Transpose	Use a letter capital...	
Correct version:	Use a capital letter...	
Align (left)	This text should be aligned to the left. It should not be indented at all.	
Correct version:	This text should be aligned to the left. It should not be indented at all.	

Using bullets

Bullet points are used in place of numbers to give emphasis to points. Look at Figure 2.17.

- The traditional bullet is slightly larger than a full stop and sits vertically in the middle of the typing line.
- The bullet should be in line with the left-hand margin.
- The text should be indented on each line to give a neat appearance.
- You can have a clear space between each bullet to separate the points.

Figure 2.17 Bullets

Depending on the software you are using you may have to set tabs and/or a temporary indent in order for the text to line up to your bullet points.

Using the spell check

Once you have finished correcting your work, you should run it through the spell check. Remember that if you have placed more than one article on the page the spell check will treat each independently. This may mean you have to set the spell check to look at both. If you do not do this it will only check the article in which you have placed the text tool.

If the spell check offers more than one alternative to a spelling error, look very carefully to see which option you should choose. Do not be tempted to take the first option without reading the text. Many errors are caused by careless use of the spell check.

Exercise 4

For the following exercises you will need to set up DTP files with the specifications given. Please note there are deliberate errors in the text which you will be asked to correct in Exercise 5 using the spell check facility.

Exercise 4.1

Set up a template with the following specifications:

Page size	A4	
Page orientation	Portrait/tall	
Number of columns	3	
Gutter space	5mm	
Margins	Left	25mm
	Right	25mm
	Top	25mm
	Bottom	25mm

Style sheet

The body text and bullet text should be formatted with a first-line indent for each paragraph.

Style name	Typeface	Point size	Alignment
Body text	Serif	12	Left
Bullet text	Serif	12	Left
Subheading	Sans serif	18	Centred
Headline	Serif	24	Centred

Ensure each style is independent and not related to another.

Text and images

Import the two text files and the image into a copy of the template and place them exactly as shown in Figure 2.18. Text file one is called: **HISTORY**. Text file two is called: **EQUIP**. The image file is called: **GLASS**.

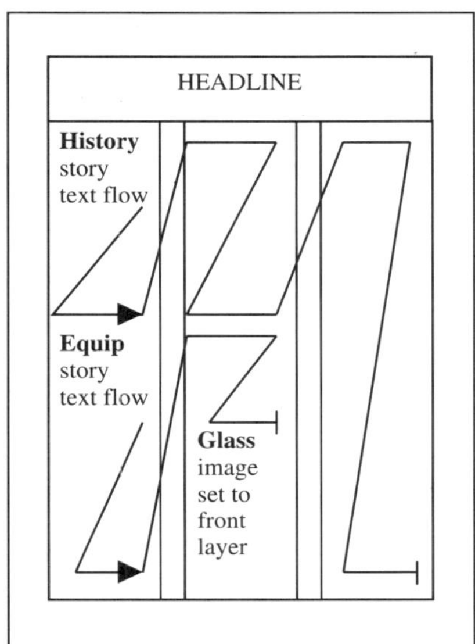

Figure 2.18 Page layout for **DRINKS**

Assigning text styles
Assign each of the styles to the relevant text.
Save your document as **DRINKS**.

Exercise 4.2

Set up a template with the following specifications:

Page size	A4	
Page orientation	Portrait/tall	
Number of columns	3	
Gutter space	5mm	
Margins	Left	25mm
	Right	25mm
	Top	25mm
	Bottom	25mm

Style sheet

The body text and bullet text should be formatted with a first-line indent for each paragraph.

Style name	Typeface	Point size	Alignment
Body text	Sans serif	10	Justified

Bullet text	Sans serif	10	Justified
Subheading	Serif, italic	16	Left
Headline	Serif	20	Left

Ensure each style is independent and not related to another.

Text and images

Import the two text files and the image into a copy of the template and place them exactly as shown in Figure 2.19. Text file one is called: **1920S**. Text file two is called: **1930S**. The image file is called: **DNK**.

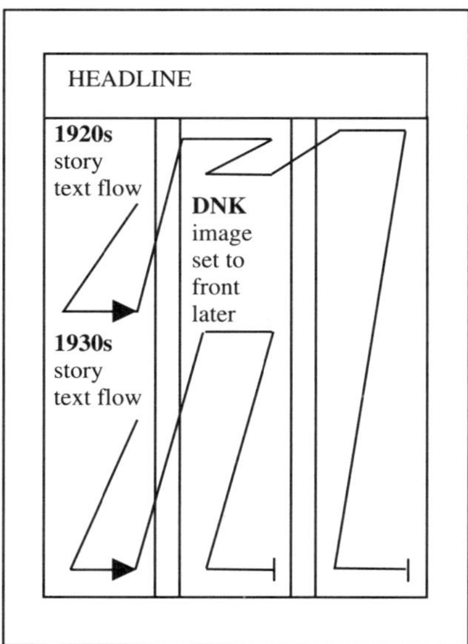

Figure 2.19 Page layout for **FASH**

Assigning text styles
Assign each of the styles to the relevant text.
Save your document as **FASH**.

Exercise 4.3

Set up a template with the following specifications:

Page size	A4	
Page orientation	Landscape/wide	
Number of columns	3	
Gutter space	5mm	
Margins	Left	25mm
	Right	25mm
	Top	30mm
	Bottom	30mm

Style sheet

The body text and bullet text should be formatted with a first-line indent for each paragraph.

Style name	**Typeface**	**Point size**	**Alignment**
Body text	Serif	12	Justified
Bullet text	Serif	12	Left
Subheading	Serif	14	Left
Headline	Serif	16	Left

Ensure each style is independent and not related to another.

Text and images

Import the two text files and the image into a copy of the template and place them exactly as shown in Figure 2.20. Text file one is called: **FENG**. Text file two is called: **HOW**. The image file is called: **FISH**.

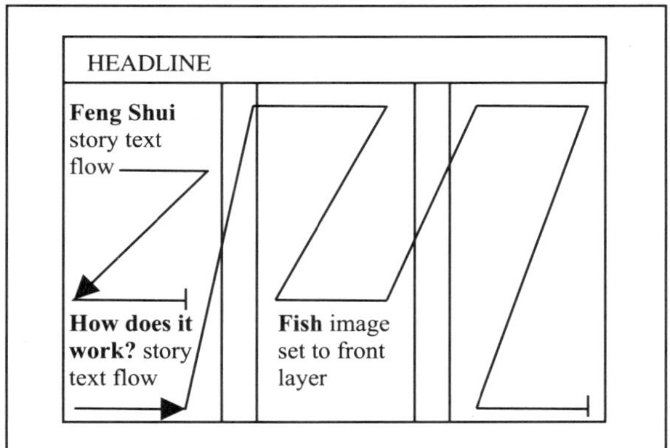

Figure 2.20 Page layout for **INTER**

Assigning text styles

Assign each of the styles to the relevant text.
Save your document as **INTER**.

Exercise 4.4

Set up a template with the following specifications:

Page size	A4	
Page orientation	Portrait/tall	
Number of columns	3	
Gutter space	5mm	
Margins	Left	25mm
	Right	25mm
	Top	25mm
	Bottom	25mm

Style sheet

The body text and bullet text should be formatted with a first-line indent for each paragraph.

Style name	**Typeface**	**Point size**	**Alignment**
Body text	Sans serif	12	Justified
Bullet text	Sans serif	12	Left
Subheading	Serif	18	Left
Headline	Serif, bold	22	Centred

Ensure each style is independent and not related to another.

Text and images

Import the two text files and the image into a copy of the template and place them exactly as shown belowin Figure 2.21. Text file one is called: **WILL**. Text file two is called: **JANE**. The image file is called: **SHAKE**.

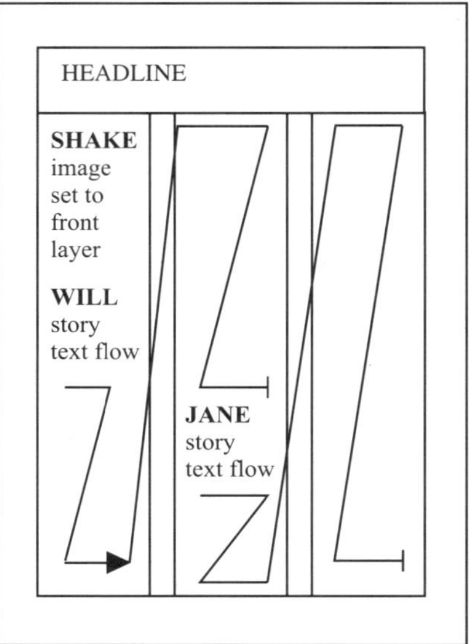

Figure 2.21 Page layout for **WRITE**

Assigning text styles
Assign each of the styles to the relevant text.
Save your document as **WRITE**.

Exercise 5

Now try the following exercises. These will give you practice on amending style sheets, making corrections and inserting bullets.

Exercise 5.1

Load the document: **DRINKS** and make the following changes to the style sheet:

Style name	Typeface	Point size	Alignment
Heading	Serif, bold	24	
Subheading	Italic	18	Left
Bullet text		12	Justified
Body text		12	Justified

Make the amendments as indicated on the proof copy on page 55.

In the **History story**, in the paragraph beginning **America is the traditional home**… highlight in **bold** the word **London**.

In the **Equipment** story insert a bullet character at the beginning of the following three paragraphs:

an ice bucket…
a juice extractor…
a sharp fruit knife…

Ensure all bullet text is indented from the bullet point.

Save the publication as: **DRINKS1** and print one copy.

Exercise 5.2

Load the document: **FASH** and make the following changes to the style sheet:

Style name	Typeface	Point size	Alignment
Heading	Bold	22	
Subheading		18	Centred
Bullet text	Serif	12	
Body text	Serif	12	

Make the amendments as indicated on the proof copy on page 56.

In the **1920s** story, in the paragraph beginning **This was the period of the**… highlight in italics the word **vamp**.

In the **1920s** story insert a bullet character at the beginning of the following five paragraphs:

pink…
light brown…
white…
soft blue…
green…

Ensure all bullet text is indented from the bullet point.

Save the publication as: **FASH1** and print one copy.

Exercise 5.3

Load the document: **INTER** and make the following changes to the style sheet:

Style name	Typeface	Point size	Alignment
Heading	Sans serif, bold	20	Centred
Subheading	Sans serif	18	Centred
Bullet text	Italic		Justified
Body text			

Make the amendments as indicated on the proof copy on page 57.

In the **Feng Shui** story, in the paragraph beginning **Although this is an…** highlight in **bold** the word **outlawed**.

In the **How does it work?** story insert a bullet character at the beginning of the following four paragraphs:

Clutter…
Throw out…
Moving water…
Place plants…

Ensure all bullet text is indented from the bullet point.

Save the publication as: **INTER1** and print one copy.

Exercise 5.4

Load the document: **WRITE** and make the following changes to the style sheet:

Style name	Typeface	Point size	Alignment
Heading	Sans serif, bold	24	Left
Subheading	Sans serif, italic	22	Centred
Bullet text		14	
Body text			

Make the amendments as indicated on the proof copy on page 58.

In the **William Shakespeare** story, in the paragraph beginning **We know...** highlight in **bold** the words **Anne Hathaway**.

In the **Jane Austen** story insert a bullet character at the beginning of the following three paragraphs:

Pride and Prejudice...
Northanger Abbey...
Mansfield Park...

Ensure all bullet text is indented from the bullet point.

Save the publication as: **WRITE1** and print one copy.

Proof copy for Exercise 5.1

COCKTAILS

History

Cocktails are becoming more popular after a few years of taking second place to foriegn beers. However, cocktails are not modern drinks, they have been in and out of fashion since 1806.

America is the traditional home of the cocktail, indeed London did not have a cocktail bar until 1910.

The cocktail was most popular during Prohibition when ingredients were blended to disquise the taste of alcohol. In the late 1930s cocktails' popularity waned and in Britain sherry parties became fashionable.

The revival of cocktail drinking began in the 1960s when people began to travel abroad for their holidays. People began to expeireince the food and drink of foreign countries and tried to re-create these new flavours at home. ~~Although they had difficulty obtaining the ingredients.~~ these days you can buy ready-made cocktails in supermarkets and off-licences. However it is much more fun to make your own.

Equipment

There are a few pieces of equipment that you will need inorder to make perfect cocktails. First of all you will need a shaker. The ingrediants and ice, if require, are placed in the shaker and then blended. The contents are then strained directly into the glass.

This leads us to the second piece of required equipment – a strainer. These can be purchased at good kitchenware stores.

If this sounds complicated then there are three part shakers that combine a strainer on the market. These are much easier to use.Another way of mixing cocktails is to stir them. For this you will need a mixing jug. Almost any jug will do, but it should have a small lip. A long bar spoon is another piece of esential equippment. This can also act as a measuring spoon as well as for stirring.

In order to add the essential 'dash' of bitters, you may wish to purchase special bottles for this purpose. These come with a nozzle that allows only a 'dash' to pour through at a time.

Other equipment that may be useful includes:

an ice bucket – these come in a variety of shapes and sizes, some being insulated. A plain bucket looks the most stylish

a juice extracter – these are used for squeezing citrus fruit when required. Fresh fruit juice should always be used. A variety of electrical juice extractors are now available

a sharp fruit knife for cutting small pieces of fruit to garnishe your drinks.

Exercise 6

Proof copy for Exercise 5.2

Fashion in the 1920s and 1930s

The 1920s

This was the period of the 'vamp', large dark eyes rimmed with kohl; turbans that came down to the eye-brows and eyelashes emphasised with mascara.

Hair took second place during this period and many women had their hair cut in a short bob. Eyebrows were either covered by turbans or bandeaux or ignored.

To complement this new look, clothes were designed to flow. Hems became shorter, waists lower and sleeves were long. In fact, the garments had a very soft, unstructured shape that was easy to wear. For the first time women were free of heavy, restrictive garments such as corsets, bodices or petticoats. With the rise in popularity of the cocktail, so dresses were designed for the cocktail hour. These tended to be a cross between a day dress and evening gown. The cut of the day dress combined with the fabric of an evening gown was not always successfull.

In 1924, the spring Paris collections showed a new and defined fashion. Hemlines just reached the calf and waistlines were moved to the hips. The fashionable figure became very boyish. Many women embraced this style and its success was great.

The most popular colours were

pink
light brown
white
soft blue
green

As the 20s moved on, so did the fashion. The bias-cut became popular. This was used in every female garment from underwear to evening gowns. A very fashionible hemline for evening gowns was ankle length at the back, rising to the knee length at the front.

1930s

At last, the outline became more feminine – a gently rounded bust and slight curve at the waist became noticeible. Hair was slightly longer and was known as a 'shingle'.

Skirts became longer and reached mid-calf. Often the hem was longer at the back. Favourite fabrics for evening wear were chiffon, silk and velvet, often with capes of the same fabric. The most popular colours were pale blues, pinks and cream. Matching gloves were an important accessory for both day and evening wear.

Cotton became a popular fabric, mostly due to Chanel who showed a cotton collection in London. Organdie and pique became fashionable alternatives to satin and silk.

During the 1930s, trousers became aceptable as beach wear for women. This trend started with the appearence of pyjama- styled trousers and were often worn as informal evening wear made from crepe de Chine or shantung. However, these soon lost popularity but the beach wear remained.

By the end of the decade fashion had changed again. The female silouette defined with small waists and padded shoulders.

Interior Design

Feng Shui

Feng Shui, pronounced Feng sh-way) is fast becoming the latest trend in interior design. It is the ancient Chinese art of placing buildings and objects so that they attract maximum posative energy as well as minimising negative energey.

Although this is an ancient Chinese art it is now outlawed in China. However, it has great respect in other far Eastern countries, and Eastern architecture students have to study it for a year as part of their courses.

This art is now becoming extremly popular in the Western world and in Britain a new magazine has been launched, that is devoted to the subject.

Feng Shui is also becoming used widely in offices and schools as well as in the home.

How does it work?

Feng Shui is based on the premise that every building and individal room has within it a microcosm of human existance, with different areas representingdifferent aspects of human life. These include career, relationships, family and health. An eight-sided grid, known as a bagua or pah kwa should be fitted over your building or room plan so that you can improve the energy flow.

For example, if you were experiencing difficulties with your career then you should look at the career areas of your home and perhaps re-arrange some of the furnature and fittings to improve the flow of the positive energy. Serious students of Feng Shui take the art a step further when dealing with their clients. They will enquire into how long the client has been living in their home, and take account of the client's Chinese horoscope. The directional and geophysical influences will also be looked at. These include the position of the house in relation to buildings and roads, the effects of ley lines, pylons and transmitters.

Many consultants say there are a few rules that can be applied to the rooms in your home. These include the following.

Clutter can block energy, so keep your rooms tidy

Throw out items that are no longer relevant to your life. This symbolically makes room for new developments

Moving water has a good influance in your wealth areas. Try placing a fish tank or indoor fountain in the wealth area of a room.

Place plants around televisions and computers as they help to absorb the electromagnetic signals.

2

GREAT WRITERS

William Shakespeare

It is assumed that William Shakespeare was born on April 23rd 1564 to a well-known Stratford family. His father, John Shakespeare was a glover and commodities dealer in leather and wool. John was made an alderman in 1565 and elected bayliff three years later. His wife, Mary was the daughter of a rich farmer Robert Arden. William was the eldest son and third of eight children.

He probably attended a grammer school from the age of seven and upon leaving he may have been apprenticed in his father's shop. We know that he married Anne Hathaway, who was also the daughter of a waelthy farmer, when he was eigteen, in 1582. William and Anne had three children, Susanna and twins, Hamnet and Judith.

Shakespeare wrote at least thirty-eight plays as well as a number of poems and sonnets. Among the most well known are Hamlet, Othello. Romeo and Juliet, and Macbeth . He died on April 23rd 1616, aged exactly fifty-two years old and was buried in the chancel of the Collegiate Church of the Holy Trinity in Stratford upon Avon.

Jane Austen

Jane Austen was born on 16th December 1775 to the Revarend George Austen and his wife Cassandra Austen. She was the seventh of eight children and was particuarly close to her sister Cassandra who was three years older than herself. She never maried, but was very fond of her many nephews and neices. The family lived in Steventon in Hampshire, where her father was the rector. Upon his retirement in 1801, the family moved to Bath where they lived until her father died. After George Austen's death, Jane and her mother went to live in Southampton for a short while before moving to a cottage near Alton.

Jane started writing when she was very young although Sense and Sensibility, her first published work, was published when she was thirty-six, in 18 11. Her other novels include
Pride and Prejudice, Northanger Abbey and Mansfield Park.

Several films and television adaptations have been made of her novels.

Jane died in 1817, aged forty-one and is buried in Winchester.

Centre No

Using layered items

You can place items on top of each other to give various effects. Look at Figures 2.22 and 2.23. Placing items to front or back is much easier than it sounds.

Figure 2.22 Layering – image at back

Figure 2.23 Layering – image at front

You must be able to see both the text and the graphic when layering items. In Figure 2.22, the graphic is rather light which enables us to clearly see the text. If the graphic was dark or of a high density, then the text might be slightly obscured. In Figure 2.23 the bird is in front of the text box and therefore obscures some of the text.

In order to layer objects you will need to be able to use the **bring to front** or **send to back** facilities that are available in most software.

Bring to front/send to back

These features allow you to show different parts of the same diagram. Look at the examples in Figure 2.24:

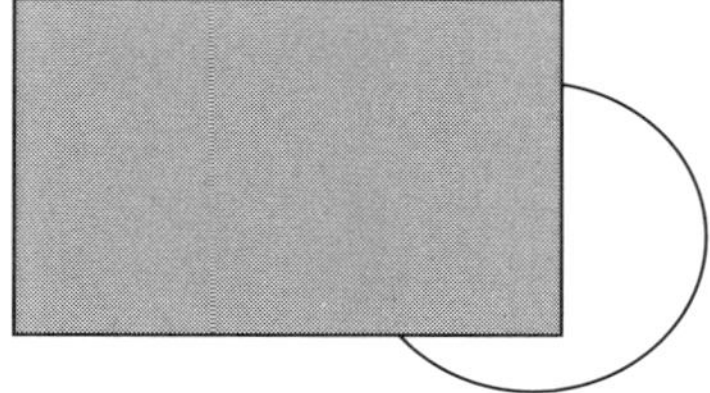

In this example, the box has been brought to the front. In order to do this, the box was selected and then the 'bring front' option was used.

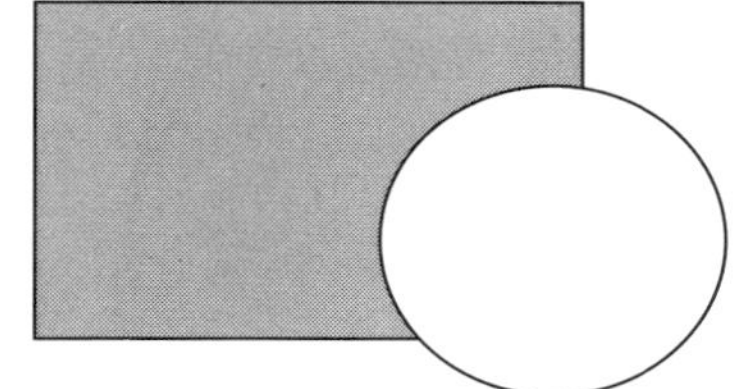

In this example, the box has been sent to the back. The box was selected and then the 'send to back' option was used.

Figure 2.24 Bring to front and send to back

The effect would have been the same had the circle been selected and then either sent to back or brought to front.

■ Using the drawing tools

You may decide to draw a line or a box to enhance your text or image. You have already looked at this in the previous section. However, you may want to set text wrap around your box to ensure that it does not touch the image or the surrounding text. Do not set the text wrap too wide – around 2mm will be sufficient.

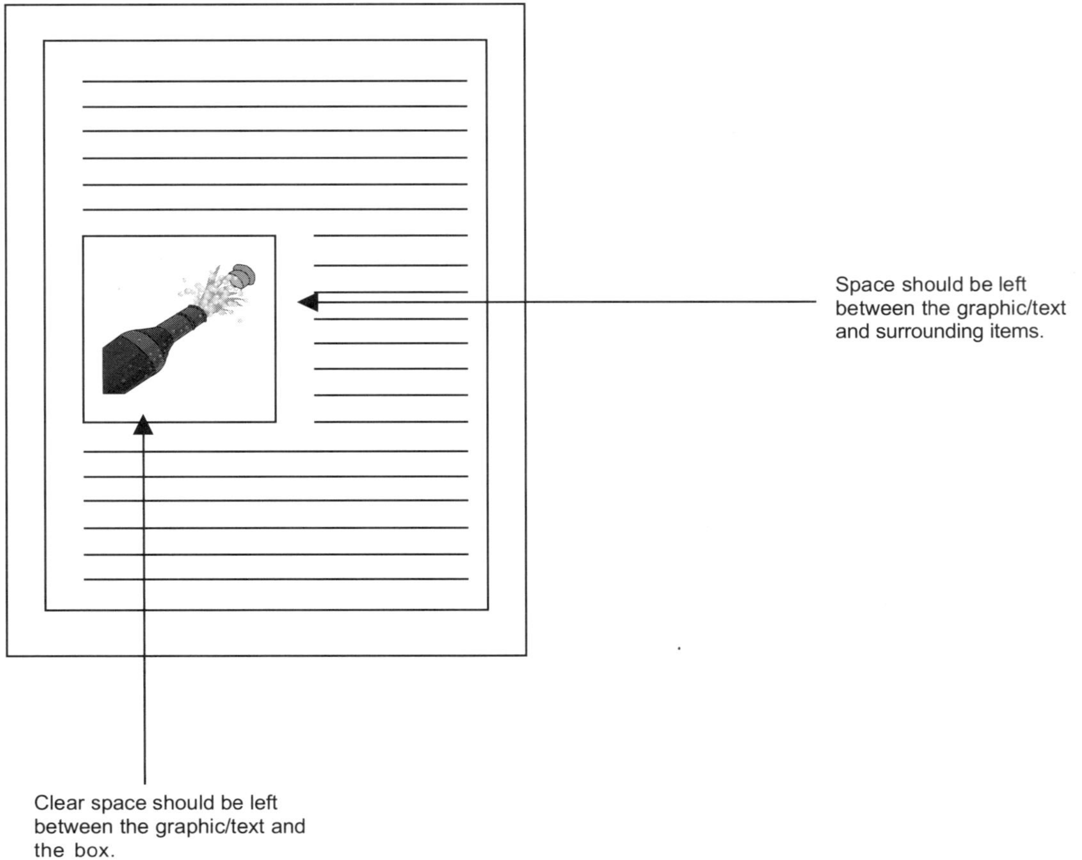

Figure 2.25 Box in document

As you can see in Figure 2.25, space must be left between the graphic or text and the box.

If your box completely obscures the graphic or text, it may be that it has a white or paper fill colour. This means that the box will blank out anything that is underneath it. In order to solve this problem, set the fill colour of the box to 'none'.

If your box moves each time you try to place it over the graphic or text, this may be because the existing text wrap is in the way. If this is the case you can do one of the following:

- Take off the text wrap of the graphic or text that will be enclosed by a box and then set text wrap for the box – this will ensure the text or other graphics will remain separate items.
- Set the text wrap boundaries for the graphic/text to a smaller size.
- If all else fails, you can make the box larger to encompass the text wrap of the graphic or text.

Changing the appearance of a box

Most software packages offer a choice of square or rounded corners for boxes. Look at Figure 2.26:

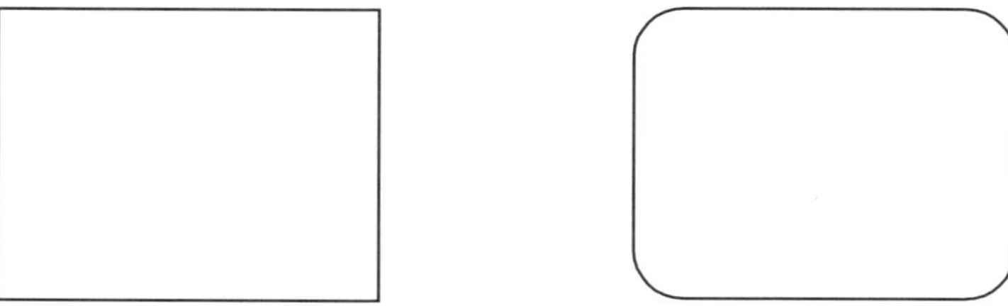

This is a square-cornered box. This is a round-cornered box.

Figure 2.26 Square and rounded corners

Exercise 6

In the following exercises, copyfit your publication to ensure that:

- headings and related text are grouped together
- one line or less of text is grouped with the rest of the related text
- text/graphics are adjusted so that they are not superimposed on other text or images (except where specified)
- paragraph spacing is consistent.

Exercise 6.1

Open the file: **DRINKS1**.

Using the spell check facility, correct the spelling errors that appear in the text.

In the **Equipment** story, overlay the text so that it is superimposed on the **GLASS** image. Ensure that the text is at the front and that the image can be seen in the background.

Draw a horizontal line across the first and second columns below the **History** story to separate it from the **Equipment** story. The line should be between 2 and 4pt rule weight. Ensure the line does not touch any text.

Place a box with **rounded** corners around the headline text, ensuring that the edges of the box do not touch the text. Ensure that the text remains centred between the margins.

Save the finished publication as: **DRINKS2** and print one copy.

Exercise 6.2

Open the file: **FASH1**.

Using the spell check facility, correct the spelling errors that appear in the text.

In the **1920s** story, overlay the text so that it is superimposed on the **DNK** image. Ensure that the text is at the front and that the image can be seen in the background.

Draw a horizontal line across the first and second columns below the **1920s** story to separate it from the **1930s** story. The line should be between 1 and 3pt rule weight. Ensure the line does not touch any text.

Place a box with **squared** corners around the headline text, ensuring that the edges of the box do not touch the text.

Save the finished publication as: **FASH2** and print one copy.

Exercise 6.3

Open the file: **INTER1**.

Using the spell check facility, correct the spelling errors that appear in the text.

In the **How does it work?** story, overlay the text so that it is superimposed on the **FISH** image. Ensure that the text is at the front and that the image can be seen in the background.

Draw a horizontal line across the first column below the **Feng Shui** story to separate it from the **How does it work?** story. The line should be between 4 and 6pt rule weight. Ensure the line does not touch any text.

Place a box with **squared** corners around the headline text, ensuring that the edges of the box do not touch the text.

Save the finished publication as: **INTER2** and print one copy.

Exercise 6.4

Open the file: **WRITE1**.

Using the spell check facility, correct the spelling errors that appear in the text.

In the **William Shakespeare** story, overlay the text so that it is superimposed on the **SHAKE** image. Ensure that the text is at the front and that the image can be seen in the background

Draw a horizontal line across the second column below the **William Shakespeare** story to separate it from the **Jane Austen** story. The line should be between 2 and 4pt rule weight. Ensure the line does not touch any text.

Place a box with **rounded** corners around the headline text, ensuring that the edges of the box do not touch the text.

Save as: **WRITE2** and print one copy.

You have now completed all the work necessary for you to be able to do the RSA Desktop Publishing Stage II exam. Try the following consolidation exercises to practice the skills you have learnt.

Consolidation 2 Part 1

2

1 Open the desktop publishing system and set up a two-page document. The paper size should be A4 and the orientation set to portrait. Specify three equal columns with a 5mm gutter. Margins should be as follows:

Left	20mm
Right	20mm
Top	20mm
Bottom	20mm

2 Set up a style sheet with the following styles:

Style Name	Typeface	Point Size	Alignment
Body text	Serif	12	Justified
Subhead	Serif, italic	18	Right
Headline	Sans serif, bold	22	Left

3 Set a header and footer as follows, using the body text typestyle:

Header

HOLIDAY PROPERTY
(right aligned)

Footer

Page No	Your initials Task 1
centred	right aligned)

Page numbering should start from page 5.

4 Save the file as a master page using the following filename: **HOLS1**.

5 Import the text file called: **HOLS**. The text should start in the left-hand column of your first page. It will fill the columns on your first page and flow onto a second page.

6 Select and apply the three different styles prepared in Step 2, to the three appropriate areas of the text.

7 Import the supplied images called: **HOUSE** (Image 1) and **COTT** (Image 2) and display them as shown in Figure 2.27. Place Image 1 at the bottom of the third column on the first page and Image 2 at the top of the first column on your second page.

8 Save your document as: **HOLS2** and print one copy.

9 Image 1 on the first page at the bottom of the third column should be resized to extend across the full width of columns 2 and 3. The image *must* be kept in proportion. Ensure that the finished publication takes no more than two pages. If necessary, Image 2 may also be resized to achieve this.

10 Copyfit your publication to ensure that:

- headings and related text are grouped together
- one line or less of text is grouped with the rest of the related text (ie there are no 'widows' and 'orphans')
- text/graphics are adjusted so that they are not superimposed on other text or images
- paragraph spacing is consistent.

11 Save your document as: **HOLS3** and print one copy.

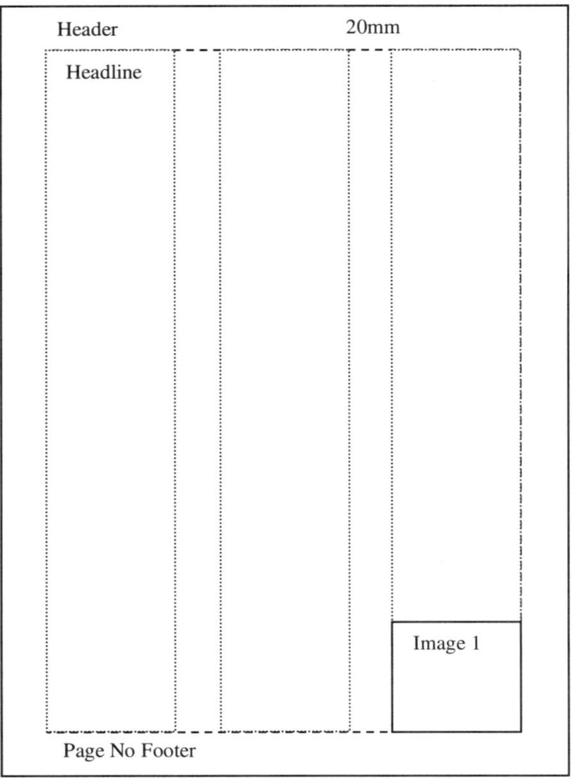

Page 5

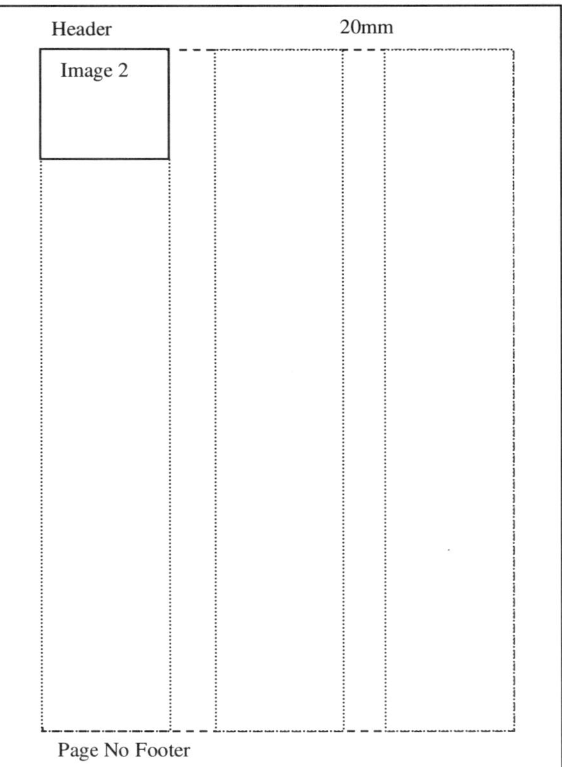

Page 6

Figure 2.27 Page layout for Consolidation 1

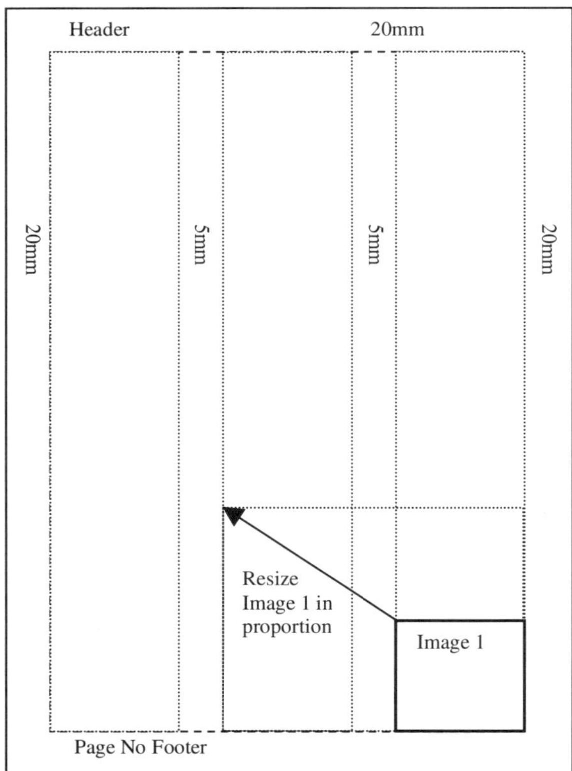

Page 5

Figure 2.28 Resize Image 1 (**HOUSE**)

Consolidation 2 Part 2

1 Set up a template with the following specifications:

Page size	A4	
Page orientation	Portrait/tall	
Number of columns	3	
Gutter space	5mm	
Margins	Left	25mm
	Right	25mm
	Top	25mm
	Bottom	25mm

Style sheet

The body text and bullet text should be formatted with a first-line indent for each paragraph.

Style name	**Typeface**	**Point size**	**Alignment**
Body text	Sans serif	10	Justified
Bullet text	Sans serif	10	Justified
Subheading	Serif	14	Left
Headline	Sans serif, bold	18	Centred

Ensure each style is independent and not related to another.

2 **Text and images**

Import the two text files and the image into a copy of the template and place them exactly as shown in Figure 2.29. Text file one is called: **MKCON**. Text file two is called: **CONGAR**. The image file is called: **POT**.

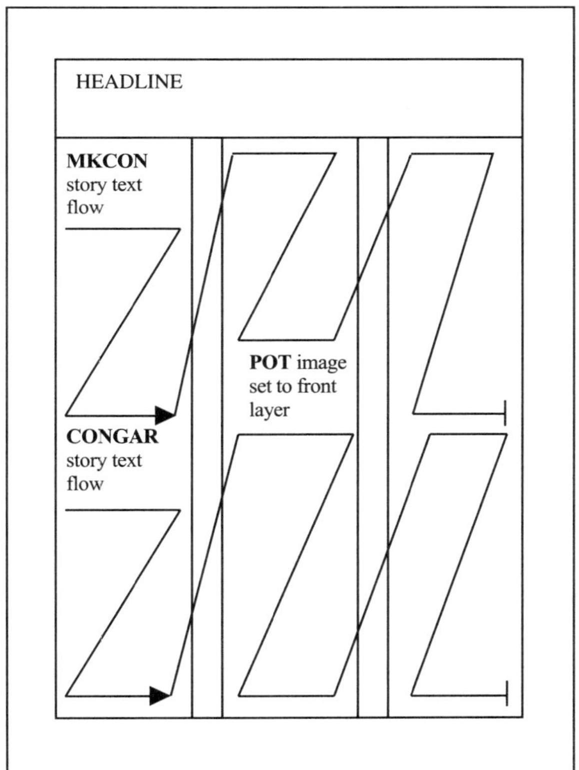

Figure 2.29 Page layout for **GARD**

3 **Assigning text styles**
Assign each of the styles to the relevant text.
Save your document as **GARD**.

Consolidation 2 Part 3

1 Load the document: **GARD**.

2 Amendments to the publication need to be made. The instructions for the amendments are indicated on the proof copy on page 68.

3 In the **Making a Container** story, insert a bullet character at the beginning of the following three paragraphs:

Ensure the plants are...
Ease the plants carefully...
Plant according...

Ensure that all bullet text is indented from the bullet point.

In the **Container Gardening** story, in the paragraph beginning **A water garden...** highlight in *italics* the words **water garden**.

4 In the **Container Gardening** story, overlay the text so that it is superimposed on the **POT** image. Ensure that the text is at the front and that the image can be seen in the background.

5 Changes to the style sheet need to be made as follows:

Style Name	Typeface	Point Size	Alignment
Body text		11	Left
Bullet text	Italic	11	Left
Subheading	Sans serif	18	
Headline		26	Left

6 Place a box with **rounded** corners around the headline text, ensuring that the edges of the box do not touch the text. (The box may extend into the left margin. Ensure that the headline remains left aligned).

7 Copyfit your publication to ensure that:

- headings and related text are grouped together
- one line or less of text is grouped with the rest of related text (ie there are no 'widows' and 'orphans')
- text/graphics are adjusted so that they are not superimposed on other text or images (except where specified)
- paragraph spacing is consistent.

8 Draw a horizontal line across the first, second and third columns below the **Container Gardening** story to separate it from the **Making a container** story. The line should be between 2 and 4pt rule weight. Ensure the line does not touch any text.

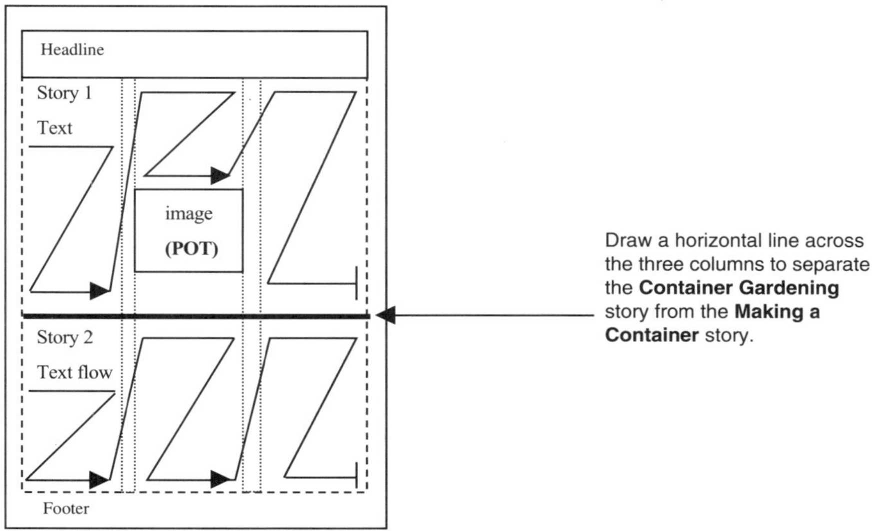

Figure 2.30 Layout for drawing line

9 Using the spell check facility of the desktop publishing system, correct the spelling errors that appear in the text.

10 Save the finished publication as: **GARD1** and print one copy.

Proof copy for Consolidation 2 Part 3

GARDENING

Container Gardening

This has become a very popular hobby in recent years and it is easy to see why. You do not need to put in hours of back breaking work digging and weeding. It is also suitable for all gardens, no matter how large or small.

You can grow a variety of plants in a container, from bulbs, bedding plants and herbs through to vegatables and fruit trees. A water garden makes an intresting container in a small garden or on a patio. Many people enjoy creating a miniture rockery or alpine garden, often using an old china kitchen sink. There is a wide variety of containers on the market. These range from plastic to the more expensive terracotta and stone. The choice is enormous as pots come in all sizes and shapes. If you feel inspired you can even make your own from pieces of wood etc. Old house hold and garden items such as wheel barrows, sinks, buckets, wicker baskets and broken watering cans can be transformed into beautiful containers. All you need is a little imagination and skill.

one of the main advantages of container gardening is that you can change the look of your garden instantly. You can have special displays, or seasonel pots to give colour all year round.

Making a container

First of all you need to prepare your container. Make sure it is clean and free from cracks. It must have a hole at the bottom for drainage. If you are using a teracotta pot then soak it in water for 5 to 10 minutes.

You need to create a drainage system in your container. To do this you will need to carefully place some drainage material at the bottom of the pot so that it covers, but does not block, the hole. Suitable material includes broken terracotta pots, polistyrene chips or large stones. You can then add some graval to cover the bottom inch or so. This is readily obtainable from most garden centres.

Now fill the pot with soil and compost. You can mix your own growing medium, but most garden centres and nurseries sell bags of ready-prepared soil at very reasonible prices. Fill to approximately 2 inches below the rim of the container.

Now you are ready to plant. Given below are a few hints to help.

Ensure the plants are well watered – do this 20 minutes before planting

Ease the plants carefully from their containers. Gently shake off excess soil and spread the roots out with your fingers

Plant according to instructions. Remember to water well each day and feed at regular intervals.

Consolidation 3

Exam Practice 2

You are now ready to try a mock examination for RSA Desktop Publishing Stage II. There are two elements of certification:

- Element 1 – set up and produce a publication
- Element 2 – edit a publication

2

You have to complete two tasks. Task 1 covers Element 1 and Task 2 covers Element 2.

In the exam, Task 2 will be supplied as a publication which has been put together by your tutor. In this book, *you* will be asked to create the publication, which will provide you with additional desktop publishing practice.

Element 1 – Set up and produce a publication

Before you start Task1 make sure you have on disk the following text file and graphic images. These need to be imported into your desktop publishing publication.

Text file is called: **EMP**

Image 1 is called: **BRIEF**

Image 2 is called: **HANDS**

Assessment Objectives

1.1a, 1.1b, 1.1c, 1.1d, 1.1e, 1.1f — Enter the desktop publishing system and create a new publication which meets the following specifications:

Number of pages	2	
Page size	A4	
Page orientation	Landscape/wide	
Number of columns	3 columns of equal width	
Gutter space	0.7cm (7mm) space between columns	
Margins	Left	2.5cm (25mm)
	Right	2.5cm (25mm)
	Top	2.5cm (25mm)
	Bottom	2.5cm (25mm)

1.2a, 1.2b, 1.2c, 1.2d, 1.2e — Prepare three styles according to the following specifications:

Style Name	**Typeface**	**Point Size**	**Alignment**
Body text	Sans serif	10	Left
Subhead	Serif	16	Centred
Headline	Serif, bold, italic	22	Centred

1.4a — Insert the following **header**:

1.4b — XXTask1 (XX being replaced by your initials) (right aligned)

1.4c	Insert the following footers: Page No # (# being replaced by auto page) (left aligned) Page numbering should start at 8. Employment (centred)
1.5a	Save the file as a master page using the filename: **EMP1** and ask your tutor to verify this.
1.6a	Import the supplied text file called: **EMP**. The text should start in the left-hand column of your first page. It will fill the columns on your first page and flow onto a second page.
1.3a	Select and apply the three different styles prepared in Step 2, to the three appropriate areas of the text.
1.7a	Import the supplied images called: **BRIEF** (Image 1) and **HANDS** (Image 2) and display these as shown in Figure 2.31. Place Image 1 at the top of the second column on the first page and Image 2 at the bottom of the second column on your second page.

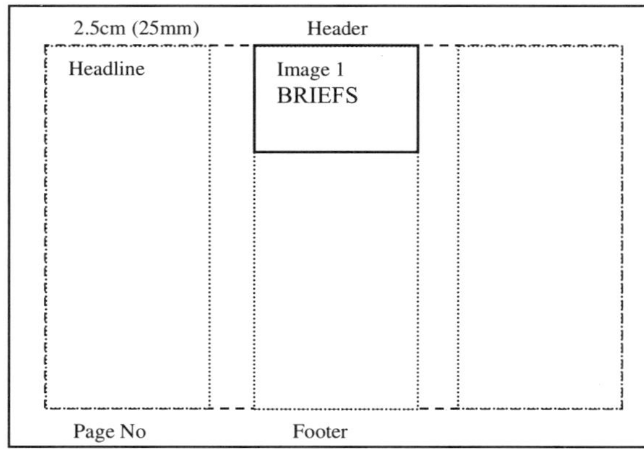

Page 8

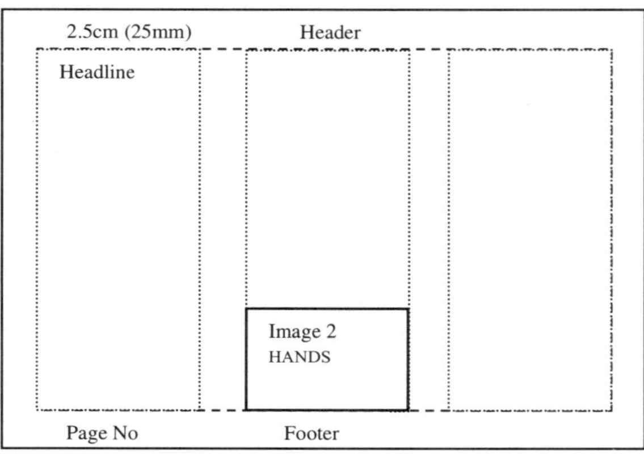

Page 9

Figure 2.31 Page layout for Element 1

1.9a	Save *two copies* of your work, using the names: **EMP2** and **EMP3**. Ask your tutor to verify this. Continue working in **EMP3**. **EMP2** can either be printed now or later as instructed by your tutor.
1.7c	Image 1 on the second page at the bottom of the second column should be resized to extend across the full width of columns 1 and 2. The image must be kept in *proportion.* Ensure that the finished publication takes no more than two pages. If necessary, Image 1 may also be resized to achieve this.

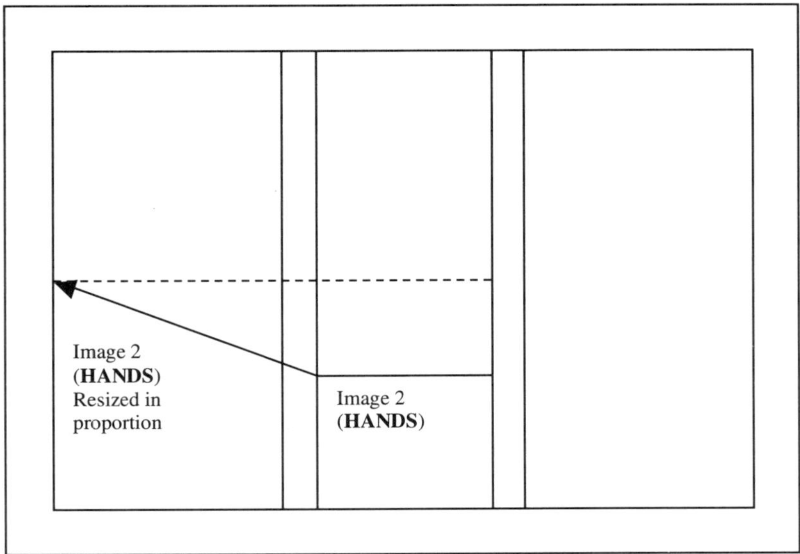

Page 9

Figure 2.32 Resize Image 2 (**HANDS**)

1.8a, 1.8b,	Copyfit your publication to ensure that:
1.8c, 1.8d	■ headings and related text are grouped together ■ one line or less of text is grouped with the rest of the related text (ie there are no 'widows' and 'orphans') ■ text/graphics are adjusted so that they are not superimposed on other text or images ■ paragraph spacing is consistent.
1.9a	Save the finished publication (**EMP3**). Ask your tutor to verify this.
1.10a	Print **EMP3** and ensure that **EMP2** is also printed as instructed by your tutor.

Element 2 – Edit a publication

Before you start Task 2, you will need to set up a DTP file with the following specifications:

Note: In the examination, your tutor will have set this file up for you.

Assessment Objectives

Set up a template with the following specifications:

Page size	A4	
Page orientation	Landscape/wide	
Number of columns	3	
Gutter space	5mm	
Margins	Left	20mm
	Right	20mm
	Top	20mm
	Bottom	20mm

Style sheet

The body text and bullet text should be formatted with a first-line indent for each paragraph.

Style name	Typeface	Point size	Alignment
Body text	Serif	10	Left
Bullet text	Serif	10	Justified
Subheading	Sans serif	16	Left
Headline	Sans serif	22	Left

Ensure each style is independent and not related to another.

Text and images

Import the two text files and the image into a copy of the template and place them exactly as shown below. Text file one is called: **HOM**. Text file two is called: **ACUP**. The image file is called: **PILLS**.

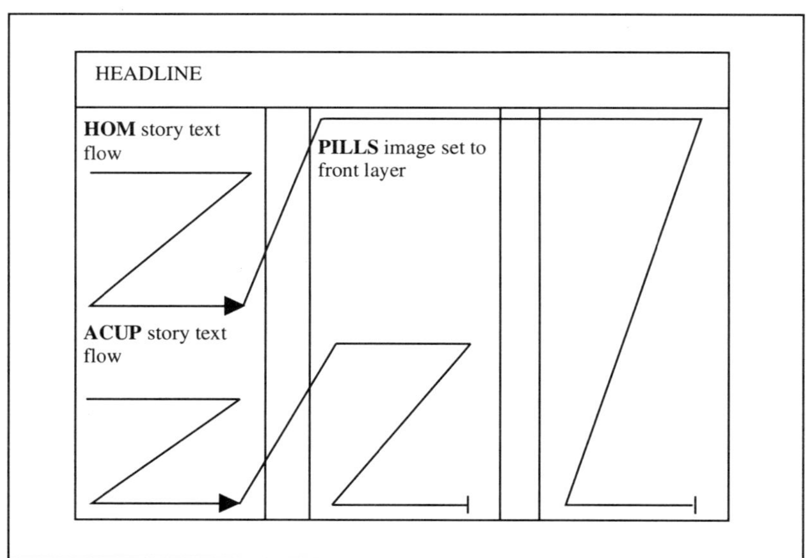

Figure 2.33 Page layout for **MED**

Assigning text styles
Assign each of the styles to the relevant text.

Save your document as **MED**.

2.1a Load the file: **MED**.

2.2a, 2.2b, Changes to the style sheet need to be made as follows:

2.2c, 2.2d, 2.2e

Style Name	Typeface	Point Size	Alignment
Body text		14	Justified
Bullet text		11	Left
Subhead		18	Right
Headling	Serif	26	

2.3a Amendments to the publication need to be made. The instructions for the amendments are indicated on the proof copy on page 74.

2.5a	In the **Homeopathy** story, insert a bullet character at the beginning of the following three paragraphs: **Holistic...** **Like Cures Like...** **Natural Treatment...**
2.5b	Ensure that all bullet text is indented from the bullet point.
2.4a	In the **Acupuncture** story, in the paragraph beginning **The basic principle...** highlight in **bold** the word **meridians**.
2.7a	In the **Homeopathy** story, overlay the text so that it is superimposed on the **PILLS** image. Ensure that the text is at the front and that the image can be seen in the background.
2.9a, 2.9b	Place a box with **squared** corners around the headline text, ensuring that the edges of the box do not touch the text. (The box may extend into the left margin. Ensure that the headline remains left aligned).
2.10a, 2.10b, 2.10c, 2.10d	Copyfit your publication to ensure that: ■ oheadings and related text are grouped together ■ one line or less of text is grouped with the rest of related text (ie there are no 'widows' and 'orphans') ■ text/graphics are adjusted to that they are not superimposed on other text or images (except where specified) ■ paragraph spacing is consistent.
2.8a	Draw a horizontal line across the first and second columns below the **Homeopathy** story to separate it from the **Acupuncture** story. The line should be between 2 and 4 pt rule weight. Ensure the line does not touch any text.

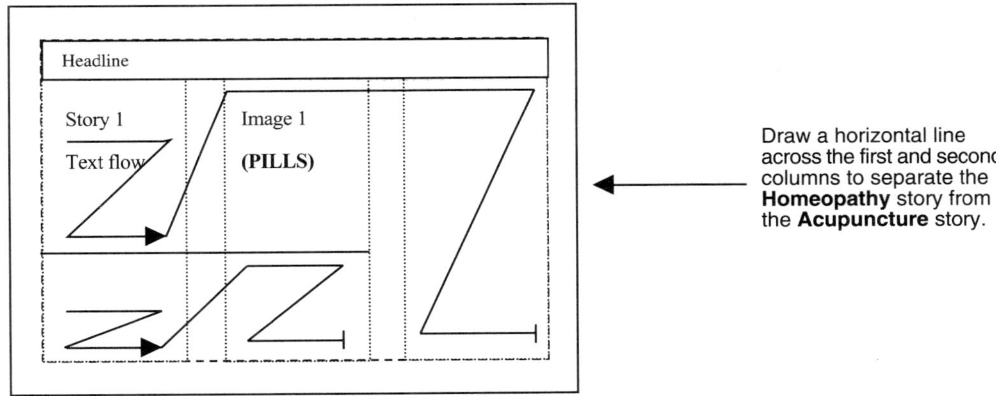

Figure 2.34 Layout for line drawing

2.6a	Using the spell check facility of the desktop publishing system, correct the spelling errors that appear in the text.
2.11a	Save the finished publication, using the filename: **MED1**, and ask your tutor to verify this.
2.12a	Print the finished publication.

ALTERNATIVE MEDICINE

Homeopathy

Homeopathy is considered an 'alternative' form of medacine, however it has been around since the end of the ninteenth century. It was originated by Samuel Hahnemann, a German physician. There are three main differences between conventional medicine and homeopathy.

Holistic. The symptoms are treated as part of a larger condition and the selected remidy will be used to treat the condition as a whole.

Like Cures Like. The remedy will be selected on its ability to start the same symptoms in a healthy person. In other words, if you are suffring from migraine, you may be given a remedy which would cause migraine in a non-sufferer.

Natural Treatment. The remedies used are completely naturel. They are derived from mineral, and plant worlds. They are safe to use. The dose given is highly diluted as this has been found to be more effective.

There are more than two thousand remedies and many can be bought at your local pharmacy. However, it is better to consult a qualified homeopath whenever possible. This is because the symptoms being displayed may not be the main cause of the disease. A trained homeopath will be able to recognise whether the obvious illness has an underlying cause. Some General Practitioners now use homeopathy alongside conventional medicine.

Acupuncture

The basic principle of acupuncture is that energy flows through certain channels in the body and that illness and pain occurs if these channels are interrupted or blocked. There are over eight hundred energy points over the body, which form a definite pattern. The lines that conect particular organs with these points are called meridians.

The acupuncturist redistributes the energy flow in the body by inserting very slender needles of pure coper, silver or gold at specific points along the meridian lines. Gold needles act as a stimulant, silver needles sedate. The number of needles used in a treatment varies from two or three to a dozen or more. the length of time the needles are kept in the body depends on the condition.

An experienced acupuncturist can detect an excess or deficiency of energy by checking the patient's pulse.

Acupuncture has had good results on disorders such as asthma, eczema, arthritis, migraine and ulcers.

Centre Number

Stage II Checklist

Did you remember to …	Assessment Objective	Consolidation 2 Part 1	Consolidation 2 Part 2	Exam Practice 2 Task 1	Exam Practice 2 Task 2
set up two pages, A4 with the orientation as specified?	1.1a 1.1b 1.1c				
select the correct number of columns and set accurate margins and gutter space?	1.1d 1.1e 1.1f				
set up the style sheet as specified, using the correct type size, font, alignment and enhancements?	1.2a 1.2b 1.2c 1.2d 1.2e				
apply the text styles correctly?	1.3a				
set up the header/footer correctly and number pages accurately?	1.4a 1.4b 1.4c				
save the blank master page?	1.5a				
import the text and images as specified in the design brief?	1.6a 1.7a 1.7b				
resize the image correctly and in proportion?	1.7c 1.7d				
copyfit the document in accordance with instructions?	1.8a, 2.10a, 1.8b, 2.10b, 1.8c, 2.10c, 1.8d, 2.10d				
save and print your document correctly?	1.9a, 2.11a 1.10a, 2.12a				
make the specified amendments to the style sheet accurately?	2.2a 2.2b 2.2c 2.2d, 2.2e				
make amendments to the text as indicated in the design brief?	2.3a 2.4a				
enhance the specified text?	2.5a 2.5b				
use bullets as appropriate and indent the text correctly?	2.6a 2.7a				

Did you remember to ...	Assessment Objective	Consolidation 2 Part 1	Consolidation 2 Part 2	Exam Practice 2 Task 1	Exam Practice 2 Task 2
use the spell check accurately?	2.6a				
layer the text and image correctly?	2.7a				
draw a line in the specified place, using the correct line weight?	2.8a 2.8b				
draw a box in the specified place using the correct corners?	2.9a 2.9b				

Exercise 2.1

Working from Home

Office Design

Many people are now turning a spare room in their home into an office. This may be because they like to keep their household accounts and business documents filed and labelled neatly in a room that also houses the family computer. It may be that a member of the family has joined the growing number of people who regularly work from home.

Whatever the reason, the office should be properly equipped and set out. If a person is planning to spend long hours in their home office then it should be subject to the same rules of planning and safety as purpose-built or commercial offices.

Ergonomics

The ergonomics of the working environment is one of the most important considerations when planning an office layout. This looks at the physical requirements of the worker – for example the way in which chairs, tables and desks are designed to take into account the requirements of the user. It also covers the way in which the office is set out.

Furniture should be designed so that the user does not have to bend or stretch unnecessarily. Desks and tables should be at the correct height for comfortable working.

Ergonomics also extends to the type of lighting in the office. Work areas must be well lit, but arranged so that glare is minimised. Adjustable lighting is extremely useful in the office and should be arranged so that close work can be carried out with the minimum of eye strain.

Keyboards should be designed so as to avoid repetitive strain injury (RSI). If you have a standard keyboard then there are wrist supports available which will help minimise the risk of RSI.

When planning the layout of your office, bear in mind how much space you have and whether you will need to use the room for any other purpose. For example, if you have to use the office as a dining room on family occasions, then you must find furniture that can easily be moved. Remember to take into account the location of electrical power points, radiators, window and doors. You may find that you will need to have extra power points installed or existing ones moved in order to accommodate all your equipment.

Furniture

As mentioned above, the furniture should be at a correct height for working, without the user having to bend or stretch unnecessarily. The desk or table should be of a size large enough to enable the user to work comfortably and to accommodate and support the equipment, such as the fax machine, telephone, computer, printer etc.

The chair that you use is also very important. It should be adjustable in height and tilt. It must also be stable. Do not be tempted to use a kitchen or dining room chair in your home office. This is particularly important if you plan to spend long periods of time working. Make sure that the chair is comfortable and supports your back properly before you purchase. Casters to avoid over-stretching are useful, as is a swivel action, which will allow easy movement. Check that it can be adjusted to the correct height for you. Many office supply shops sell a range of reasonably priced chairs that look good and will cover all these requirements.

As this is also your home, it is important that you have enough storage units. Make

Task1 Page No 8 Sharon Spencer

Exercise 2.1 continued

sure that at the end of each day you can put away all your papers so that the office becomes part of the home again. There is a wide variety of storage equipment on the market today, with such a range of styles that you are sure to find something that fits in with your home decoration and existing furniture.

Flooring

As the office will be a part of your home, you may wish to keep it carpeted. However, bear in mind that carpets should be anti-static if you have computers and other electrical equipment in the room. A plain wooden floor looks very stylish and is more practical in the office.

Computers

If you are working from home using a computer, you must bear in mind the Display Screen Equipment Regulations of 1992. There is less distraction at home, particularly if you are alone in the house during the day. This means than you may be spending a much longer period of time looking at the computer screen that you would if you were at the office.

Try to incorporate rest breaks at regular intervals. Just going to make a cup of tea will give you a break from looking at the computer screen. Occasionally stop and carry out another work activity such as making a telephone call, or reading through your papers.

The position of your computer is important. Try to ensure that you minimise glare on the computer screen and that the work area is well lit. Do not position the computer near to radiators or windows.

The display screen or monitor of your computer should be clear and without glare. You should be able to adjust the contrast and brightness of the display.

Remember to arrange regular eye checks and update your glasses prescription whenever necessary.

Data Protection Act

If you are working from home then you should be aware that the Data Protection Act of 1984 applies to you. This Act protects the use of data which is held on computer. It does not apply to paper records.

Basically, personal data must be obtained and processed lawfully and held only for specified and lawful purposes. It must not be kept for longer than is necessary. The storage of information must not allow unauthorised access, loss or destruction.

You should check that your work does not require you to register under the Data Protection Act, you can ask your local business centre or Citizen's Advice Bureau.

Task1 Page No 9 Sharon Spencer

Exercise 2.2

Banking Today

Banking has changed a great deal over the past fifty years. In those days only the wealthy had bank accounts. Most people were paid weekly in cash and had no need of the financial services offered by modern-day banks. Women were not encouraged to have their own bank accounts and even in the 1960s, single women had to ask a male relative to guarantee her financial affairs before being allowed to open an account.

These days most people have a bank account into which their salary is paid. Even Saturday job wages are paid direct into a bank account. Banks are targeting young children to open accounts that change to meet their needs as they grow older.
The range of services banks offer today is diverse, from share dealing to arranging travel insurance.

Current Accounts

Customers who keep their current accounts in credit do not have to pay bank charges. A cheque guarantee card that also acts as a cashpoint card is generally provided after an initial period. This will guarantee to pay the recipient of the cheque even if sufficient funds are not in the customer's account. Cheque guarantee cards usually cover sums between fifty and one hundred pounds per cheque.

Cheque guarantee cards may also be used as a form of debit card. This works by swiping the card through a machine and electronically transferring the sum from one account to another. The amount transferred can be as much as required, up to the amount of money held in the current account.

Salaries are generally paid into a current account. Standing orders and direct debits can be arranged so that mortgages and household bills can be paid direct from the current account. This means that bills are paid on time with little inconvenience.

Deposit Accounts

These generally take the form of savings accounts and attract high rates of interest.

Unlike current accounts, access to your money may not be instant, depending on the conditions of the account. Interest is paid on a regular basis and it may be possible to have this monthly, giving a regular income.

If you are a tax payer, you may have to deduct tax from the interest you are paid.

Travel Services

Banks now offer a range of travel services for their customers, from travel insurance to buying and selling foreign currency. Travel insurance rates are generally competi-

tive and can cover all your arrangements, cancellation, health and personal belongings.

Buying and selling foreign currency could not be easier, and most can be purchased without notice. However, if you are going to an exotic location, check that your bank will be able to supply the currency without notice.

Pension Plans

It is never too early to start planning for your retirement. On average, you will need a pension of at least half your present salary in order to maintain a reasonable standard of living.

There are at present tax benefits for monies that are paid into pension plans. Most banks have pensions advisers who

Exercise 2.2 continued

specialise in assisting customers plan for their retirement.

Mortgages

There are many different types of mortgage available today and the choice can be very confusing. Repayment mortgages are now growing in popularity after being unfashionable for a number of years. These allow the repayment of the loan and interest within an agreed time. You will require a life assurance policy that covers the sum of the loan so that the mortgage can be repaid in the event of your death.

Endowment mortgages cover the interest payable at the end of the agreed length of the mortgage. This has two purposes; to pay off the capital sum at the end of the mortgage and to provide life assurance.

PEP mortgages work in the same way as an endowment mortgage, but in this instance, monies are held in a savings plan rather than an insurance policy. Pension mortgages can also be arranged with the capital element being repaid from the lump sum available upon maturity of the pension.

A range of different interest rates will also be available. You may choose from variable, capped or fixed. Variable rates alter in line with the banks base rate. When economic conditions fluctuate, so do the mortgage interest rates.

Capped rates work on a system whereby the maximum interest rate is fixed, but should the variable rate drop below the capped rate, then this will also fall.

Fixed rates will last for an agreed period of time, regardless of the performance of the variable rate. This often gives the borrower peace of mind, but if interest rates fall below the fixed rate, there is little customers can do to alter this situation.

Share Dealing

Most major branches of banks offer a share dealing and portfolio administration service. You may arrange just the buying and selling of shares through the bank, or you may ask the bank to advise you on the best deals on the market.

Statements will be sent on a regular basis so that you can assess the performance of your investments. Commission is generally payable on the deals that you make.

Telephone Banking

Many banks now offer a 24-hour, 7-days a-week banking service. Just make a simple telephone call and you can set up and alter direct debits, transfer cash from one account to another and even arrange a loan or overdraft.

Many banks now advertise their services on the Internet. Will this be the main method of financial transactions in the not too distant future?

Exercise 2.3

Page No 3

Auctions

Going to an auction is an interesting experience. It can be great fun to pick out an item you take a liking to and then bid against others in order to secure your purchase.

It is possible to pick up some incredible bargains at an auction, especially if you are looking to furnish a new home. Collectors of unusual and specific items such as 1950s memorabilia or clockwork toys may also strike lucky at an auction.

There is a temptation however to buy items that you cannot afford, or do not really want because of the excitement of bidding. It would be as well to follow the few simple guidelines given below.

To find our where your nearest auction rooms are, look in your local newspaper or telephone directory. General sales are usually held on a regular basis, perhaps monthly. Notice will normally be published in the local newspaper, giving details of the prior viewing arrangements. General household sales are the most common and sell everything from furniture to bric a brac.

Property auctions are generally held every few months and can cover quite a large area. These are often advertised by local estate agents. If you are interested in attending these, you should register your interest with estate agents in your areas.

Specialist sales are held less frequently and take place in major towns and cities. These cover fine art, jewellery, antiques and collectors' items.

Catalogues

Each auction will have a catalogue listing all the items, or lots as they are known, to be auctioned. A short description of each item will be listed, together with the lot number and any reserve price. A reserve price is the minimum price at which an item is to be sold. If an item does not reach its reserve price in the sale, then it will normally be withdrawn.

Most auction rooms make a small charge for the catalogue. However, you may find that the specialist auctions charge as much as £15 - £20 for a full colour catalogue.

It is useful to buy a catalogue before the day of the sale. You can then check the items carefully making a note of the lot number and any reserve price. It is usually possible to purchase catalogues by post if it is not convenient for you to collect one in person.

Viewing

It is usually possible to view the lots of sale a few days before the auction is due to be held. It is strongly recommended that you do this as

once you have made a successful bid, the transaction is legally binding. You may not retract your offer to buy once the auctioneer accepts your bid.

When you view the various lots make a note of the numbers of any in which you are interested. Decide on a maximum price that you are willing to pay for the item. it may be worthwhile researching current prices elsewhere so that you do not end up paying more than the item is actually worth. Check the item extremely carefully for wear and tear or damage.

If possible, view the items again on the day of the sale to check that you are still willing to purchase the goods.

Buying Property

If you wish to purchase a property through auction, it is particularly important that you

Sharon Spencer Task3

Exercise 2.3 continued

Page No 4

inspect it thoroughly before attending the sale. If you are successful in bidding for a property you must pay a ten per cent deposit immediately. As with other purchases, the contract made at the auction is legally binding and you are obliged to complete the purchase, even if you later find the property has structural problems.

If you require a mortgage to complete the property purchase, this must be arranged before you bid. Talk to your bank or building society manager immediately you find a property in which you are interested. They will arrange for the necessary structural survey to take place. You will have to pay for these in advance and if you are unsuccessful in your bid, you will lose this money.

A solicitor will also need to be appointed before the day of the sale to arrange the necessary land searches and registrations. These must also be completed before the day of the sale.

Quite often, your bank or building society manager will want to accompany you to the sale to ensure that you do not exceed your budget.

Commission

If you are successful in your bid you will have to pay a deposit before you leave the auction rooms. You will also have to pay a sales commission to the auction rooms which is based on a percentage of the purchase price. Ensure you find out the rate charged and add this to your maximum price before you start to bid.

Sale Day

On the day of the sale, try to arrive a little early. Have another look at the items you wish to purchase and check the lot numbers again.

When the bidding commences, ensure that you can hear the auctioneer clearly. Before you enter the bidding, check that you are competing for the correct article. This sounds obvious, but you may find you end up purchasing a completely unsuitable item because you confused the catalogue numbers. Ensure that you do not get carried away with the excitement of the sale and bid in excess of your maximum price.

If you cannot attend the sale in person, you will be able to leave a bid with the auction rooms who will ensure that this is included at the appropriate time. You may also, in some specialist sales, make telephone bids. If you are successful you will be contacted by telephone after the sale has finished.

As already mentioned, if you are successful in your bidding, you will have to pay a deposit before you leave the auction rooms. You will also have to arrange for the balance of the purchase price to be paid, and the items to be collected. This is usually to be within two or three days. Items that are not collected within this time may be subject to storage fees.

Why not try visiting an auction to see for yourself how exciting it can be to bid against others in order to make a purchase?

Sharon Spencer Task3

Exercise 2.4

Shopping

Loyalty Shopping

Super Supermarkets have introduced a loyalty shopper scheme. You will be receiving full details in the post within the next few weeks. Basically, the system works like this: for every pound you spend you will be awarded a bonus point. Collect five hundred bonus points and you will receive a £5 voucher, which can be exchanged either as money-off vouchers for your shopping or a gift from our exclusive catalogue.

How can I register?

Registering in our loyalty shopping scheme is easy. Just complete and return the form which will be posted to your home, or fill in an application form at any one of our stores. You will then be issued with a loyalty card printed with your personal number.

Ensure you register by the end of next month in order to receive the benefits of this new scheme immediately.

Collecting Bonus Points

Collecting bonus points could not be easier. When you pay for your goods, give your loyalty card to the assistant. The amount you spend will be recorded and for every pound you spend a point will be awarded. The total number of points awarded will be clearly shown on your till receipt.

A number of goods will be awarded extra bonus points each week. Purchase these and you will soon build up the amount of vouchers you can claim.

Claiming Bonus Points

If you wish to claim your bonus points in money-off vouchers, this can be done at the same time as you pay for your goods. Just inform the assistant that you wish to claim your bonus points and vouchers will be given to the value of your points. You can then use these against your shopping bill. Remember, points can be claimed in blocks of 500. For each 500 bonus points you claim, you will receive a voucher to the value of £5.

Gift Catalogue

If you would rather, you may choose a gift from our exciting new catalogue. This will be sent to you upon registration. Choose from a wide selection of goods including the following:

Household goods – this section includes kitchen appliances such as ice-cream makers, toasters, kettles, tableware and table linen. There is something to suit all tastes and gifts start from as little as 2500 bonus points.

Leisure items – choose from sportswear and equipment, books, videos and CDs. All the latest in sports equipment will be found in the catalogue. If you decide to exchange your vouchers for videos or CDs, then ask for our supplementary list. An up to date list will be sent to you immediately.

You can even save your vouchers to exchange for a colour television set, video player or CD system. Gifts start from 3000 bonus points.

Garden items – If you are a keen gardener you will appreciate the range of gifts on offer. From garden seats to stylish plant holders there is something for everyone. We will even supply the plants from our seasonal plant list. Gifts start from 1500 points.

Sharon Spencer Page No 6

Exercise 2.4 continued

Shopping

Holidays – If you would like a break away from home, we can help. You can use your vouchers against a number of travel agents' brochures to give discounts. The usual £5 per 500 points applies. We are also featuring short breaks in the catalogue, which you may book direct with us. A romantic weekend in Paris or 3-day breaks in Dublin are included in these offers.

If you prefer to make your own holiday arrangements, let us help. Bonus points can be exchanged for part payment on ferry or air tickets. The amount of discount available depends upon the date of travel. However a £35 voucher towards a ferry trip to France is yours for just 3500 points.

Gifts for your friends and family – a selection of fresh flowers, chocolates and fine wines can be sent direct to your friends and family. Make someone's day special with a bouquet or hamper. Delivery is included and gifts start from 2000 points.

Helping Others

Super Supermarkets have arranged for national charities to benefit from our bonus points scheme. If you wish, you may donate your bonus points to any one of a number of national charities. Each voucher that is donated will be worth £6 to the charity – an extra £1 from Super Supermarkets.

At present, we are compiling a list of charities that will be involved with the scheme. Full details will be issued to customers within the next few months.

Educational Programme

Our educational programme helps many hundreds of schools in this country. We give over £250,000 every year towards educational projects. Now you can join us in helping schools and colleges. Just nominate the school(s) you would like to help and we will give them 2 bonus points for each £1 you spend.

These bonus points can be exchanged for any of the extensive range of school equipment featured in our special educational catalogue. Over 8,500 schools have received free equipment in the past few years. Make sure your child's school is included in this great give-away. A special education pack is available from our head office.

Special Offers

From time to time, Super Supermarkets will be offering extra points and gifts. Make sure you check the in-store displays to find out the latest offers. If you prefer, we can send details of our special promotions to you. Please tick the relevant box on the application form to make sure you do not miss out.

Sharon Spencer Page No 7

Exercise 3.1

Working from Home

Office Design

Many people are now turning a spare room in their home into an office. This may be because they like to keep their household accounts and business documents filed and labelled neatly in a room that also houses the family computer. It may be that a member of the family has joined the growing number of people who regularly work from home.

Whatever the reason, the office should be properly equipped and set out. If a person is planning to spend long hours in their home office then it should be subject to the same rules of planning and safety as purpose-built or commercial offices.

Ergonomics

The ergonomics of the working environment is one of the most important considerations when planning an office layout. This looks at the physical requirements of the worker – for example the way in which chairs, tables and desks are designed to take into account the requirements of the user. It also covers the way in which the office is set out.

Furniture should be designed so that the user does not have to bend or stretch unnecessarily. Desks and tables should be at the correct height for comfortable working.

Ergonomics also extends to the type of lighting in the office. Work areas must be well lit, but arranged so that glare is minimised. Adjustable lighting is extremely useful in the office and should be arranged so that close work can be carried out with the minimum of eye strain.

Keyboards should be designed so as to avoid repetitive strain injury (RSI). If you have a standard keyboard then there are wrist supports available which will help minimise the risk of RSI.

When planning the layout of your office, bear in mind how much space you have and whether you will need to use the room for any other purpose. For example, if you have to use the office as a dining room on family occasions, then you must find furniture that can easily be moved. Remember to take into account the location of electrical power points, radiators, window and doors. You may find that you will need to have extra power points installed or existing ones moved in order to accommodate all your equipment.

Furniture

As mentioned above, the furniture should be at a correct height for working, without the user having to bend or stretch unnecessarily. The desk or table should be of a size large enough to enable the user to work comfortably and to accommodate and support the equipment, such as the fax machine, telephone, computer, printer etc.

The chair that you use is also very important. It should be adjustable in height and tilt. It must also be stable. Do not be tempted to use a kitchen or dining room chair in your home office. This is particularly important if you plan to spend long periods of time working. Make sure that the chair is comfortable and supports your back properly before you purchase. Casters to avoid over-stretching are useful, as is a swivel action, which will allow easy movement. Check that it can be adjusted to the correct height for you. Many office supply shops sell a range of reasonably priced chairs that look good and will cover all these requirements.

As this is also your home, it is important that you have enough storage units. Make sure that at the end of each day you can put away all your papers so that the office becomes part of the home again. There is a wide variety of storage equipment on the market today, with such a range of styles that you are sure to find something that fits in with your home decoration and existing furniture.

Task1 Page No 8 Sharon Spencer

Exercise 3.1 continued

Working from Home

Flooring

As the office will be a part of your home, you may wish to keep it carpeted. However, bear in mind that carpets should be anti-static if you have computers and other electrical equipment in the room. A plain wooden floor looks very stylish and is more practical in the office.

Computers

If you are working from home using a computer, you must bear in mind the Display Screen Equipment Regulations of 1992. There is less distraction at home, particularly if you are alone in the house during the day. This means that you may be spending a much longer period of time looking at the computer screen and than you would if you were at the office.

Try to incorporate rest breaks at regular intervals. Just going to make a cup of tea will give you a break from looking at the computer screen. Occasionally stop and carry out another work activity such as making a telephone call, or reading through your papers.

The position of your computer is important. Try to ensure that you minimise glare on the computer screen that the work area is well lit. Do not position the computer near to radiators or windows.

The display screen or monitor of your computer should be clear and without glare. You should be able to adjust the contrast and brightness of the display.

Remember to arrange regular eye checks and update your glasses prescription whenever necessary.

Data Protection Act

If you are working from home then you should be aware that the Data Protection Act of 1984 applies to you. This Act protects the use of data which is held on computer. It does not apply to paper records.

Basically, personal data must be obtained and processed lawfully and held only for specified and lawful purposes. It must not be kept for longer than is necessary. The storage of information must not allow unauthorised access, loss or destruction.

You should check that your work does not require you to register under the Data Protection Act, you can ask your local business centre or Citizen's Advice Bureau.

Task1 Page No 9 Sharon Spencer

Exercise 3.2

Banking Today

Banking has changed a great deal over the past fifty years. In those days only the wealthy had bank accounts. Most people were paid weekly in cash and had no need of the financial services offered by modern-day banks. Women were not encouraged to have their own bank accounts and even in the 1960s, single women had to ask a male relative to guarantee her financial affairs before being allowed to open an account.

These days most people have a bank account into which their salary is paid. Even Saturday job wages are paid direct into a bank account. Banks are targeting young children to open accounts that change to meet their needs as they grow older.
The range of services banks offer today is diverse, from share dealing to arranging travel insurance.

Current Accounts

Customers who keep their current accounts in credit do not have to pay bank charges. A cheque guarantee card that also acts as a cashpoint card is generally provided after an initial period. This will guarantee to pay the recipient of the cheque even if sufficient funds are not in the customer's account. Cheque guarantee cards usually cover sums between fifty and one hundred pounds per cheque.

Cheque guarantee cards may also be used as a form of debit card. This works by swiping the card through a machine and electronically transferring the sum from one account to another. The amount transferred can be as much as required, up to the amount of money held in the current account.

Salaries are generally paid into a current account. Standing orders and direct debits can be arranged so that mortgages and household bills can be paid direct from the current account. This means that bills are paid on time with little inconvenience.

Deposit Accounts

These generally take the form of savings accounts and attract high rates of interest. Unlike current accounts, access to your money may not be instant, depending on the conditions of the account. Interest is paid on a regular basis and it may be possible to have this monthly, giving a regular income.

If you are a tax payer, you may have to deduct tax from the interest you are paid.

Travel Services

Banks now offer a range of travel services for their customers, from travel insurance to buying and selling foreign currency. Travel insurance rates are generally competi-

tive and can cover all your arrangements, cancellation, health and personal belongings.

Buying and selling foreign currency could not be easier, and most can be purchased without notice. However, if you are going to an exotic location, check that your bank will be able to supply the currency without notice.

Pension Plans

It is never too early to start planning for your retirement. On average, you will need a pension of at least half your present salary in order to maintain a reasonable standard of living.

There are at present tax benefits for monies that are paid into pension plans. Most banks have pensions advisers who

Exercise 3.2 continued

specialise in assisting customers plan for their retirement.

Mortgages

There are many different types of mortgage available today and the choice can be very confusing. Repayment mortgages are now growing in popularity after being unfashionable for a number of years. These allow the repayment of the loan and interest within an agreed time. You will require a life assurance policy that covers the sum of the loan so that the mortgage can be repaid in the event of your death.

Endowment mortgages cover the interest payable at the end of the agreed length of the mortgage. This has two purposes; to pay off the capital sum at the end of the mortgage and to provide life assurance.

PEP mortgages work in the same way as an endowment mortgage, but in this instance, monies are held in a savings plan rather than an insurance policy. Pension mortgages can also be arranged with the capital element being repaid from the lump sum available upon maturity of the pension.

A range of different interest rates will also be available. You may choose from variable, capped or fixed. Variable rates alter in line with the banks base rate. When economic conditions fluctuate, so do the mortgage interest rates.

Capped rates work on a system whereby the maximum interest rate is fixed, but should the variable rate drop below the capped rate, then this will also fall.

Fixed rates will last for an agreed period of time, regardless of the performance of the variable rate. This often gives the borrower peace of mind, but if interest rates fall below the fixed rate, there is little customers can do to alter this situation.

Share Dealing

Most major branches of banks offer a share dealing and portfolio administration service. You may arrange just the buying and selling of shares through the bank, or you may ask the bank to advise you on the best deals on the market.

Statements will be sent on a regular basis so that you can assess the performance of your investments. Commission is generally payable on the deals that you make.

Telephone Banking

Many banks now offer a 24-hour, 7-days a-week banking service. Just make a simple telephone call and you can set up and alter direct debits, transfer cash from one account to another and even arrange a loan or overdraft.

Many banks now advertise their services on the Internet. Will this be the main method of financial transactions in the not too distant future?

Exercise 3.3

Page No 3

Auctions

Going to an auction is an interesting experience. It can be great fun to pick out an item you take a liking to and then bid against others in order to secure your purchase.

It is possible to pick up some incredible bargains at an auction, especially if you are looking to furnish a new home. Collectors of unusual and specific items such as 1950s memorabilia or clockwork toys may also strike lucky at an auction.

There is a temptation however to buy items that you cannot afford, or do not really want because of the excitement of bidding. It would be as well to follow the few simple guidelines given below.

To find our where your nearest auction rooms are, look in your local newspaper or telephone directory. General sales are usually held on a regular basis, perhaps monthly. Notice will normally be published in the local newspaper, giving details of the prior viewing arrangements. General household sales are the most common and sell everything from furniture to bric a brac.

Property auctions are generally held every few months and can cover quite a large area. These are often advertised by local estate agents. If you are interested in attending these, you should register your interest with estate agents in your areas.

Specialist sales are held less frequently and take place in major towns and cities. These cover fine art, jewellery, antiques and collectors' items.

Catalogues

Each auction will have a catalogue listing all the items, or lots as they are known, to be auctioned. A short description of each item will be listed, together with the lot number and any reserve price. A reserve price is the minimum price at which an item is to be sold. If an item does not reach its reserve price in the sale, then it will normally be withdrawn.

Most auction rooms make a small charge for the catalogue. However, you may find that the specialist auctions charge as much as £15 - £20 for a full colour catalogue.

It is useful to buy a catalogue before the day of the sale. You can then check the items carefully making a note of the lot number and any reserve price. It is usually possible to purchase catalogues by post if it is not convenient for you to collect one in person.

Viewing

It is usually possible to view the lots of sale a few days before the auction is due to be held. It is strongly

Sharon Spencer

Task3

Exercise 3.3 continued

Page No 4

recommended that you do this as once you have made a successful bid, the transaction is legally binding. You may not retract your offer to buy once the auctioneer accepts your bid.

When you view the various lots make a note of the numbers of any in which you are interested. Decide on a maximum price that you are willing to pay for the item. it may be worthwhile researching current prices elsewhere so that you do not end up paying more than the item is actually worth. Check the item extremely carefully for wear and tear or damage.

If possible, view the items again on the day of the sale to check that you are still willing to purchase the goods.

Buying Property

If you wish to purchase a property through auction, it is particularly important that you inspect it thoroughly before attending the sale. If you are successful in bidding for a property you must pay a ten per cent deposit immediately. As with other purchases, the contract made at the auction is legally binding and you are obliged to complete the purchase, even if you later find the property has structural problems.

If you require a mortgage to complete the property purchase, this must be arranged before you bid. Talk to your bank or building society manager immediately you find a property in which you are interested. They will arrange for the necessary structural survey to take place. You will have to pay for these in advance and if you are unsuccessful in your bid, you will lose this money.

A solicitor will also need to be appointed before the day of the sale to arrange the necessary land searches and registrations. These must also be completed before the day of the sale.

Quite often, your bank or building society manager will want to accompany you to the sale to ensure that you do not exceed your budget.

Commission

If you are successful in your bid you will have to pay a deposit before you leave the auction rooms. You will also have to pay a sales commission to the auction rooms which is based on a percentage of the purchase price. Ensure you find out the rate charged and add this to your maximum price before you start to bid.

Sale Day

On the day of the sale, try to arrive a little early. Have another look at the items you wish to purchase and check the lot numbers again.

When the bidding commences, ensure that you can hear the auctioneer clearly. Before you enter the bidding, check that you are competing for the correct article. This sounds obvious, but you may find you end up purchasing a completely unsuitable item because you confused the catalogue numbers. Ensure that you do not get carried away with the excitement of the sale and bid in excess of your maximum price.

If you cannot attend the sale in person, you will be able to leave a bid with the auction rooms who will ensure that this is included at the appropriate time. You may also, in some specialist sales, make telephone bids. If you are successful you will be contacted by telephone after the sale has finished.

As already mentioned, if you are successful in your bidding, you will have to pay a deposit before you leave the auction rooms. You will also have to arrange for the balance of the purchase price to be paid, and the items to be collected. This is usually to be within two or three days. Items that are not collected within this time may be subject to storage fees.

Why not try visiting an auction to see for yourself how exciting it can be to bid against others in order to make a purchase?

Sharon Spencer

Task3

Exercise 3.4

Loyalty Shopping

Super Supermarkets have introduced a loyalty shopper scheme. You will be receiving full details in the post within the next few weeks. Basically, the system works like this: for every pound you spend you will be awarded a bonus point. Collect 500 bonus points and you will receive a £5 voucher, which can be exchanged either as money off vouchers for your shopping or a gift from our exclusive catalogue.

How can I register?

Registering in our loyalty shopping scheme is easy. Just complete and return the form which will be posted to your home, or fill in an application form at any one of our stores. You will then be issued with a loyalty card printed with your personal number.

Ensure you register by the end of next month in order to receive the benefits of this new scheme immediately.

Collecting Bonus Points

Collecting bonus points could not be easier. When you pay for your goods, give your loyalty card to the assistant. The amount you spend will be recorded and for every pound you spend a point will be awarded. The total number of points awarded will be clearly shown on your till receipt.

A number of goods will be awarded extra bonus points each week. Purchase these and you will soon build up the amount of vouchers you can claim.

Claiming Bonus Points

If you wish to claim your bonus points in money-off vouchers, this can be done at the same time as you pay for your goods. Just inform the assistant that you wish to claim your bonus points and vouchers will be given to the value of your points. You can then use these against your shopping bill. Remember, points can be claimed in blocks of 500. For each 500 bonus points you claim, you will receive a voucher to the value of £5.

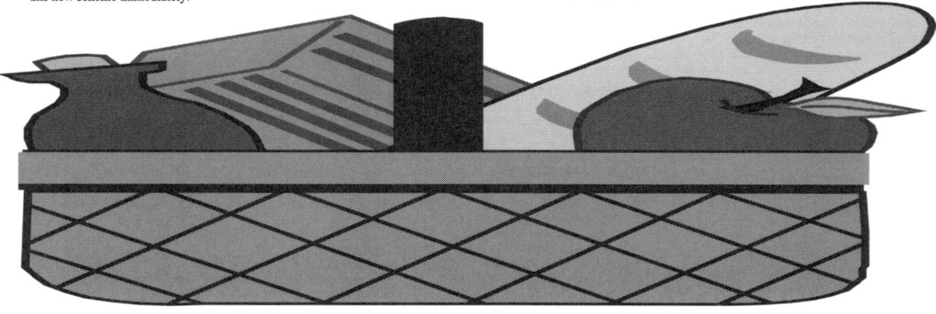

Exercise 3.4 continued

Gift Catalogue

If you would rather, you may choose a gift from our exciting new catalogue. This will be sent to you upon registration. Choose from a wide selection of goods including the following:

Household goods – this section includes kitchen appliances such as ice-cream makers, toasters, kettles, tableware and table linen. There is something to suit all tastes and gifts start from as little as 2500 bonus points.

Leisure items – choose from sportswear and equipment, books, videos and CDs. All the latest in sports equipment will be found in the catalogue. If you decide to exchange your vouchers for videos or CDs, then ask for our supplementary list. An up to date list will be sent to you immediately.

You can even save your vouchers to exchange for a colour television set, video player or CD system. Gifts start from 3000 bonus points.

Garden items – If you are a keen gardener you will appreciate the range of gifts on offer. From garden seats to stylish plant holders there is something for everyone. We will even supply the plants from our seasonal plant list. Gifts start from 1500 points.

Holidays – If you would like a break away from home, we can help. You can use your vouchers against a number of travel agents' brochures to give discounts. The usual £5 per 500 points applies. We are also featuring short breaks in the catalogue, which you may book direct with us. A romantic weekend in Paris or 3-day breaks in Dublin are included in these offers.

If you prefer to make your own holiday arrangements, let us help. Bonus points can be exchanged for part payment on ferry or air tickets. The amount of discount available depends upon the date of travel. However a £35 voucher towards a ferry trip to France is yours for just 3500 points.

Gifts for your friends and family – a selection of fresh flowers, chocolates and fine wines can be sent direct to your friends and family. Make someone's day special with a bouquet or hamper. Delivery is included and gifts start from 2000 points.

Helping Others

Super Supermarkets have arranged for national charities to benefit from our bonus points scheme. If you wish, you may donate your bonus points to any one of a number of national charities. Each voucher that is donated will be worth £6

to the charity – an extra £1 from Super Supermarkets.

At present, we are compiling a list of charities that will be involved with the scheme. Full details will be issued to customers within the next few months.

Educational Programme

Our educational programme helps many hundreds of schools in this country. We give over £250,000 every year towards educational projects. Now you can join us in helping schools and colleges. Just nominate the school(s) you would like to help and we will give them 2 bonus points for each £1 you spend.

These bonus points can be exchanged for any of the extensive range of school equipment featured in our special educational catalogue. Over 8,500 schools have received free equipment in the past few years. Make sure your child's school is included in this great give-away. A special education pack is available from our head office.

Special Offers

From time to time, Super Supermarkets will be offering extra points and gifts. Make sure you check the in-store displays to find out the latest offers. If you prefer, we can send details of our special promotions to you. Please tick the relevant box on the application form to make sure you do not miss out.

Exercise 5.1

COCKTAILS

History

Cocktails are becoming more popular after a few years of taking second place to foriegn beers. However, cocktails are not modern drinks, they have been in and out of fashion since 1806.

America is the traditional home of the cocktail, indeed **London** did not have a cocktail bar until 1910.

The cocktail was most popular during Prohibition when ingredients were blended to disguise the taste of alcohol. In the late 1930s cocktails' popularity waned and in Britain sherry parties became fashionable.

The revival of cocktail drinking began in the 1960s when people began to travel abroad for their holidays. People began to expeirence the food and drink of foreign countries and tried to re-create these new flavours at home.

These days you can buy ready-made cocktails in supermarkets and off-licences. However it is much more fun to make your own.

Equipment

There are a few pieces of equipment that you will need in order to make perfect cocktails. First of all you will need a shaker. The ingrediants and ice, if required, are placed in the shaker and then blended. The contents are then strained directly into the glass.

This leads us to the second piece of required equipment – a strainer. These can be purchased at good kitchenware stores.

If this sounds complicated then there are three-part shakers that include a strainer on the market. These are much easier to use.

Another way of mixing cocktails is to stir them. For this you will need a mixing jug. Almost any jug will do, but it should have a small lip. A long bar spoon is another piece of esential equippment. This can also act as a measuring spoon as well as for stirring.

In order to add the essential 'dash' of bitters, you may wish to purchase special bottles for this purpose. These come with a nozzle that allows only a 'dash' to pour through at a time.

Other equipment that may be useful includes:

- an ice bucket – these come in a variety of shapes and sizes, some being insulated. A plain bucket looks the most stylish
- a juice extracter – these are used for squeezing citrus fruit when required. Fresh fruit juice should always be used. A variety of electrical juice extractors are now widely available
- a sharp fruit knife for cutting small pieces of fruit to garnishe your drinks.

Sharon Spencer Exercise 6

Exercise 5.2

Fashion in the 1920s and 1930s

The 1920s

This was the period of the *'vamp'*, large dark eyes rimmed with kohl; turbans that came down to the eyebrows and eyelashes emphasised with mascara.

Hair took second place during this period and many women had their hair cut in a short bob.

To complement this new look, clothes were designed to flow. Hems became shorter, waists lower and sleeves were long. In fact, the garments had a very soft, unstructured shape that was easy to wear. For the first time women were free of heavy, restrictive garments such as corsets, bodices or petticoats.

With the rise in popularity of the cocktail, so dresses were designed for the cocktail hour. These tended to be a cross between a day dress and evening gown. The cut of the day dress combined with the fabric of an evening gown was not always successfull.

In 1924, the spring Paris collections showed a new and defined fashion. Hemlines just reached the calf and waistlines were moved to the hips. The fashionable figure became very boyish. Many women embraced this style and its success was great.

The most popular colours were

- pink
- light brown
- white
- soft blue
- green

As the 20s moved on, so did the fashion. The bias-cut became popular. This was used in every female garment from underwear to evening gowns. A very fashionible hemline for evening gowns was ankle length at the back, rising to the knee length at the front. This was a very elegant look.

1930s

At last, the outline became more feminine – a gently rounded bust and slight curve at the waist became noticeible. Hair was slightly longer and was known as a 'shingle'.

Skirts became longer and reached mid-calf. Often the hem was longer at the back. Favourite fabrics for evening wear were chiffon, silk and velvet, often with capes of the same fabric. The most popular colours were pale blues, pinks and cream. Matching gloves were an important accessory for both day and evening wear.

Cotton became a popular fabric, mostly due to Chanel who showed a cotton collection in London. Organdie and pique became fashionable alternatives to satin and silk.

During the 1930s, trousers became aceptable as beach wear for women. This trend started with the appearence of pyjama-styled trousers and were often worn as informal evening wear made from crepe de Chine or shantung. However, these soon lost popularity but the beach wear remained.

By the end of the decade fashion had changed again. The female silouette defined with small waists and padded shoulders was now the style.

Sharon Spencer

Exercise 5.4

GREAT WRITERS

William Shakespeare

It is assumed that William Shakespeare was born on April 23rd 1564 to a well-known Stratford family. His father, John Shakespeare was a glover and commodities dealer in leather and wool. John was made an alderman in 1565 and elected bailiff three years later. His wife, Mary was the daughter of a rich farmer Robert Arden. William was the eldest son and third of eight children.

He probably attended a grammar school from the age of seven and upon leaving he may have been apprenticed in his father's shop.

We know that he married **Anne Hathaway**, who was also the daughter of a wealthy farmer, when he was eighteen, in 1582. William and Anne had three children, Susanna and twins, Hamnet and Judith.

Shakespeare wrote at least thirty eight plays as well as a number of poems and sonnets. Among the most well known are , Othello, Hamlet, Romeo and Juliet, and Macbeth . He died on April 23rd 1616, aged exactly fifty-two years old and was buried in the chancel of the Collegiate Church of the Holy Trinity in Stratford upon Avon.

Jane Austen

Jane Austen was born on 16th December 1775 to the Reverend George Austen and his wife Cassandra Austen. She was the seventh of eight children and was particularly close to her sister Cassandra who was three years older than herself. She never married, but was very fond of her many nephews and nieces. The family lived in Steventon in Hampshire, where her father was the rector. Upon his retirement in 1801, the family moved to Bath where they lived until her father died. After George Austen's death, Jane and her mother went to live in Southampton for a short while before moving to a cottage near Alton.

Jane started writing when she was very young although Sense and Sensibility, her first published work, was published when she was 36, in 1811. Her other novels include

- Pride and Prejudice,
- N o r t h a n g e r Abbey and
- Mansfield Park.

Several films and television adaptations have been made of her novels.

Jane died in 1817, aged forty-one and is buried in Winchester.

Sharon Spencer Centre No

Exercise 5.3

Interior Design

Feng Shui

Feng Shui (pronounced Feng sh-way), is fast becoming the latest trend in interior design. It is the ancient Chinese art of placing buildings and objects so that they attract maximum posative energy as well as minimising negative energey.

Although this is an ancient Chinese art it is now **outlawed** in China. However, it has great respect in other Far Eastern countries, and Eastern architecture students have to study it for a year as part of their courses.

This art is now becoming extremly popular in the Western world and in Britain a new magazine has been launched, that is devoted to the subject.

Feng Shui is also becoming widely used in offices and schools as well as in the home.

How does it work?

Feng Shui is based on the premise that every building and individual room has within it a microcosm of human existance, with different areas representing different aspects of human life. These include career, relationships, family and health. An eight-sided grid, known as a bagua or pah kwa should be fitted over your building or room plan so that you can improve the energy flow.

For example, if you were experiencing difficulties with your career then you should look at the career areas of your home and perhaps re-arrange some of the furnature and fittings to improve the flow of the positive energy.

Serious students of Feng Shui take the art a step further when dealing with their clients. They will enquire into how long the client has been living in their home, and take account of the client's Chinese horoscope. The directional and geophysical influences will also be looked at. These include the position of the house in relation to buildings and roads, the effects of ley lines, pylons and transmitters.

Many consultants say there are a few rules that can be applied to the rooms in your home to increase positive energy. These include the following.

- *Clutter can block energy, so keep your rooms tidy*
- *Throw out items that are no longer relevant to your life. This symbolically makes room for new developments*
- *Moving water has a good influance in your wealth areas. Try placing a fish tank or indoor fountain in the wealth area of a room.*
- *Place plants around televisions and computers as they help to absorb the electromagnetic signals.*

Sharon Spencer

Exercise 6.1

COCKTAILS

History

Cocktails are becoming more popular after a few years of taking second place to foreign beers. However, cocktails are not modern drinks, they have been in and out of fashion since 1806.

America is the traditional home of the cocktail, indeed **London** did not have a cocktail bar until 1910.

The cocktail was most popular during Prohibition when ingredients were blended to disguise the taste of alcohol. In the late 1930s cocktails' popularity waned and in Britain sherry parties became fashionable.

The revival of cocktail drinking began in the 1960s when people began to travel abroad for their holidays. People began to experience the food and drink of foreign countries and tried to re-create these new flavours at home.

These days you can buy ready-made cocktails in supermarkets and off-licences. However it is much more fun to make your own.

Equipment

There are a few pieces of equipment that you will need in order to make perfect cocktails. First of all you will need a shaker. The ingredients and ice, if required, are placed in the shaker and then blended. The contents are then strained directly into the glass.

This leads us to the second piece of required equipment – a strainer. These can be purchased at good kitchenware stores.

If this sounds complicated then there are three part shakers that include a strainer on the market. These are much easier to use.

Another way of mixing cocktails is to stir them. For this you will need a mixing jug. Almost any jug will do, but it should have a small lip. A long bar spoon is another piece of essential equipment. This can also act as a measuring spoon as well as for stirring.

In order to add the essential 'dash' of bitters, you may wish to purchase special bottles for this purpose. These come with a nozzle that allows only a 'dash' to pour through at a time.

Other equipment that may be useful includes:

- an ice bucket – these come in a variety of shapes and sizes, some being insulated. A plain bucket looks the most stylish
- a juice extractor – these are used for squeezing citrus fruit when required. Fresh fruit juice should always be used. A variety of electrical juice extractors are now widely available
- a sharp fruit knife for cutting small pieces of fruit to garnish your drinks.

Sharon Spencer Exercise 6

Exercise 6.2

Fashion in the 1920s and 1930s

The 1920s

This was the period of the *'vamp'*, large dark eyes rimmed with kohl; turbans that came down to the eyebrows and eyelashes emphasised with mascara.

Hair took second place during this period and many women had their hair cut in a short bob. To complement this new look, clothes were designed to flow. Hems became shorter, waists lower and sleeves were long. In fact, the garments had a very soft, unstructured shape that was easy to wear. For the first time women were free of heavy, restrictive garments such as corsets, bodices or petticoats.

With the rise in popularity of the cocktail, so dresses were designed for the cocktail hour. These tended to be a cross between a day dress and evening gown. The cut of the day dress combined with the fabric of an evening gown was not always successful.

In 1924, the spring Paris collections showed a new and defined fashion. Hemlines just reached the calf and waistlines were moved to the hips. The fashionable figure became very boyish. Many women embraced this style and its success was great.

The most popular colours were

- pink
- light brown
- white
- soft blue
- green

As the 20s moved on, so did the fashion. The bias-cut became popular. This was used in every female garment from underwear to evening gowns. A very fashionable hemline for evening gowns was ankle length at the back, rising to the knee length at the front. This was a very elegant look.

1930s

At last, the outline became more feminine – a gently rounded bust and slight curve at the waist became noticeable. Hair was slightly longer and was known as a 'shingle'.

Skirts became longer and reached mid-calf. Often the hem was longer at the back. Favourite fabrics for evening wear were chiffon, silk and velvet, often with capes of the same fabric. The most popular colours were pale blues, pinks and cream. Matching gloves were an important accessory for both day and evening wear.

Cotton became a popular fabric, mostly due to Chanel who showed a cotton collection in London. Organdie and pique became fashionable alternatives to satin and silk.

During the 1930s, trousers became acceptable as beach wear for women. This trend started with the appearance of pyjama-styled trousers and were often worn as informal evening wear made from crepe de Chine or shantung. However, these soon lost popularity but the beach wear remained.

By the' end of the decade fashion had changed again. The female silhouette defined with small waists and padded shoulders was now the style.

Sharon Spencer

Exercise 6.3

Feng Shui

Feng Shui (pronounced Feng sh-way), is fast becoming the latest trend in interior design. It is the ancient Chinese art of placing buildings and objects so that they attract maximum posative energy as well as minimising negative energey.

Although this is an ancient Chinese art it is now **outlawed** in China. However, it has great respect in other Far Eastern countries, and Eastern architecture students have to study it for a year as part of their courses.

This art is now becoming extremly popular in the Western world and in Britain a new magazine has been launched, that is devoted to the subject.

Feng Shui is also becoming widely used in offices and schools as well as in the home.

How does it work?

Feng Shui is based on the premise that every building and individal room has within it a microcosm of human existance, with different areas representing different aspects of human life. These include career, relationships, family and health. An eight-sided grid, known as a bagua or pah kwa should be fitted over your building or room plan so that you can improve the energy flow.

For example, if you were experiencing difficulties with your career then you should look at the career areas of your home and perhaps re-arrange some of the furnature and fittings to improve the flow of the positive energy.

Serious students of Feng Shui take the art a step further when dealing with their clients. They will enquire into how long the client has been living in their home, and take account of the client's Chinese horoscope. The directional and geophysical influences will also be looked at. These include the position of the house in relation to buildings and roads, the effects of ley lines, pylons and transmitters.

Many consultants say there are a few rules that can be applied to the rooms in your home to increase positive energy. These include the following:

- *Clutter can block energy, so keep your rooms tidy*
- *Throw out items that are no longer relevant to your life. This symbolically makes room for new developments*
- *Moving water has a good influance in your wealth areas. Try placing a fish tank or indoor fountain in the wealth area of a room.*
- *Place plants around televisions and computers as they help to absorb the electromagnetic signals.*

Interior Design

Sharon Spencer

Exercise 6.4

GREAT WRITERS

William Shakespeare

It is assumed that William Shakespeare was born on April 23rd 1564 to a well-known Stratford family. His father, John Shakespeare was a glover and commodities dealer in leather and wool. John was made an alderman in 1565 and elected bailiff three years later. His wife, Mary was the daughter of a rich farmer Robert Arden. William was the eldest son and third of eight children.

He probably attended a grammar school from the age of seven and upon leaving he may have been apprenticed in his father's shop.

We know that he married **Anne Hathaway**, who was also the daughter of a wealthy farmer, when he was eighteen, in 1582. William and Anne had three children, Susanna and twins, Hamnet and Judith.

Shakespeare wrote at least thirty eight plays as well as a number of poems and sonnets. Among the most well known are , Othello, Hamlet, Romeo and Juliet, and Macbeth . He died on April 23rd 1616, aged exactly fifty-two years old and was buried in the chancel of the Collegiate Church of the Holy Trinity in Stratford upon Avon.

Jane Austen

Jane Austen was born on 16th December 1775 to the Reverend George Austen and his wife Cassandra Austen. She was the seventh of eight children and was particularly close to her sister Cassandra who was three years older than herself. She never married, but was very fond of her many nephews and nieces. The family lived in Steventon in Hampshire, where her father was the rector. Upon his retirement in 1801, the family moved to Bath where they lived until her father died. After George Austen's death, Jane and her mother went to live in Southampton for a short while before moving to a cottage near Alton.

Jane starting writing when she was very young although Sense and Sensibility, her first published work, was published when she was thirty-six, in 1811. Her other novels include

- Pride and Prejudice,
- Northanger Abbey and
- Mansfield Park.

Several films and television adaptations have been made of her novels.

Jane died in 1817, aged forty-one and is buried in Winchester.

Sharon Spencer Centre No

Consolidation 2 Part 1 – HOLS2

Holiday Homes

Do you own a second property that would be suitable as a holiday home? Would you like to see your property occupied for most of the year, saving you money and at the same time bringing in an income?

If so, consider letting your home through our booking agency. We are a long-established booking agency that has properties all over the country. Each year we deal with over 800 properties.

This leaflet aims to tell you about our agency and to give you information on how to turn your second home into a successful business.

About us

We have been in the holiday business for over 20 years. Starting as a family firm we have expanded over the years and now employ over 50 full time staff.

Each year we produce a full-colour brochure detailing over 800 properties. Each one is featured in a full-colour photograph together with a professionally written description. We aim to make the most of your property.

We can take the worry out of letting your home as we deal with the clients on your behalf. Our wide experience of the holiday industry means we can give our expert opinion as to the potential of your holiday property.

We can also advise you on the amount of rent you can realistically expect to receive.

By choosing us as your booking agent, you can be assured of receiving a first-class service. Our competent staff deal with all the details on your behalf.

Marketing

We make the most of our properties and the results of this can be seen in the high level of bookings each of our homes receive each year.

The full-colour brochure is subject to a hard-selling, high profile advertising campaign. Each year we receive over 250,000 enquiries.

Our offices are open from 8.00 am to 8.00 pm Monday to Friday, and 10.00 am to 6.00 pm at weekends. The offices are manned by people, not answerphones so clients can discuss their requirements straight away. This means you will never miss an opportunity to let your property.

Grading

We request that each property undergoes a Tourist Board inspection on a yearly basis. This is so we can assure our customers that the properties we let are of the highest possible standard. The Tourist Board grades properties on a scale of 1 – 5, grade 5 being the highest. We only accept properties that have been awarded a grade 4 or 5. This is because we like to give our customers peace of mind. They must be able to rely on the property they book to be comfortable and well equipped.

The report prepared by the Tourist Board provides excellent feedback on your property and gives helpful suggestions on how to improve and upgrade your home. In order to achieve a high grade, the property must be in excellent condition. The furniture and fittings must be of a high standard and free from signs of wear and tear. Obviously the property must be clean and tidy. Special attention is paid to the kitchen and bathroom.

Extra marks will be awarded for the provision of luxury items, such as dishwashers, washing machines, freezers, microwave ovens, CD players etc. Good quality furniture will also command extra marks.

Insurance

As well as the usual buildings insurance, we request that you take out Public Liability insurance. We strongly advise property owners to take out accidental damage and loss insurance on the contents of the property. This will ensure that any problems can be dealt with quickly, with the minimum of expense and worry. We have made arrangements

Consolidation 2 Part 1 – HOLS2 continued

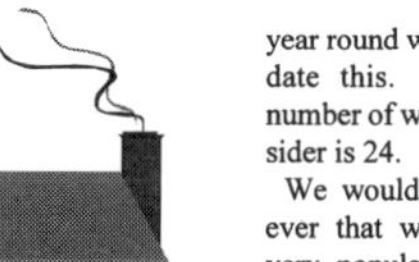

with a local insurance company who will give you the best possible rates. If you decide to place your property with us, our insurance broker will contact you to discuss your insurance requirements in detail.

When our customers book a holiday property, we request that they take out cancellation insurance. This means that should a booking be cancelled because of ill-health, etc, you will receive 85% of the booking fee. This assures you of some income should a customer be forced to cancel a booking.

Private Holidays

You will probably wish to take some weeks for yourself, family and friends. We ask you to limit this to 2 weeks during the peak holiday season of July and August. Up to a total of 4 additional weeks can be booked out during the low and high season. These conditions are for property owners who wish to let their homes for the entire year.

If you do not wish your property to be available all year round we can accommodate this. The minimum number of weeks we can consider is 24.

We would point out however that winter breaks are very popular with our customers, in particular the Christmas and New Year periods.

If a booking is cancelled for any reason and we are unable to re-let, we will give you first refusal to take the week for yourself or your family. These weeks do not count towards your entitlement.

Commission

We feel our commission rates are extremely competitive. A basic rate of 15% of the rental value, plus VAT is charged for each booking. If you are registered for VAT you may be able to claim this back. This fees covers all advertising, administration and fee collection and is very good value for money.

The Tourist Board inspection report fee must also be paid by the property owners. Currently the charges are £75 per visit.

Consolidation 2 Part 1 – HOLS3

Holiday Homes

Do you own a second property that would be suitable as a holiday home? Would you like to see your property occupied for most of the year, saving you money and at the same time bringing in an income?

If so, consider letting your home through our booking agency. We are a long-established booking agency that has properties all over the country. Each year we deal with over 800 properties.

This leaflet aims to tell you about our agency and to give you information on how to turn your second home into a successful business.

About us

We have been in the holiday business for over 20 years. Starting as a family firm we have expanded over the years and now employ over 50 full time staff.

Each year we produce a full-colour brochure detailing over 800 properties. Each one is featured in a full-colour photograph together with a professionally written description. We aim to make the most of your property.

We can take the worry out of letting your home as we deal with the clients on your behalf. Our wide experience of the holiday industry means we can give our expert opinion as to the potential of your holiday property.

We can also advise you on the amount of rent you can realistically expect to receive.

By choosing us as your booking agent, you can be assured of receiving a first-class service. Our competent staff deal with all the details on your behalf.

Marketing

We make the most of our properties and the results of this can be seen in the high level of bookings each of our homes receive each year.

The full-colour brochure is subject to a hard-selling, high profile advertising campaign. Each year we receive over 250,000 enquiries.

Our offices are open from 8.00 am to 8.00 pm Monday to Friday, and 10.00 am to 6.00 pm at weekends. The offices are manned by people, not answerphones so clients can discuss their requirements straight away. This means you will never miss an opportunity to let your property.

Grading

We request that each property undergoes a Tourist Board inspection on a yearly basis. This is so we can assure our customers that the properties we let are of the highest possible standard. The Tourist Board grades properties on a scale of 1 – 5, grade 5 being the highest. We only accept properties that have been awarded a grade 4 or 5. This is because we like to give our customers peace of mind. They must be able to rely on the property they book to be comfortable and well equipped.

Consolidation 2 Part 1 – HOLS3 continued

The report prepared by the Tourist Board provides excellent feedback on your property and gives helpful suggestions on how to improve and upgrade your home. In order to achieve a high grade, the property must be in excellent condition. The furniture and fittings must be of a high standard and free from signs of wear and tear. Obviously the property must be clean and tidy. Special attention is paid to the kitchen and bathroom.

Extra marks will be awarded for the provision of luxury items, such as dishwashers, washing machines, freezers, microwave ovens, CD players etc. Good quality furniture will also command extra marks.

Insurance

As well as the usual buildings insurance, we request that you take out Public Liability insurance. We strongly advise property owners to take out accidental damage and loss insurance on the contents of the property. This will ensure that any problems can be dealt with quickly, with the minimum of expense and worry. We have made arrangements with a local insurance company who will give you the best possible rates. If you decide to place your property with us, our insurance broker will contact you to discuss your insurance requirements in detail.

When our customers book a holiday property, we request that they take out cancellation insurance. This means that should a booking be cancelled because of ill-health, etc, you will receive 85% of the booking fee. This assures you of some income should a customer be forced to cancel a booking.

Private Holidays

You will probably wish to take some weeks for yourself, family and friends. We ask you to limit this to 2 weeks during the peak holiday season of July and August. Up to a total of 4 additional weeks can be booked out during the low and high season. These conditions are for property owners who wish to let their homes for the entire year.

If you do not wish your property to be available all year round we can accommodate this. The minimum number of weeks we can consider is 24.

We would point out however that winter breaks are very popular with our customers, in particular the Christmas and New Year periods.

If a booking is cancelled for any reason and we are unable to re-let, we will give you first refusal to take the week for yourself or your family. These weeks do not count towards your entitlement.

Commission

We feel our commission rates are extremely competitive. A basic rate of 15% of the rental value, plus VAT is charged for each booking. If you are registered for VAT you may be able to claim this back. This fees covers all advertising, administration and fee collection and is very good value for money.

The Tourist Board inspection report fee must also be paid by the property owners. Currently the charges are £75 per visit.

Consolidation 2 Part 2 – GARD1

GARDENING

Container Gardening

This has become a very popular hobby in recent years and it is easy to see why. You do not need to put in hours of back breaking work digging and weeding. It is also suitable for all gardens, no matter how large or small.

You can grow a variety of plants in a container, from bulbs, bedding plants and herbs through to vegetables and fruit trees.

A *water garden* makes an interesting container in a small garden or on a patio. Many people enjoy creating a miniature rockery or alpine garden, often using an old china kitchen sink.

There is a wide variety of containers on the market. These range from inexpensive plastic to the more expensive terracotta and stone. The choice is enormous as pots come in all shapes and sizes. If you feel inspired you can even make your own from pieces of wood etc. Old household and garden items such as wheelbarrows, sinks, buckets, wicker baskets and broken watering cans can be transformed into beautiful containers. All you need is a little imagination and skill.

One of the main advantages of container gardening is that you can change the look of your garden instantly. You can have special displays, or seasonal pots to give colour all year round.

Making a container

First of all you need to prepare your container. Make sure it is clean and free from cracks. It must have a hole at the bottom for drainage. If you are using a terracotta pot then soak it in water for 5 to 10 minutes.

You need to create a drainage system in your container. To do this you will need to carefully place some drainage material at the bottom of the pot so that it covers, but does not block, the hole. Suitable material includes broken terracotta pots, polystyrene chips or large stones. You can then add some gravel to cover the bottom inch or so. This is readily obtainable from most garden centres.

Now fill the pot with soil and compost. You can mix your own growing medium, but most garden centres and nurseries sell bags of ready-prepared soil at very reasonable prices. Fill to approximately 2 inches below the rim of the container.

Now you are ready to plant. Given below are a few hints to help.

- *Ensure the plants are well watered – do this 20 minutes before planting*
- *Ease the plants carefully from their containers. Gently shake off excess soil and spread the roots out with your fingers*
- *Plant according to instructions. Remember to water well each day and feed at regular intervals.*

Sharon Spencer Consolidation 3

Exam Practice 2 – EMP2

SLSTask1

Finding Employment

If you are trying to find work it can often seem an impossible task. You scan the job advertisements in the local paper each day, send off an application form or CV and then wait for a reply. You may be lucky enough to be asked to attend for an interview, or you may receive the dreaded 'thanks, but no thanks' letter. How can you improve your chances of success in the job market? Try some of the following hints.

Finding the vacancies

The first place to start your search is your local newspaper. Most local papers have a 'job night' where several pages are devoted to advertisements. Make sure you collect your copy as early as possible during the day. Read through the vacancies very carefully and ring or write for application forms as soon as possible.

The local job centre will also display job vacancies. These vacancies change rapidly so you may need to visit on a regular basis. The job centre staff will be pleased to advise you of any of the jobs they have listed.

Employment agencies will also be able to advise you on local vacancies. They may be able to offer you temporary work. This is often a good way to find a permanent position.

National newspapers also advertise job vacancies. These tend to be more specialised. For example, it may be that accounting jobs are advertised on Thursdays, secretarial jobs on Tuesdays etc. You do not need to buy these papers yourself, your local library will have these each day.

For professional and technical work you may need to look in specialist or trade magazines. These can also be found at your local library or job centre.

Preparing a CV

Your CV is your advertisement and so it must be well-written, informative, interesting and relevant. There are many ways to present your CV, but however you choose to present yours ensure that it is aimed towards the type of work you are looking for. As a general rule, do not make your CV more than 2 sides of A4. Employers are busy people and do not have the time, or inclination to wade through masses of paper.

The presentation is essential to success. Badly typed CVs full of spelling errors will not impress any potential employer. Ensure that you check your CV again and again so that there are no mistakes. If you know your proofreading skills are poor then ask a friend to help you. If you are using a word processor to produce your CV then do not try to do anything too fancy. This is not the time to experiment with ornate fonts and the use of the bold and underscore keys.

If you cannot type your own CV then it is well worth paying a professional to produce one for you. They will be able to help with grammar and spelling and should produce a CV that can be copied and used again and again. Look in your local telephone directory for agencies that will provide this service.

What to include in your CV

The traditional method of writing a CV starts with a section on personal details. You should include your name, address, telephone number and contact number. Some people also include their date of birth and marital status. If you hold a clean, current driving licence it is useful to include this in the personal details section.

A list of educational qualifications and schools attended may follow. Start with the last secondary school you attended – there is

Page No 8 Employment

Exam Practice 2 – EMP2 continued

SLSTask1

no need to give the name and address of your primary school. List the qualifications you attained, together with the respective grades. It is usual to indicate when the exam was taken, for example, June 1995. Start with GCSE's or O-Levels and then carry on to A-Levels if applicable.

Once you have finished listing your school qualifications then you can add any qualifications gained through higher or further education. Evening classes, where a qualification has been attained should of course be included.

If you have received any formal training through your work, for example if you are a teacher and have attended some courses, then these should be listed.

Now for the section on work history. List your most recent employment first, and then working down in order. Some people like to give details of what the job entailed and their duties and responsibilities. However, if you are changing careers then this information may not be relevant.

If you have had little work experience or are returning to work after a break you may wish to consider starting your CV with a personal profile. This lists the personal qualities and life skills that you have gained that will be useful in the world of work. For example, if you have taken a break from work to raise your family you have probably gained multi-tasking and organisational skills. These are extremely useful in the workplace. This type of CV often starts with a paragraph of skills and experience and then goes into the more 'tradtional' CV with educational qualifications, career history etc listed separately.

Don't forget to mention any work experience you have had whilst at school, college or training course. This is particularly important if you are applying for your first job. Saturday and part time work should also be included.

If you have any hobbies then do include them. These show that you are interested in other activities and you may well have special talents that are not always used in the workplace, for example if you are a competitive swimmer.

You may also include any other activities you participate in. For example, if you are a leading member of the PTA or a school governor.

The names of two referees may be included on your CV, however, one should always be the name of your most recent employer. If

you are still in employment you may not wish to do this. It is quite acceptable to give the names of referees but to request that contact is not made until your permission has been granted. Referees should of course have been asked if they are prepared to act as such before the CV is prepared.

Once you have completed your CV, you will be able to start applying for work. Good luck!

Page No 9

Employment

Exam Practice 2 – EMP3

SLSTask1

Finding Employment

If you are trying to find work it can often seem an impossible task. You scan the job advertisements in the local paper each day, send off an application form or CV and then wait for a reply. You may be lucky enough to be asked to attend for an interview, or you may receive the dreaded 'thanks, but no thanks' letter. How can you improve your chances of success in the job market? Try some of the following hints.

Finding the vacancies

The first place to start your search is your local newspaper. Most local papers have a 'job night' where several pages are devoted to advertisements. Make sure you collect your copy as early as possible during the day. Read through the vacancies very carefully and ring or write for application forms as soon as possible.

The local job centre will also display job vacancies. These vacancies change rapidly so you may need to visit on a regular basis. The job centre staff will be pleased to advise you of any of the jobs they have listed.

Employment agencies will also be able to advise you on local vacancies. They may be able to offer you temporary work. This is often a good way to find a permanent position.

National newspapers also advertise job vacancies. These tend to be more specialised. For example, it may be that accounting jobs are advertised on Thursdays, secretarial jobs on Tuesdays etc. You do not need to buy these papers yourself, your local library will have these each day.

For professional and technical work you may need to look in specialist or trade magazines. These can also be found at your local library or job centre.

Preparing a CV

Your CV is your advertisement and so it must be well-written, informative, interesting and relevant. There are many ways to present your CV, but however you choose to present yours ensure that it is aimed towards the type of work you are looking for. As a general rule, do not make your CV more than 2 sides of A4. Employers are busy people and do not have the time, or inclination to wade through masses of paper.

The presentation is essential to success. Badly typed CVs full of spelling errors will not impress any potential employer. Ensure that you check your CV again and again so that there are no mistakes. If you know your proofreading skills are poor then ask a friend to help you. If you are using a word processor to produce your CV then do not try to do anything too fancy. This is not the time to experiment with ornate fonts and the use of the bold and underscore keys.

If you cannot type your own CV then it is well worth paying a professional to produce one for you. They will be able to help with grammar and spelling and should produce a CV that can be copied and used again and again. Look in your local telephone directory for agencies that will provide this service.

What to include in your CV

The traditional method of writing a CV starts with a section on personal details. You should include your name, address, telephone number and contact number. Some people also include their date of birth and marital status. If you hold a clean, current driving licence it is useful to include this in the personal details section.

Page No 8

Employment

Exam Practice 2 – EMP3 continued

SLSTask1

A list of educational qualifications and schools attended may follow. Start with the last secondary school you attended – there is no need to give the name and address of your primary school. List the qualifications you attained, together with the respective grades. It is usual to indicate when the exam was taken, for example, June 1995. Start with GCSE's or O-Levels and then carry on to A-Levels if applicable.

Once you have finished listing your school qualifications then you can add any qualifications gained through higher or further education. Evening classes, where a qualification has been attained should of course be included.

If you have received any formal training through your work, for example if you are a teacher and have attended some courses, then these should be listed.

Now for the section on work history. List your most recent employment first, and then working down in order. Some people like to give details of what the job entailed and their duties and responsibilities. However, if you are changing careers then this information may not be relevant.

If you have had little work experience or are returning to work after a break you may wish to consider starting your CV with a personal profile. This lists the personal qualities and life skills that you have gained that will be useful in the world of work. For example, if you have taken a break from work to raise your family you have probably gained multi-tasking and organisational skills. These are extremely useful in the workplace. This type of CV often starts with a paragraph of skills and experience and then goes into the more 'tradtional' CV with educational qualifications, career history etc listed separately.

Don't forget to mention any work experience you have had whilst at school, college or training course. This is particularly important if you are applying for your first job. Saturday and part time work should also be included.

If you have any hobbies then do include them. These show that you are interested in other activities and you may well have special talents that are not always used in the workplace, for example if you are a competitive swimmer.

You may also include any other activities you participate in. For example, if you are a leading member of the PTA or a school governor.

The names of two referees may be included on your CV, however, one should always be the name of your most recent employer. If you are still in employment you may not wish to do this. It is quite acceptable to give the names of referees but to request that contact is not made until your permission has been granted. Referees should of course have been asked if they are prepared to act as such before the CV is prepared.

Once you have completed your CV, you will be able to start applying for work. Good luck!

Page No 9 Employment

Exam Practice 2 – MED1

ALTERNATIVE MEDICINE

Homeopathy

Homeopathy is considered an 'alternative' form of medicine, however it has been around since the end of the nineteenth century. It was originated by Samuel Hahnemann, a German physician. There are three main differences between conventional medicine and homeopathy.

- Holistic. The symptoms are treated as part of a larger condition and the selected remedy will be used to treat the condition as a whole.
- Like Cures Like. The remedy will be selected on its ability to start the same symptoms in a healthy person. In other words, if you are suffering from migraine, you may be given a remedy which would cause migraine in a non-sufferer.
- Natural Treatment. The remedies used are completely natural. They are derived from animal, mineral, and plant worlds. They are safe to use. The dose given is highly diluted as this has been found to be more effective.

There are more than two thousand remedies and many can be bought at your local pharmacy. However, it is better to consult a qualified homeopath whenever possible. This is because the symptoms being displayed may not be the main cause of the disease. A trained homeopath will be able to recognise whether the obvious illness has an underlying cause. Some General Practitioners now use homeopathy alongside conventional medicine.

Acupuncture

The basic principle of acupuncture is that energy flows through certain channels in the body and that illness and pain occurs if these channels are interrupted or blocked. There are over eight hundred energy points over the body, which form a definite pattern. The lines that connect particular organs with these points are called **meridians.**

The acupuncturist redistributes the energy flow in the body by inserting very slender needles of pure copper, silver or gold at specific points along the meridian lines. Gold needles act as a stimulant, silver needles sedate.

The number of needles used in a treatment varies from two or three to a dozen or more. The length of time the needles are kept in the body depends on the condition.

An experienced acupuncturist can detect an excess or deficiency of energy by checking the patient's pulse.

Acupuncture has had good results on disorders such as eczema, asthma, arthritis, migraine and ulcers.

Sharon Spencer Centre Number

Section 3

Advanced Desktop Publishing

Before you start this section make sure you can:

- open the desktop publishing software
- set up master pages
- create a new document
- open an existing file
- save and print documents
- set up page layouts
- set up column guides
- set up style sheets
- import text and images
- resize images in proportion
- insert lines and boxes
- copyfit your work
- multi-layer text and images.

In this section you will learn how to:

- format tables
- use advanced copyfitting tools
- create an alternative layout for a publication
- crop graphics
- use irregular text wrap
- set up non-standard paper sizes
- use shading and reverse text
- prepare documents for colour printing.

Section 3A

This section will help you to produce highly professional work, using a variety of layouts and with an element of design.

Section 3B

You will learn how to set up non-standard page sizes and prepare documents for colour printing in this section.

Designing a page layout

In Section 2 of this book you looked at creating documents using specified measurements for margins, gutters and style sheets. You are now going to try designing your own documents from a design brief.

In the workplace, as in examinations, you may be given a sketch of the page layout with various instructions dotted around the page to work from. Use this as a checklist and mark each instruction as you complete it.

It may be that you will be able to choose the margins and gutter space. If this is the case, look at the amount of text and graphics you have to place and keep the margins and guides to a minimum size. A gutter space of 5mm is acceptable.

You may have to key in some text, for example, the headline. If you are unsure as to how it should be displayed, the design brief should give you some guidance. For example, if the headline has been written on the design brief in capitals, then key it in capitals. The alignment of the text can also be seen from the design brief. If it is clear that the heading stretches from margin to margin, then make sure you do the same. Once you have finished keying in the headline, or any text, check it carefully for typographical errors.

Setting up tables

The text that you import may contain a table, or you might have to key in a table yourself.

How you set up a table depends on the software you are using. If the table is fairly short, for example, in the region of five or six lines, there is probably no need to use the more complicated table editors.

Keying in the table

If your software is of a complicated type, then the example given below is probably the easiest way to key in a table. However, if you are using a software such as Microsoft Publisher, then the insert table tool can be very useful. Follow the on-screen instructions for Microsoft Publisher to find out how to do this.

If you are not going to use a table editor then key in the text, pressing the tab key between each entry as in Figure 3.1. Remember to use the same text style as for the body text.

(type) Heading 1 (press tab) (type) Heading 2 (press tab) (type) Heading 3 (press return)

(type) Text (press tab) (type) Text (press tab) (type) Text (press return)
(type) Text (press tab) (type) Text (press tab) (type) Text (press return)
(type) Text (press tab) (type) Text (press tab) (type) Text (press return)
(type) Text (press tab) (type) Text (press tab) (type) Text (press return)
(type) Text (press tab) (type) Text (press tab) (type) Text (press return)

Figure 3.1 Creating a table

Now highlight the text and set some tabs. With the text highlighted you will easily be able to line up the columns with a minimum of two clear spaces between. If you are using software such as Microsoft Publisher, you may be able to use the above example to place into a table grid. However, in order for it to work, you must have a tab, comma or paragraph mark between each section of text.

Your table should now look like Figure 3.2.

Heading 1	Heading 2	Heading 3
Text	Text	Text
Text	Text	Text
Text	Text	Text
Text	Text	Text
Text	Text	Text

Figure 3.2 Finished table

■ Using existing text

If you are to form a table from text that is contained within one of the articles, you will approach this in a slightly different way. If you are using Microsoft Publisher or similar software, you can still use the insert table facility, but you will have to ensure that a tab, a comma or paragraph mark is inserted between each entry as in the example above. Once these have been inserted then you can follow the on-screen help to achieve the desired effect.

If you do not have this facility on your software, then place the cursor between each entry and press tab as in Figure 3.3.

Heading 1 (press tab) Heading 2 (press tab) Heading 3

Text (press tab) Text (press tab) Text
Text (press tab) Text (press tab) Text
Text (press tab) Text (press tab) Text
Text (press tab) Text (press tab) Text
Text (press tab) Text (press tab) Text

Figure 3.3 Creating a table using existing text

You will then be able to highlight the text and set tabs in the correct places.

■ Aligning your table

You should always try to ensure that your table alignment is consistent. This is to ensure that your work looks as professional as possible. It does not matter whether you decide to centre, left or right align each column as long as they are all the same. If you are using a table editor of some description this is a simple operation. You can just highlight the text and choose the alignment. If you have followed the above method then the text will have to remain left aligned. This is perfectly acceptable.

Creating dropped capitals

You may wish to set up dropped capital(s). Look at Figure 3.4.

> This is a dropped capital. You may have noticed these in newspapers and magazines

Figure 3.4 Dropped capital

Two things are important when setting dropped capitals:

- The space between the dropped capital and the rest of the text. In Figure 3.4 a space of 1mm was set. This makes a neat margin.
- The number of lines the capital is dropped. In the example above three lines was set.

Keeping the text flow around dropped capitals consistent

So that your work looks professional the text flow around the dropped capitals should be consistent. This means that the text should be indented neatly and not touching the dropped capital. The line spacing should also be consistent with the body text, ie the leading should be the same.

Generally if you are working on an up-to-date version of your software, this should not cause any problems as the dropped capital facility will do this automatically. However, if you have to create the dropped capital manually, then you will have to take care to avoid these problems.

Advanced copyfitting tools

You looked at some ways of copyfitting your material in Section 2. However, there are a few more advanced tools that you can use to ensure your work looks neat and tidy.

Displaying the material on one page

In the workplace, you may often have to ensure that your work fits on one page. This is common sense, as a leaflet that extended just a few lines onto a second page would look unprofessional and untidy. In order to keep your work on one page, you can try one or more of the following:

- Change your point sizes so that the text fits on the page. Remember to keep the sizes within the specified range given on the design brief.
- Change the size of the image(s).
- Adjust the **tracking**. See below for more information on tracking.
- Adjust the **leading**. See below for more information on leading.

Tracking

Tracking is the space between characters. The default setting for this is usually 'none' or 'normal'. Look at Figure 3.5 to see how tracking works.

This is a sentence typed in a size 12, serif font. The tracking is on the default setting of normal.

This is a sentence typed in a size 12, serif font. The tracking has been set to very loose.

This is a sentence typed in a size 12, serif font. The tracking has been set to very tight.

Figure 3.5 Tracking

As you can see, adjusting the tracking can make a great deal of difference. However, if you decide to alter the tracking, then remember that the text must still be legible.

Adjust the leading

Leading is the technical term for the space between lines of text. It can be adjusted to give different effects. Look at Figure 3.6.

This is a sentence typed in a 12-point serif font. The leading is set on automatic and the words are easy to read from line to line. As a general rule, an automatic leading setting for a 12-point font size would be between 12 and 14 points.

To condense the lines slightly we can alter the leading so that the space between the lines of text is smaller. This example has used a 12-point serif font and leading of 10 points.

To expand the lines we can alter the leading so that the space between the lines of text is larger. This example has used a 12-point serif font and leading of 18 points.

Figure 3.6 Leading

Note: the text set with a 10-point leading has been slightly clipped. This is not acceptable; it would have been better to use an 11-point leading.

Consistency of leading

It is important that the leading is kept consistent throughout the publication. The best place to adjust the leading is within your style sheet if this is possible. This will ensure that all the body text will have the same leading. Do not forget to include any tables or other text that has been keyed in as a separate story.

The leading may be slightly different for headings and subheadings, although these should also be consistent. It would be difficult, for example if the headline was in 20 point and the body text in 10 point to achieve a leading that would suit both.

Removing hyphenation

Work that has many hyphens at the right-hand margin can be difficult to read and can look untidy. This is particularly relevant when you are using justified or force-justified alignment. You can switch off the hyphenation feature within your style sheet. It is easier if you do so at this point as it means you will not be trying to alter your publication once you have completed it.

■ White space

The areas around graphics/text and at the top and bottom of the page or columns are known as white space. Look at the example in Figure 3.7.

As you can see, the white space in this example is uneven at the top and bottom of columns and around the graphic. The columns should be neatly aligned where possible, with only the third column having white space at the bottom, although this should not be more than 10mm. In order to ensure that this is the case you can do any of the following:

- enlarge or reduce the size of the graphic
- adjust the leading to ensure a neat fit
- adjust the tracking to ensure a neat fit
- ensure the text flow is from the top to the bottom of each column – in Figure 3.7, the text box does not stretch from the top to the bottom in the 2nd and 3rd columns.

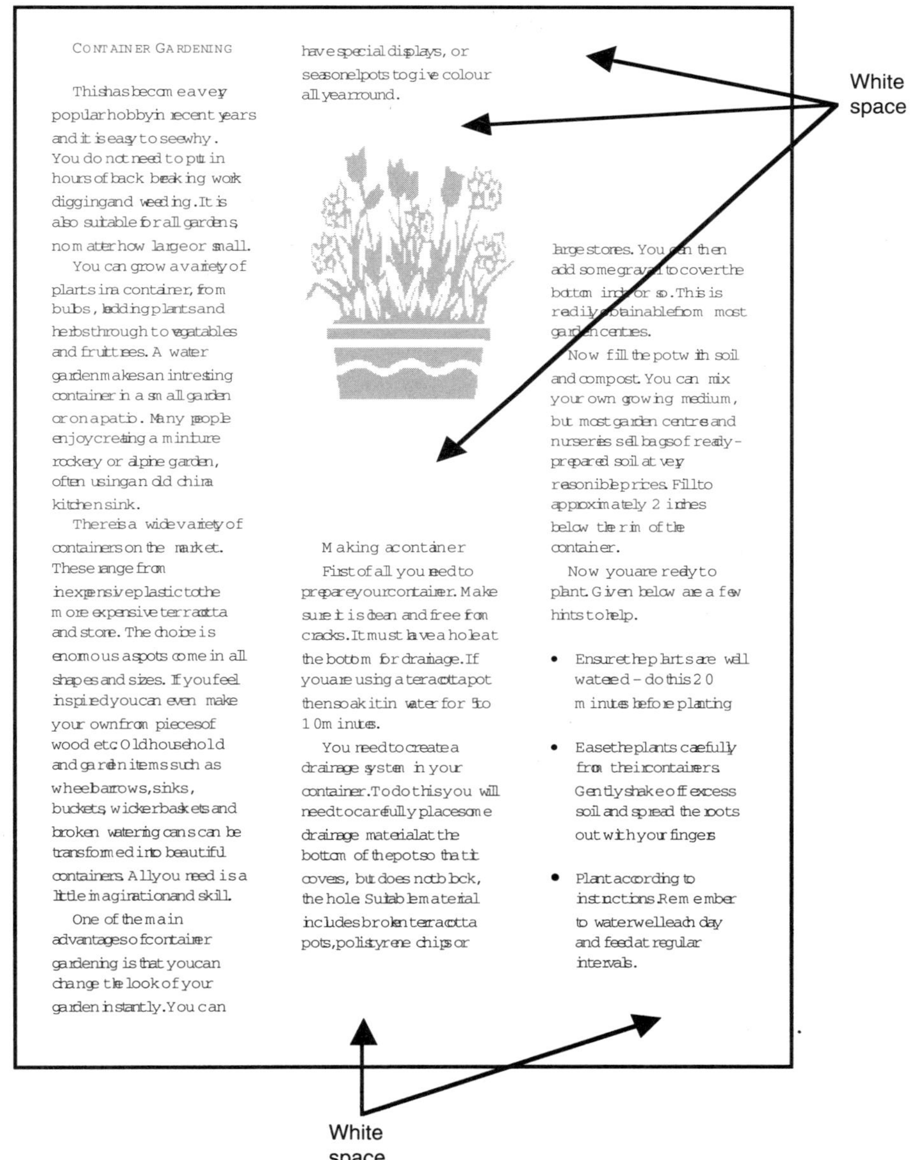

CONTAINER GARDENING

This has becom e a very popular hobby in recent years and it is easy to see why. You do not need to put in hours of back breaking work digging and weeding. It is also suitable for all gardens, no matter how large or small.

You can grow a variety of plants in a container, from bulbs, bedding plants and herbs through to vegatables and fruit trees. A water garden makes an intresting container in a small garden or on a patio. Many people enjoy creating a minture rockery or alpine garden, often using an old china kitchen sink.

There is a wide variety of containers on the market. These range from inexpensive plastic to the more expensive terracotta and stone. The choice is enormous as pots come in all shapes and sizes. If you feel inspired you can even make your own from pieces of wood etc. Old household and garden items such as wheelbarrows, sinks, buckets, wicker baskets and broken watering cans can be transformed into beautiful containers. All you need is a little imagiration and skill.

One of the main advantages of container gardening is that you can change the look of your garden instantly. You can have special displays, or seasonel pots to give colour all year round.

Making a container

First of all you need to prepare your container. Make sure it is clean and free from cracks. It must have a hole at the bottom for drainage. If you are using a teracotta pot then soak it in water for 5 to 10 minutes.

You need to create a drainage system in your container. To do this you will need to carefully place some drainage material at the bottom of the pot so that it covers, but does not block, the hole. Suitable material includes broken terracotta pots, polistyrene chips or large stones. You can then add some gravel to cover the bottom inch or so. This is readily obtainable from most garden centres.

Now fill the pot with soil and compost. You can mix your own growing medium, but most garden centre and nurseries sell bags of ready-prepared soil at very resonible prices. Fill to approximately 2 inches below the rim of the container.

Now you are ready to plant. Given below are a few hints to help.

- Ensure the plants are well watered – do this 20 minutes before planting
- Ease the plants carefully from their containers. Gently shake off excess soil and spread the roots out with your fingers
- Plant according to instructions. Remember to water well each day and feed at regular intervals.

Figure 3.7 White space

Exercise 1

Now try the following exercises. You must copyfit your publications to ensure:

- all material is displayed on one page
- text/graphics/lines are not superimposed on each other
- headings and related text are grouped together
- one line or less of text is grouped with the rest of related text
- paragraph spacing is consistent
- leading is consistent
- no more than 5 hyphenated line endings on page
- no more than 10mm (vertical) white space unless specified in the design brief.

Exercise 1.1

Create an A4 size publication following the given design brief, page 102. Gutter space can be as you wish. Use lines/rules where indicated in the design brief.

Set up a style sheet for headline, subhead and body text as shown in the design brief. Choose point sizes to fill the publication. Import the text files: **BOOK**, **COMP** and **HOME** and apply the appropriate styles.

In the **Competition Winners** article, insert the following new paragraph between the first and second paragraphs:

A display of these pictures is in the main hall and will be there until the end of term. Parents are welcome to visit the display after school each day.

You must format the table at the end of the **Competition Winners** article. Set up three columns, left aligned, with column headings:

Place, **Name** and **Class**

Produce dropped capitals for the first letter of **each** article. Maintain consistent text flow of the body text around the dropped capitals.

Place the two image files: **BOOKS** and **HMWRK** as indicated in the design brief, maintaining the original proportions.

Save as: **SCHOOL1** and print the publication.

Exercise 1.2

Create an A4 size publication following the given design brief, page 102. Gutter space can be as you wish. Use lines/rules where indicated in the design brief.

Set up a style sheet for headline, subhead and body text as shown in the design brief. Choose point sizes to fill the publication. Import the text files: **SAFE**, **HAZ** and **ACC** and apply the appropriate styles.

In the **How to Prevent Accidents** article, insert the following table at the end of the article. You must format the table. Set up two columns, left aligned with column headings, **Room** and **Hazard**.

Room	**Hazard**
Bathroom	Slippery surfaces
Bathroom	Electrical points
Kitchen	Sharp objects
Kitchen	Boiling water
Kitchen	Hot surfaces
Living room	Worn carpets
Stairs	Worn carpets
Stairs	Poor lighting
Garden	Poisonous plants

Produce dropped capitals for the first letter of **each** article. Maintain consistent text flow of the body text around the dropped capitals.

Place the two image files: **MATCH** and **LAWN** as indicated in the design brief, maintaining the original proportions.

Save as: **SAFETY1** and print the publication.

Design Brief for Exercise 1.1

Design Brief for Exercise 1.2

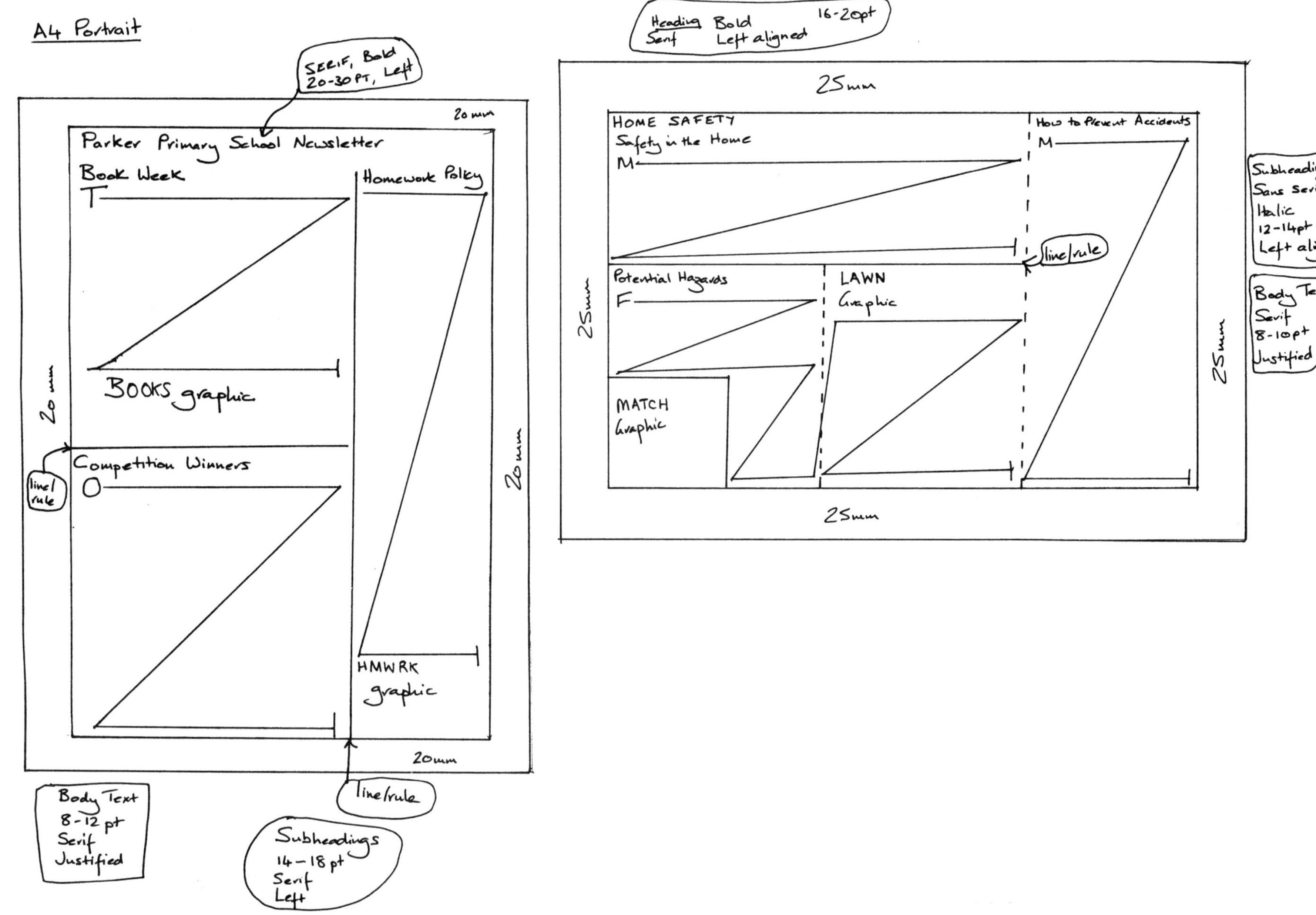

Exercise 1.3

Create an A4 size publication following the given design brief on page 104. Gutter space may be as you wish. Use lines/rules where indicated in the design brief.

Set up a style sheet for headline, subhead and body text as shown in the design brief. Choose point sizes to fill the publication. Import the text files: **DAYOUT**, **EVENTS** and **KNOCK** and apply the appropriate styles.

In the **It's a Knockout Tournament** article, insert the following new paragraph between the third and fourth paragraphs:

The matches will consist of three games. The winner will go on to the next round and so on. The tournament winners will receive a £50 sports voucher.

You must format the table in the **Forthcoming Events** article. Set up two columns, left aligned, with column headings **Date** and **Act**.

Produce dropped capitals for the first letter of **each** article. Maintain consistent text flow of the body text around the dropped capitals.

Place the two image files: **JAZZ** and **TROPHY** as indicated in the design brief, maintaining the original proportions.

Save as: **CLUB1** and print the publication.

Exercise 1.4

Create an A4 size publication following the given design brief on page 104. Gutter space can be as you wish. Use lines/rules where indicated in the design brief.

Set up a style sheet for headline, subhead and body text as shown in the design brief. Choose point sizes to fill the publication. Import the text files: **PROC**, **PROP** and **FIN** and apply the appropriate styles.

In the **Finance** article, insert the following new paragraph between the second paragraph and the table:

Make sure that you can easily meet the monthly repayments before entering into a loan. Keep in mind that if interest rates rise, the monthly repayments on the mortgage will also increase.

You must format the table at the end of the **Finance** article. Set up two columns, left aligned, with column headings **Income** and **Amount of Loan.**

Produce dropped capitals for the first letter of each article. Maintain consistent text flow of the body text around the dropped capitals.

Place the image file: **HSE** as indicated in the design brief, maintaining the original proportions.

Save as: **BUYHM1** and print the publication.

Design Brief for Exercise 1.3

Design Brief for Exercise 1.4

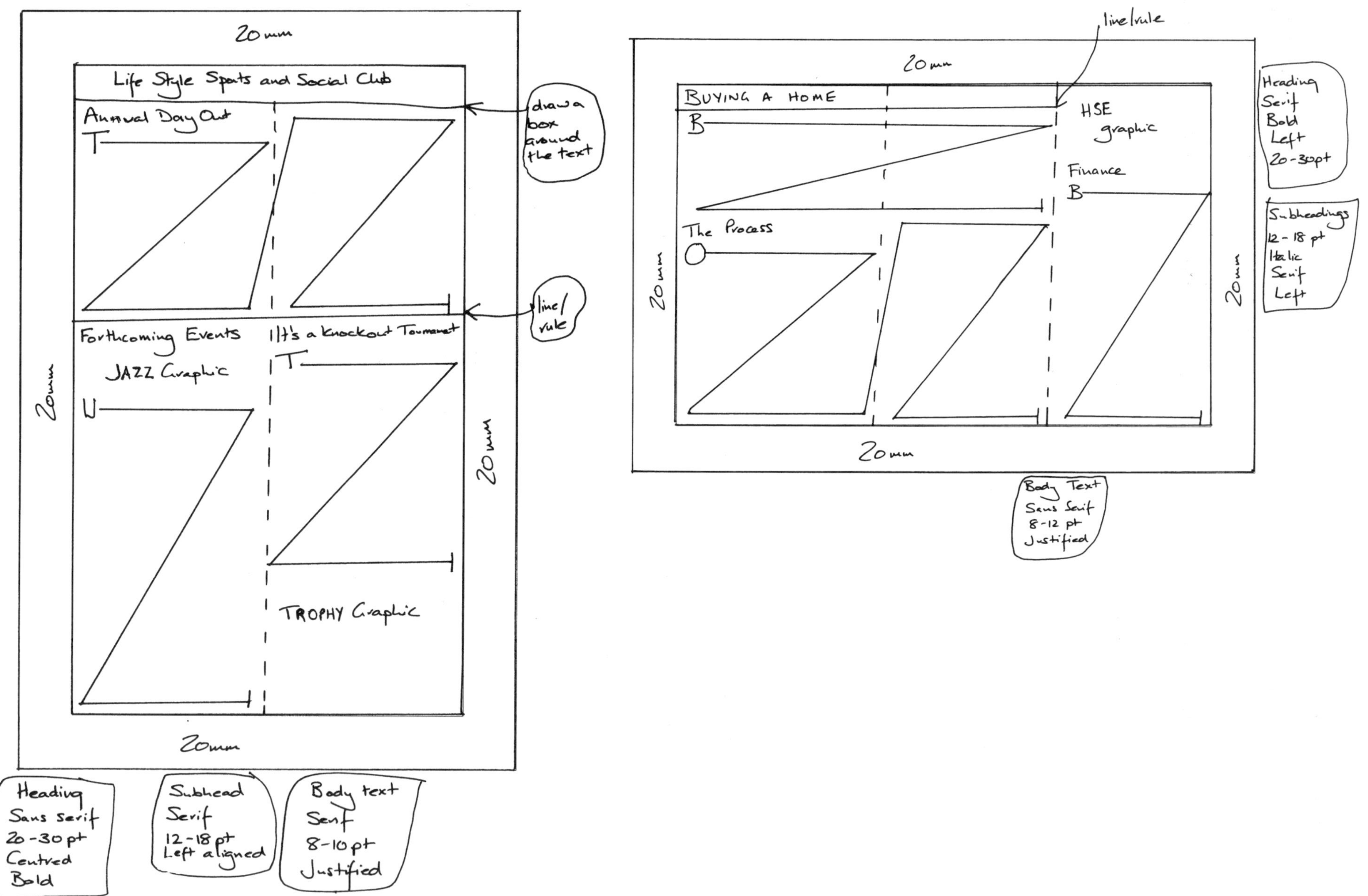

Producing an alternative version of a publication

You may decide that you would like to see an alternative version of a document you have created, or perhaps your boss would like to see several ideas on a page layout.

You may wish to work on a copy of the document you have already created or start again. It does not matter which option you choose. However, if you decide to work on your existing publication, you must ensure that you are working on a copy and that the original publication is saved.

You may be given a second design brief to work from for the alternative layout. Some of the new layout may be specified, for example, placing one of the stories first. You can then choose how to set out the rest of the publication. Remember that you must not change the fonts or font sizes in an examination.

It may be that you will have to delete some of the text. Ensure you take out only the text specified, no more, no less.

Cropping graphics

Cropping graphics means that you cut some of the graphic out. Look at Figure 3.8:

This is the original graphic

This graphic has been cropped to remove the hat on the right

Figure 3.8 Cropping graphics

You will need to use the graphic cropping tool which may either be found in your toolbox if you are using a software such as Aldus PageMaker, or be part of the toolbar options if you are using a software such as Microsoft Publisher.

To use the cropping tool, you need to place the tool over one off the handles of the graphic and then drag either horizontally or vertically to crop the graphic. This takes a little practice to get right. Make sure that you do not cut too much off the graphic or leave any little bits. If you are working on a page view or 75% view, you may need to zoom in so that you can see if there are any dots left behind.

Although the graphic appears to be cut, the full graphic is in fact still there. If you make a mistake, or wish to see the full graphic again, then just place the cropping tool back over the relevant handle and drag the mouse out again. You will see that the graphic reappears in its full form.

■ Creating irregular text wrap

It is possible to set irregular text wrap around the graphic so that the text is actually set around the shape of the graphic rather than in a square box. Look at Figure 3.9.

The text wrap has been set to wrap around the graphic thus making an interesting page layout. Depending on the software you are using, this may be a simple operation or a rather time-consuming exercise. You should not have any hyphenated words around the graphic, and the leading and tracking should also remain even. Full details on how to achieve this are given below.

Figure 3.9 Irregular text wrap

As you can see the text is brought in to fit around the graphic rather than have a box effect. How you achieve this depends on the software you are using. It may be that you are given the option for irregular text wrap with the normal wrapping options. If so, it should be simple and easy to use.

If, however, you do not have this option, you will need to create the irregular text wrap for yourself. In order to do this, you will need to click on the handles of the text wrap and pull it towards the graphic. As it works in straight lines, you will need to create more handles that can be pulled in to fit around the graphic.

This is the original text wrap – square shaped – around the cropped graphic.

New handles have been created on the text wrap so that they can be pulled in to fit around the graphic. You can create the black handles by clicking on the dotted line. Do not create too many or you will end up with too much text wrap.

Figure 3.10 Creating irregular text wrap

■ Turning off the hyphenation around wrapped text

If you switch off hyphenation in the text-formatting menu, or style sheet, this should also apply to the text wrapped around the graphic and will look much neater.

If, however this does not work, you will need to ensure that the size of the graphic and the text wrap surrounding it are such that no hyphenation occurs. This is achievable, but it may take some time to get exactly right.

Amending kerning

The kerning is the spacing between individual characters. There are pairs of letters that when put together have a small amount of space between them. For example, if we type the letters **Aw** you can see that there is a small space between. If these letters are magnified to a size that might be used in a newsletter, logo or heading, you can see that this can look untidy (see Figure 3.11).

You can see the difference between the space separating the **a** and the **w** and that separating the **t** and the **r**.

Figure 3.11 No kerning

Kerning can be used to tidy up the gap between the two letters, or it can be used to expand the letters as in the examples below:

Aw **t r**

How you use the kerning facility depends on your software, but remember that when you are kerning two letters, you should place the cursor between them, or in the case of some software programs, highlight the two letters, before you alter the kerning value.

Exercise 2

Now try the following exercises. You will need to design an alternative page layout for the exercises you created earlier. You must copyfit your publications to ensure:

- all material is displayed on one page
- text/graphics/lines are not superimposed on each other
- headings and related text are grouped together
- one line or less of text is grouped with the rest of the related text
- paragraph spacing is consistent
- leading is consistent
- no more than 5 hyphenated line endings on a page
- no more than 10mm (vertical) white space unless specified

Exercise 2.1

Open the file: **SCHOOL1** and save as: **SCHOOL2**.

Design a landscape layout based on the alternative page sketch on page 109.

Delete from the **Book Week** article, the paragraph **A local author…**

Note that the first article must now be **Homework Policy**.

You must use the same fonts and the same point sizes that you chose in Exercise1.1, page 100.

Crop the **BOOKS** graphic to remove the book on the right-hand side. Use irregular text wrap around the **BOOKS** image. Do not include any hyphenation in text that wraps around the graphic.

In the headline text, in the word **School**, amend the kerning of the two letters **o** so that they touch each other.

Ensure that the publication fills the page by changing the leading of the body text.

Save and print the publication.

Exercise 2.2

Open the file: **SAFETY1** and save as: **SAFETY2**.

Design a portrait layout based on the alternative page sketch, page 109.

Delete from the **How to Prevent Accidents** article, the table at the end of the story.

Note that the first article must be **Safety in the Home**.

You must use the same fonts and the same point sizes that you chose in Exercise 1.2, page 101.

Crop the **LAWNMOWER** graphic to remove the grass on the right-hand side. Use irregular text wrap around the **LAWNMOWER** image. Do not include any hyphenation in text that wraps around the graphic.

In the headline text, in the words **Home Safety**, amend the kerning of the two words so that they extend to a third of the page.

Ensure that the publication fills the page by changing the leading of the body text.

Save and print the publication.

Alternative Page Sketch for Exercise 2.1

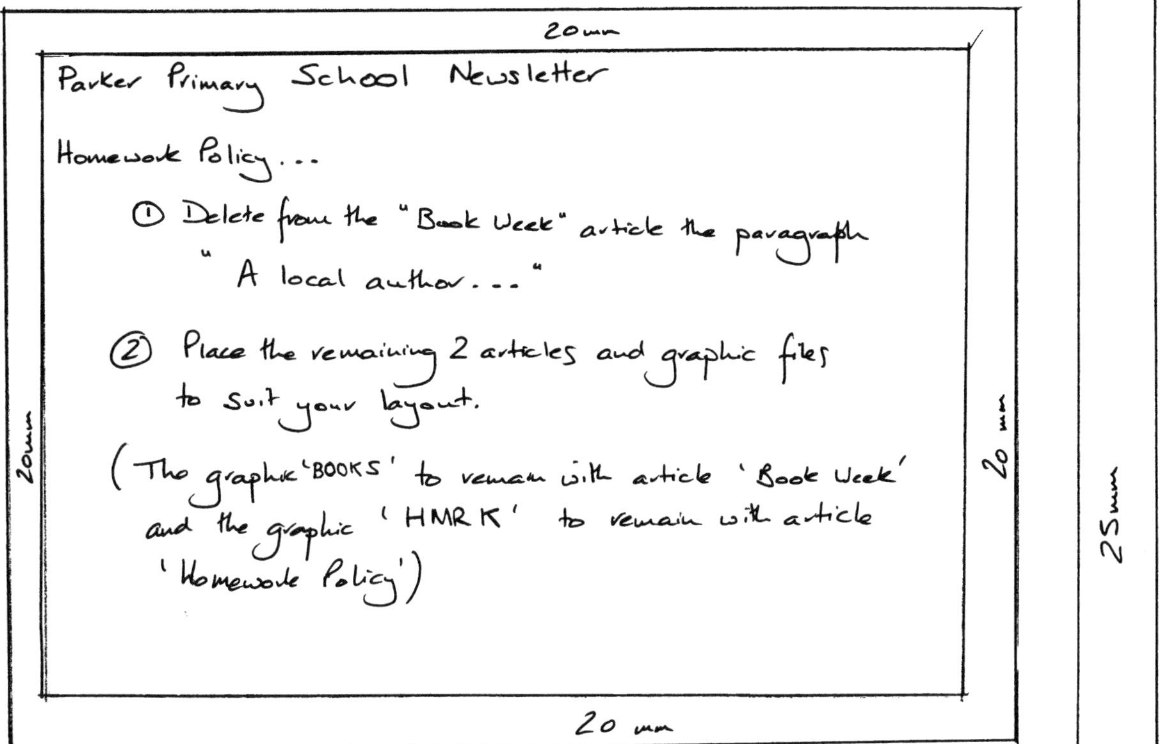

Alternative Page Sketch for Exercise 2.2

25mm

25mm

HOME SAFETY

Safety in the Home

① Delete from the 'How to Prevent Accidents' the table.

② Place the remaining 2 articles and graphic files to suit your layout.

25mm

25mm

3

Exercise 2.3

Open the file: **CLUB1** and save as: **CLUB2**.

Design a landscape layout based on the alternative page sketch on page 111.

Delete from the **Annual Day Out** article, the paragraph **Bath is also home of course,...**

Note that the first article must now be **Forthcoming Events**.

You must use the same fonts and the same point sizes that you chose in Exercise 1.3, page 103.

Crop the **TROPHY** graphic to remove the stand at the bottom. Use irregular text wrap around the **TROPHY** image. Do not include any hyphenation in text that wraps around the graphic.

In the headline text, amend the kerning of the headline so that it stretches across the entire width of the publication.

Ensure that the publication fills the page by changing the leading of the body text.

Save and print the publication.

Exercise 2.4

Open the file: **BUYHM1** and save as: **BUYHM2**.

Design a portrait layout based on the alternative page sketch on page 111.

Delete the table from the **Finance** article.

Note that the first article must now be **Finance**.

You must use the same fonts and the same point sizes that you chose in Exercise 1.4, page 103.

Crop the **HOUSE** graphic to remove the smoke from the chimney. Use irregular text wrap around the **HOUSE** image. Do not include any hyphenation in text that wraps around the graphic.

In the headline text, amend the kerning of the headline so that it stretches to halfway across the publication.

Ensure that the publication fills the page by changing the leading of the body text.

Save and print the publication.

Alternative Page Sketch for Exercise 2.3

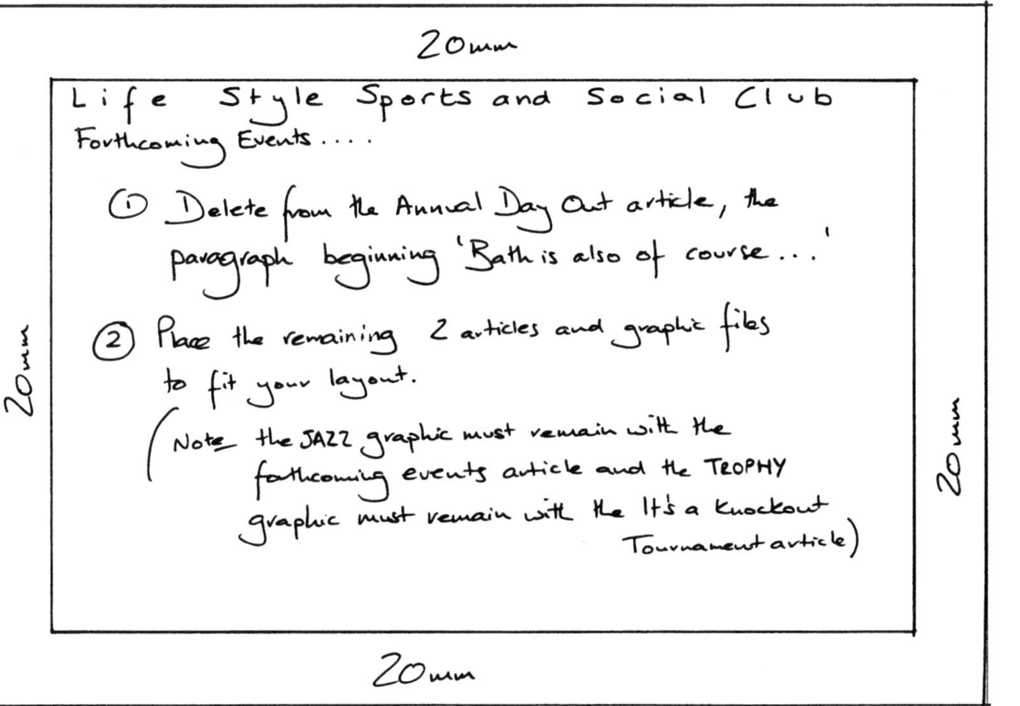

Alternative Page Sketch for Exercise 2.4

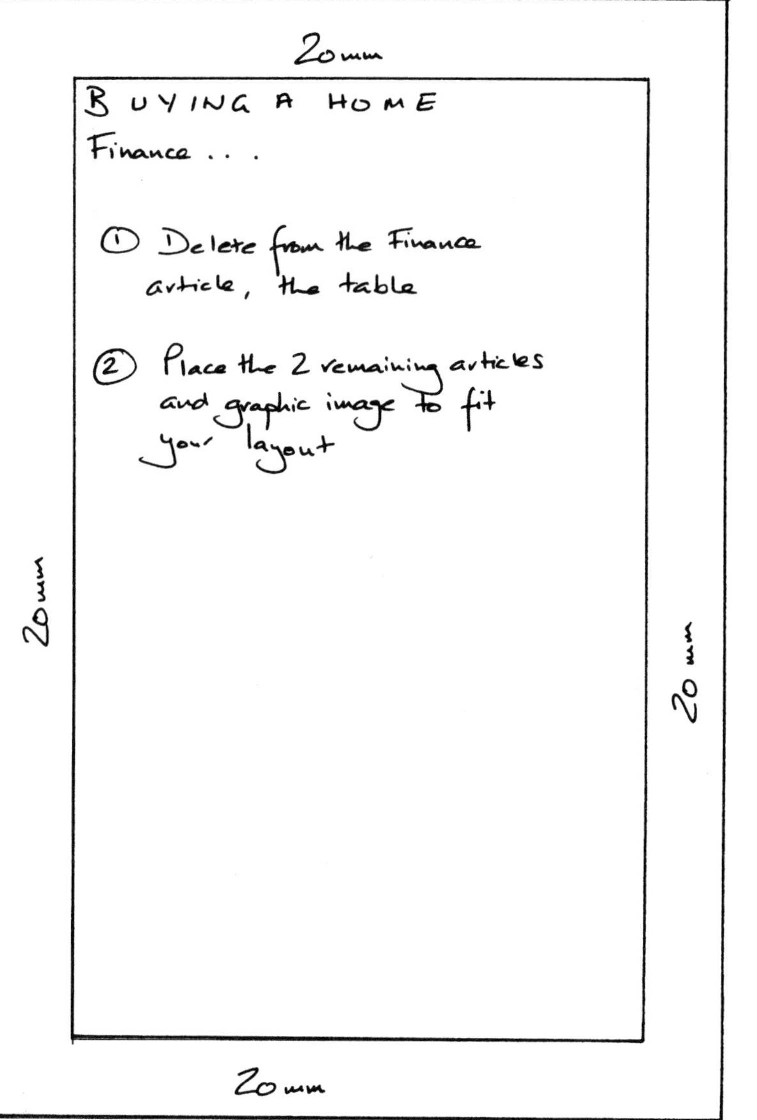

Using a non-standard page size

Non-standard page sizes may be used in the workplace to produce posters, business cards, index cards, leaflets etc. For the purposes of this book, you will be defining the page measurements for a page smaller than A4.

This should not cause too many problems. In the page setup menu, you will need to change the paper size to 'custom' and then type in the relevant measurements. Type in exactly the measurements you require.

Using crop marks

Crop marks are used to show the printing area of a sheet of paper. In the print process, printing is carried out on standard-size sheets of paper and then cut to the required size. The crop marks show exactly where the cuts need to be made. Look at Figure 3.12.

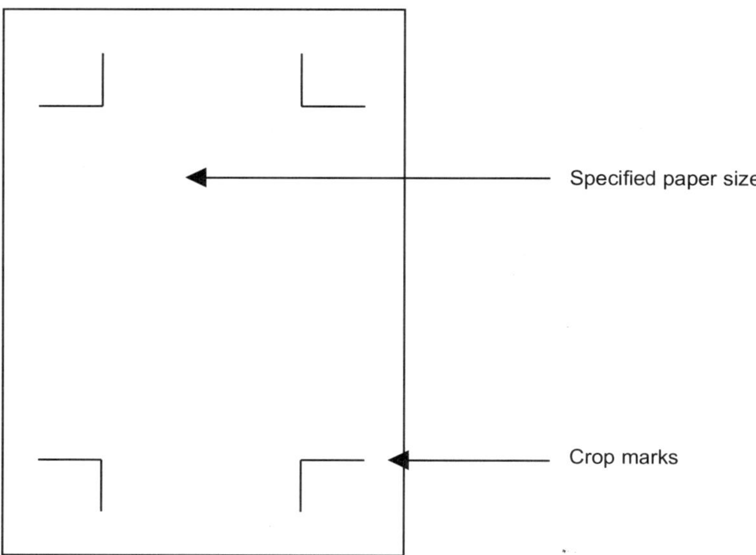

Figure 3.12 Crop marks

Some software packages will also insert the date and time of the document, just outside of the crop marks.

You will normally have to specify that you require crop marks in your software program. This may be contained within the print options. Find out how to set crop marks on your software now.

Unfortunately, most software programs do not show crop marks on screen, even in print preview. Ensure that when you print your publication they can be seen.

Designing your document

If you are producing a leaflet or newsletter you will want your document to be eye-catching. There are a number of ways in which you can achieve this. For example:

- use of fonts and sizes
- use of bold and/or italic
- using boxes and lines to draw attention to parts of the text

- placing the graphics and text in an eye-catching way
- using shading for boxes
- multi-layering boxes/text/images
- using reversed text
- using rotated text
- using bullets
- repeating text and/or images.

You have already looked at most of these. However, there are still a few to learn.

3

Shading

It is still possible to read the text through shading. Beware, however, of making your shade colour too dark. Look at Figure 3.13.

This box is shaded using a 25% grey fill. Note that you can still read the text.	This box is shaded using a 50% grey fill. It is much more difficult to read the text

Figure 3.13 Shading

Reverse text

Reverse text is different to shaded text. Look at Figure 3.14.

Reversed text means white text on a black background. This can be very effective when used as a design feature in a publication.

Figure 3.14 Reverse text

How you achieve this effect depends on your software. You may have a text style in the format or text style menu that just states reverse text. Alternatively, you may need to set up a text box and use a black fill with white text. Find out how to reverse text on your software now.

Repeating text and/or images

Quite often a leaflet will repeat the company logo on each page or repeat the same information in a bid to get us to remember it. If you wish to repeat items then copying them is a quick alternative to importing them separately. This is particularly true if you have set up a multi-layered item and then wish to repeat it.

Generally, in order to copy items, you will need to select the item first by clicking on it, then use the copy facility – usually found in the edit menu. You will also find any shortcut keys that can be used. For example, in Microsoft Publisher, the shortcut key is **CTRL** + **C**.

The items then need to be pasted into a different location. To do this, return to the edit menu and choose the paste facility. This will then bring a second copy of your item onto screen which can be dragged into position. There is usually a shortcut key for the paste facility too.

You may wish to copy layered items. If this is the case you can do this in three ways:

1 Copy and paste each item separately and then use the mouse to position correctly.
2 Click on the handles of each item whilst holding down the **SHIFT** key. With the handles selected you can follow the usual copy and paste procedures to paste the layered items together.
3 By grouping the items first. This means that the items will be grouped together to form just one item. To do this, click on the handles of all items, holding down the **SHIFT** key at the same time. Then select the **group** command. The various items will form one item and then you can follow the usual copy and paste procedures. If you wish to ungroup the items later, for example to amend one or more of them, then there will be an ungroup facility to do this. However, if you decide to ungroup an image, remember that when all the handles are highlighted, all the items will be selected. If you accidentally press delete then you will lose all the items from your page. As soon as you have ungrouped, click the mouse button once in a clear space to deselect the items.

Rotated text

Rotated text can give an interesting effect. Look at Figure 3.15.

Figure 3.15 Rotated text

Rotating text is usually a simple operation. You will need to use the rotation drawing tool. Click on the text box to bring forward a handle and then using the rotation tool pull the box around to the correct position. Alternatively, you may have a value box in which you can type the amount of rotation in degrees. If you use this you will not need to move the text manually.

Printing colour separations

Printing your publication using colour-separation techniques is not nearly as difficult as it sounds as your software will probably be able to do this automatically. However, before you do this, you need to decide which items to have as black, and which to have as the specified colour. It does not matter which you choose, however, you must ensure that all the items on the page are assigned a colour. If you do not do this then they will either not be printed at all, or will be printed on both pages. To do this, just select each object and assign it to either a colour or black.

In the printing process, colours are printed separately and so in order to print a two-page publication we will end up with four separate pages – two for each page of our two-page publication. Look at Figure 3.16, which shows the process for a two colour separation – red and black:

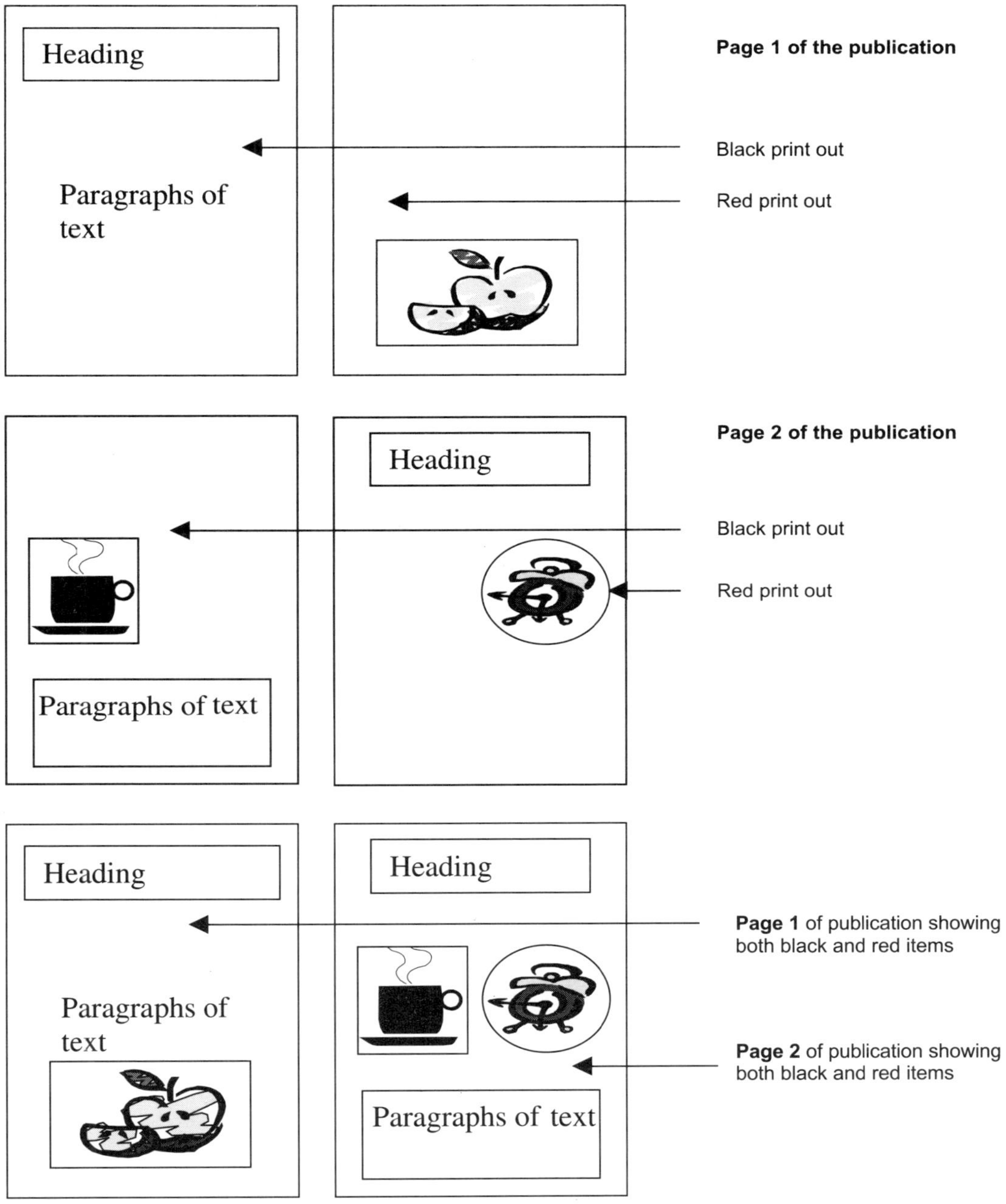

Figure 3.16 Colour separations

You do not need a colour printer to do this as both separations can be printed in black. The reason for this is that each sheet prints only the items that are to be in its own colour. The above example shows how this works.

There must be some way of showing the reader which sheets correspond with each colour. Some software programs will do this automatically. If this is not the case, then you should insert a footer or text box outside the crop marks which gives the colour and page number for each sheet.

Exercise 3

Try the following exercises.

Exercise 3.1

Produce the publication from the page layout sketches on page 117. Follow the orientation and measurements given.

The text files for this exercise are: **SNOW**, **STALLS** and **SANTA**. The image files for this exercise are: **SNOWMAN**, **TREE** and **SAN**.

Design the layout of the pages from the page layout sketches on page 117. Use 25mm margins.

You will need to key in the text which appears on the page layout sketches, as this text is not included in your text files.

Ensure that you follow all the instructions on the page layout sketches.

Save as: **XMAS1**.

You must produce two printouts of each page, one for each colour. You may choose which images/parts of text are to be pink, and which black. Be careful to ensure that each item of the publication appears on either the pink or the black printout. Please note that the worked examples show the final composite pages and not the colour separations.

Ensure that crop marks are included on the colour-separated pages and indicate which page and colour is which (ie Page 1 – Black, Page 1 – pink, etc).

Exercise 3.2

Produce the publication from the page layout sketches on page 118. Follow the orientation and measurements given.

The text files for this exercise are: **NEWENG**, **TOURS** and **CITY**. The image files for this exercise are: **FLAG**, **SKY** and **STATUE**.

Design the layout of the pages from the page layout sketches on page 118. Use 25mm margins.

You will need to key in the text which appears on the page layout sketches, as this text is not included in your text files.

Ensure that you follow all the instructions on the page layout sketches.

Save as: **USA1**.

You must produce two printouts of each page, one for each colour. You may choose which images/parts of text are to be pink, and which black. Be careful to ensure that each item of the publication appears on either the pink or the black printout.

Ensure that crop marks are included on the colour-separated pages and indicate which page and colour is which (ie Page 1 – Black, Page 1 – pink, etc).

Page 1 Layout for Exercise 3.1

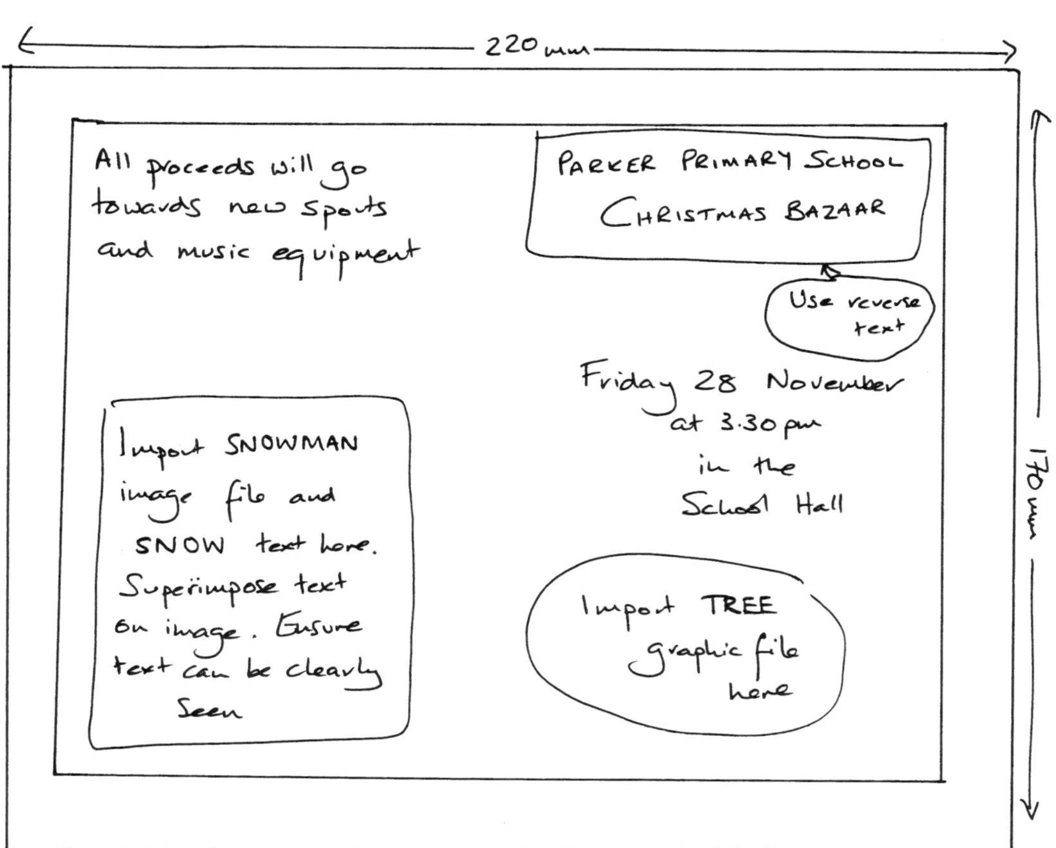

3

Page 2 Layout for Exercise 3.1

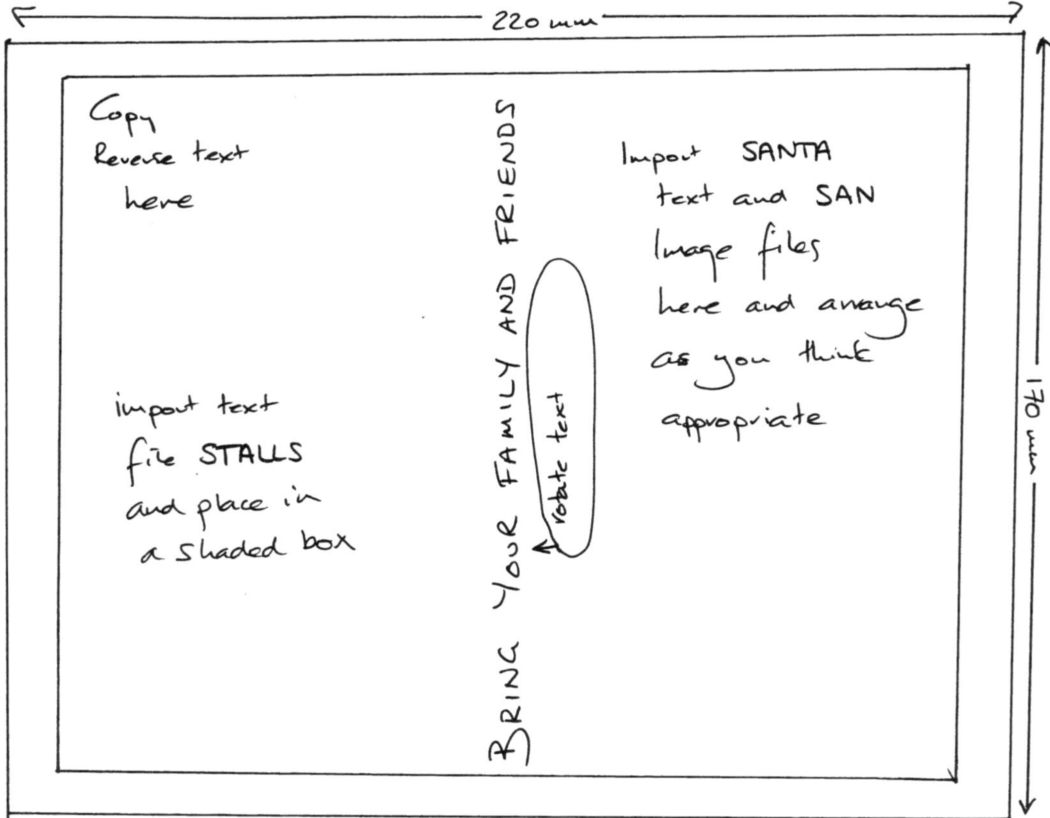

Page 1 Layout for Exercise 3.2

160mm

190mm

Import FLAG image here

Import NEW ENG text here

Use reverse text

Tour America with USA TODAY

Import STATUE image here

Import TOURS text here

Visit us on the Web on http://www/tours.co.uk

Use rotated text here

Page 2 Layout for Exercise 3.2

160mm

190mm

Import CITY text file and SKY image and arrange as you think appropriate

Copy STATUE image here

New for this year...
ACCOMMODATION SERVICE
We have found a number of luxury properties for you to rent. These can be booked for a minimum of 2 nights and can be slotted into your tour.
Ask XXXX for more details.

Replace XXXX with your name. Create a shaded box for this text.

Exercise 3.3

12000. Follow the orientation and measurements given.

The text files for this exercise are: **PARTY**, **THEME** and **DETAILS**. The image files for this exercise are: **HATS**, **CAKE** and **BLN**.

Design the layout of the pages from the attached page layout sketches on page 120. Use 25mm margins.

You will need to key in the text which appears on the page layout sketches, as this text is not included in your text files.

Ensure that you follow all the instructions on the page layout sketches.

Save as: **PARTY1**.

You must produce two printouts of each page, one for each colour. You may choose which images/parts of text are to be pink, and which black. Be careful to ensure that each item of the publication appears on either the pink or the black printout.

Ensure that crop marks are included on the colour-separated pages and indicate which page and colour is which (ie Page 1 – Black, Page 1 – pink, etc).

Exercise 3.4

Produce the publication from the page layout sketches on page 120. Follow the orientation and measurements given.

The text files for this exercise are: **BATH**, **OUTING**; and **TIMES**. The image files for this exercise are: **SEWING** and **PIN**.

Design the layout of the pages from the page layout sketches on page 121. Use 25mm margins.

You will need to key in the text which appears on the page layout sketches, as this text is not included in your text files.

Ensure that you follow all the instructions on the page layout sketches.

Save as: **SEW1**.

You must produce two printouts of each page, one for each colour. You may choose which images/parts of text are to be pink, and which black. Be careful to ensure that each item of the publication appears on either the pink or the black printout.

Ensure that crop marks are included on the colour-separated pages and indicate which page and colour is which (ie Page 1 – Black, Page 1 – pink, etc).

Page 1 Layout for Exercise 3.3

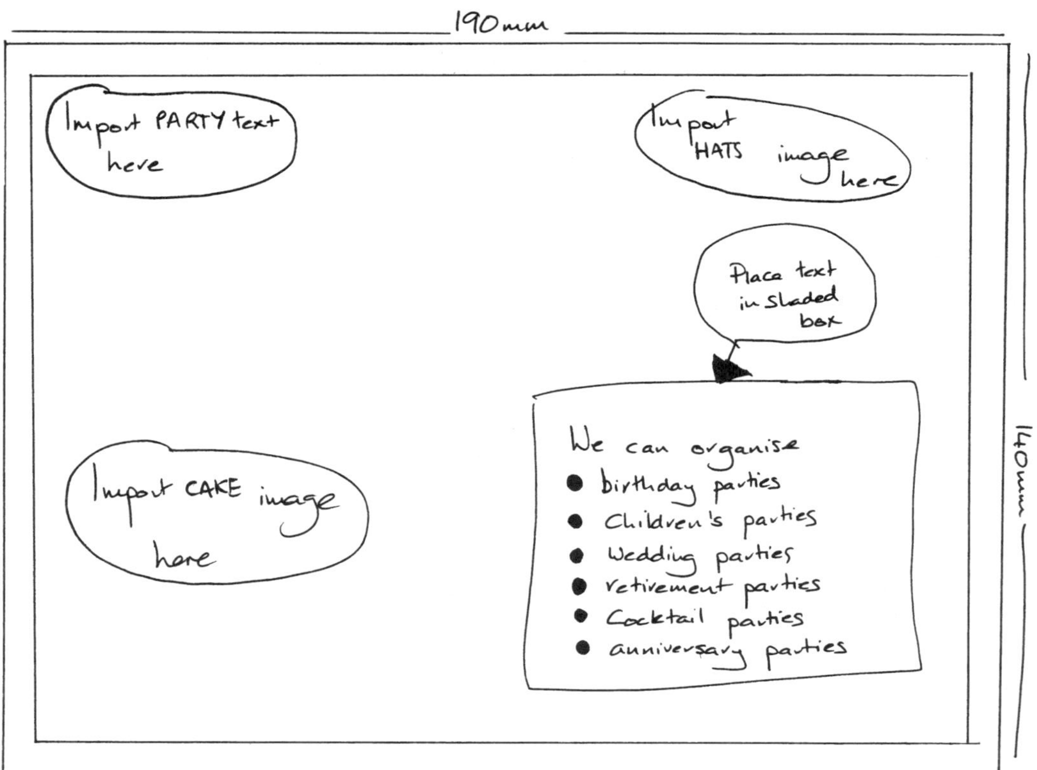

Page 2 Layout for Exercise 3.3

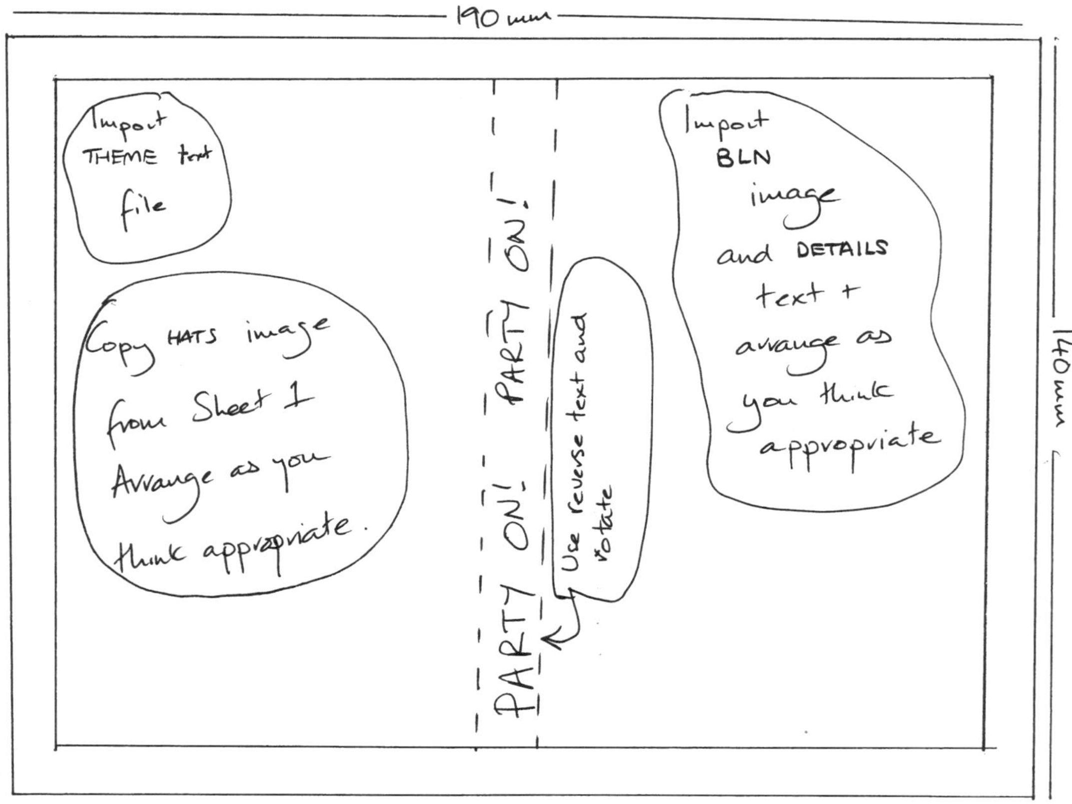

Page 1 Layout for Exercise 3.4

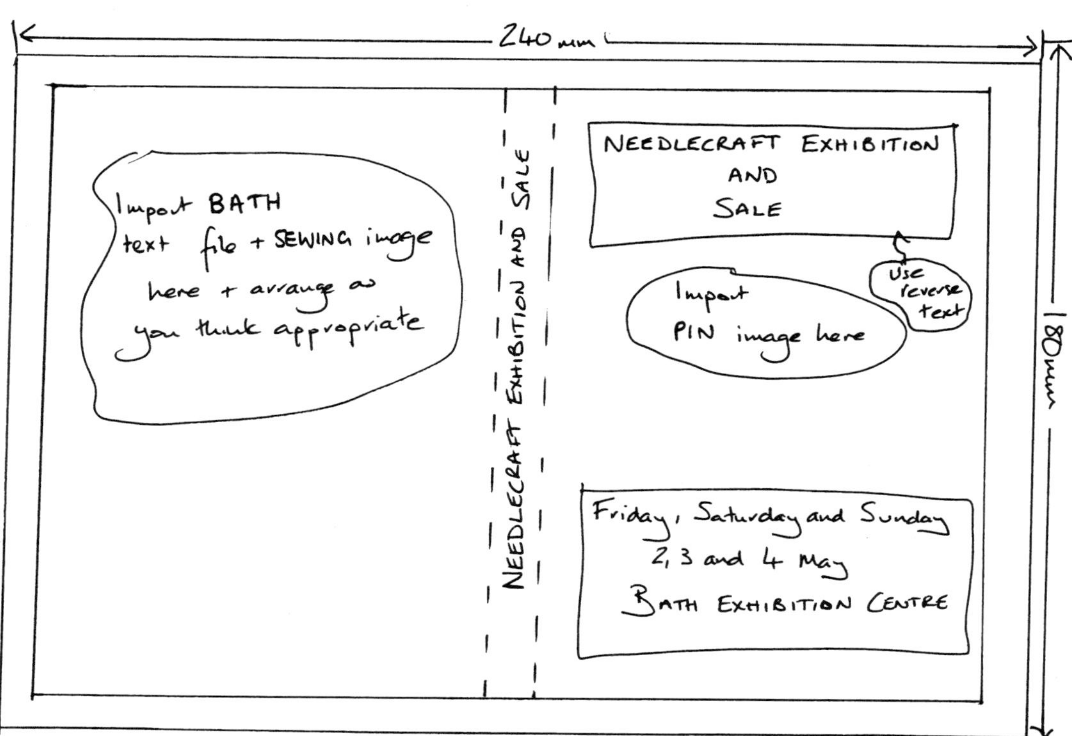

Page 2 Layout for Exercise 3.4

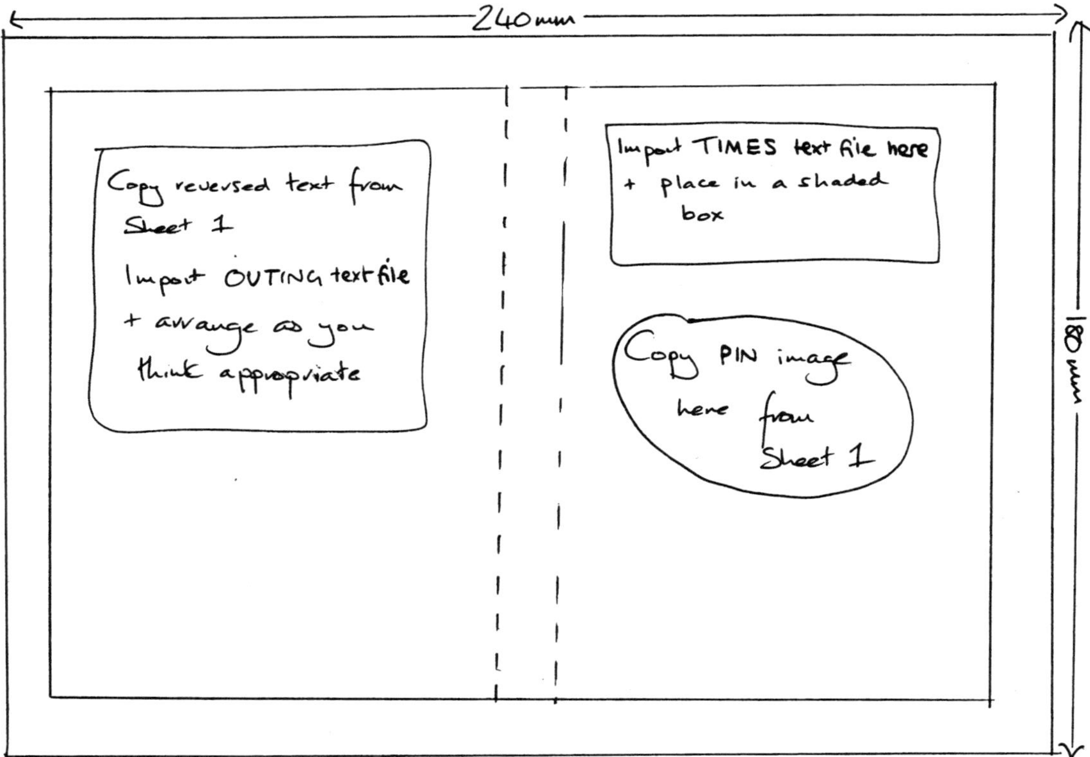

You have now completed all the work necessary for you to be able to do the RSA Desktop Publishing Stage III exam. Try the following consolidation exercises to practice the skills you have learnt.

3

Consolidation 3 Part 1

Before you start Task 1, ensure you have on disk the following text and image files. These must be imported into your DTP publication.

Text files: **MEMB**; **GOODS**; **ORDER**

Image files: **BK**; **STEREO**

1. Create an A4 size publication following the design brief on page 123. Gutter space may be as you wish. Use lines/rules where indicated in the design brief.
2. Set up a style sheet for Headline, Subhead and Body Text as shown in the design brief. Choose point sizes to fill the publication. Import the text files and apply the appropriate styles.
3. In the 'Ordering Details' article, insert the following new paragraph between the second and third paragraphs:

   All our goods should reach you in perfect condition within 28 days of ordering. If you decide, after examination, that you do not wish to keep the goods, you may return them for a full refund.
4. You must format the table within the 'Range of Goods' article. Set up two columns, left aligned, with column headings: 'Age of Child' and 'Category'.
5. Produce dropped capitals for the first letter of **each** article. Maintain consistent text flow of the body text around the dropped capitals.
6. Place the two image files as indicated in the design brief, maintaining the original proportions.
7. Copyfit your publication to ensure:
   - all material is displayed on one page
   - text/graphics/lines are not superimposed on each other
   - headings and related text are grouped together
   - one line or less of text is grouped with the rest of the related text
   - paragraph spacing is consistent
   - leading is consistent
   - no more than 5 hyphenated line endings on a page
   - no more than 1cm (10mm) (vertical) white space unless specified in the design brief.
8. Save as **MYPL1** and print the publication.

Design Brief for Consolidation 3 Part 1

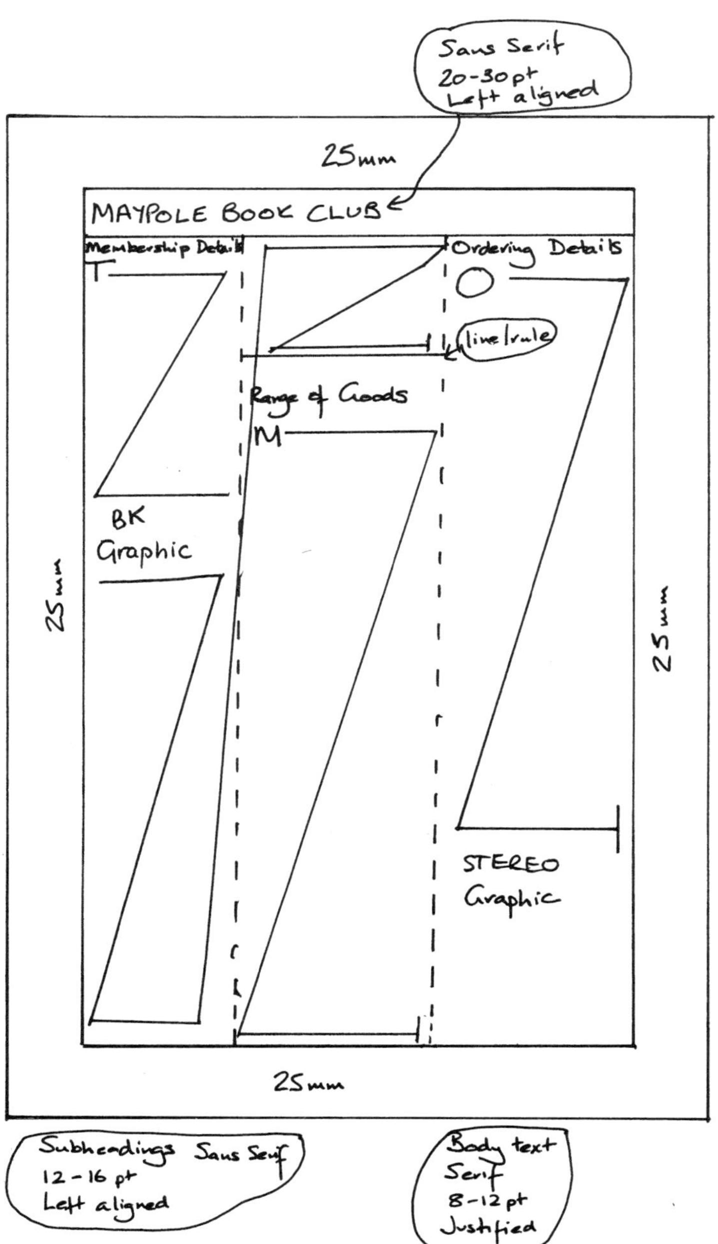

Consolidation 3 Part 2

You are required to produce an alternative version of the publication from Element One (**MYPL1**).

1 Design a landscape layout based on the alternative page layout sketch on page 124.

Delete, from the 'Range of Goods' article, the table.

Note that the first article must remain 'Membership Details'.

You must use the same fonts and the same point sizes that you chose in Part 1.

2 Crop the **STEREO** graphic to remove the headphones.

3 Use irregular text wrap around the **STEREO** image. Do not include any hyphenation in text that wraps around the graphic.

4 In the Headline text, in the word 'BOOK' amend the kerning of the two letters 'O' so that they cross each other.

5 Ensure the publication fills the page by changing the leading of the body text.

6 Copyfit your publication to ensure:

- all material is displayed on one page
- text/graphics/lines are not superimposed on each other
- headings and related text are grouped together
- one line or less of text is grouped with the rest of the related text
- paragraph spacing is consistent
- leading is consistent
- no more than 5 hyphenated line endings on a page
- no more than 1cm (10mm) (vertical) white space unless specified in the design brief.

7 Save as **MYPL2** and print the publication.

Page Layout for Consolidation 3 Part 2

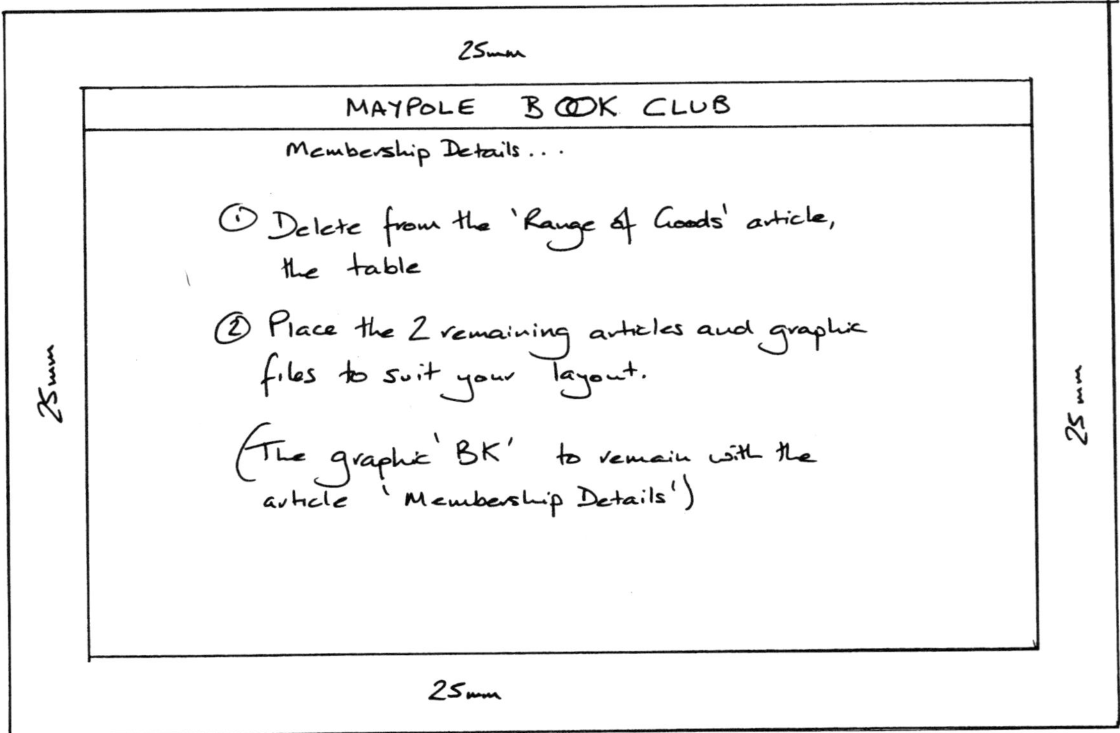

Consolidation 3 Part 3

For this task you are required to produce a leaflet consisting of 2 pages. The publication should be designed and set up to produce a two-colour leaflet in blue and black. However, you do not need a colour printer.

Text files: **HLFTRM**; **TEDDY**; **SAND**

Image files: **SUN**; **TED**; **YACHT**; **JACK**

1 Produce the publication from the page layout sketches on page 126. Follow the orientation and measurements given.

2 Design the layout of the pages from the page layout sketches on page 126. Use 25mm margins.

3 You will need to key in the text which appears on the page layout sketches, as this text is not included in your text files.

4 Ensure that you follow all the instructions on the page layout sketches.

5 Save the document as: **TOY1**.

You must produce two printouts of each page, one for each colour. You may choose which images/parts of text are to be blue, and which black. Be careful to ensure that each item of the publication appears on either the blue or the black printout.

Ensure that crop marks are included on the colour separated pages and indicate which page and colour is which (ie Page 1 – Black, Page 1 – Blue, etc).

Page Layout for Consolidation 3 Part 3 – Page 1

180 mm

210 mm

Import SUN image here

TOY CHEST NEWS
Summer Edition

Free to Customers

Create + use reverse text

Import HLFTRM text file here

Import TEDDY text file + TED image here (Arrange as you think appropriate)

Create a shaded ellipse as background to this text.

Page Layout for Consolidation 3 Part 3 – Page 2

180 mm

210 mm

Import SAND text file

Import YACHT image

Rotate text

Import JACK image here

Just IN
A brand new range of quality wooden toys. See the new range in Selected shops

Call 0182 388299 for a Mail order Catalogue

Coming Soon . . .
Watch out for the Autumn issue of Toy Chest News. We will be featuring some great new toys for Christmas.

Copy here, from Sheet 1 the shaded ellipse and text

Exam Practice 3

Element 1 – Create a pre-press publication from a design brief

Before you start Task 1, ensure you have on disk the following text files and image files. These must be imported into your DTP publication.

Text files: **DOOR**; **VOL**; **GREEN**

Image files: **BOXES**; **COURIER**

3

Assessment objectives	
1.1a	Create an A4 size publication following the design brief on page 128. Gutter space may be as you wish. Use lines/rules where indicated in the design brief.
1.2a	Set up a style sheet for Headline, Subhead and Body Text as shown in the design brief. Choose point sizes to fill the publication. Import the text files and apply the appropriate styles.
1.5a	In the 'Volunteers Required' article, insert the following new paragraph between the first and second paragraphs: Volunteers are now required to join in our working parties. This can be during the week or at weekends. If you can spare a few hours and would like to meet new people, keep fit and work for a deserving cause, then please contact us.
1.3a	You must format the table at the end of the 'Green Stationery' article. Set up three columns, left aligned, with column headings: 'Item', 'Quantity' and 'Price'.
1.4a, 1.4b	Produce dropped capitals for the first letter of each article. Maintain consistent text flow of the body text around the dropped capitals.
1.1a	Place the two image files as indicated in the design brief, maintaining the original proportions.
1.6a, 1.6b, 1.6c, 1.6d, 1.6e, 1.6f, 1.6g, 1.6h	Copyfit your publication to ensure: ■ all material is displayed on one page ■ text/graphics/lines are not superimposed on each other. ■ headings and related text are grouped together ■ one line or less of text is grouped with the rest of the related text ■ paragraph spacing is consistent ■ leading is consistent ■ no more than 5 hyphenated line endings on a page ■ no more than 1cm (10mm) (vertical) white space unless specified in the design brief.
1.7a	Save as **ENV1** and print the publication.

Design Brief for Exam Practice 3 Element 1

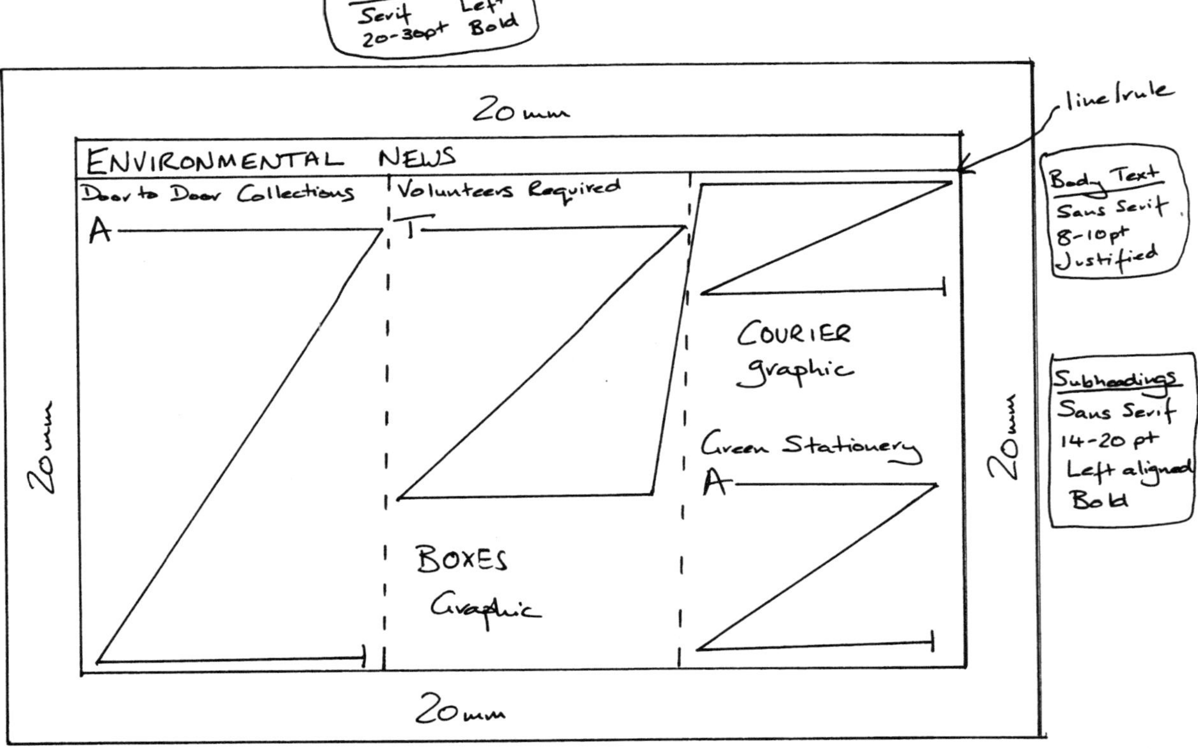

Element 2 – Produce alternative version of a publication

You are required to produce an alternative version of the publication from Element One (**ENV1**).

Assessment objectives

2.1a	Design a portrait layout based on the alternative page layout sketch on page 129. Delete, from the 'Green Stationery' article, the paragraph beginning 'Customers who visit the store by the end of June…' Note that the first article must remain 'Door to Door Collections'. You must use the same fonts and the same point sizes that you chose in Element 1.
2.2a	Crop the **BOXES** graphic to remove the box on the right-hand side.
2.3a, 2.3b	Use irregular text wrap around the **BOXES** image. Do not include any hyphenation in text that wraps around the graphic.
2.4a	In the Headline text, amend the kerning of the headline so that the letters touch each other.
2.5a	Ensure the publication fills the page by changing the leading of the body text.
2.6a, 2.6b,	Copyfit your publication to ensure:

2.6c, 2.6d, 2.6e, 2.6f, 2.6g, 2.6h	■ all material is displayed on one page ■ text/graphics/lines are not superimposed on each other ■ headings and related text are grouped together ■ one line or less of text is grouped with the rest of the related text ■ paragraph spacing is consistent ■ leading is consistent ■ no more than 5 hyphenated line endings on a page ■ no more than 1cm (10mm) (vertical) white space unless specified in the design brief.
2.7a	Save as **ENV2** and print the publication.

Page Layout for Exam Practice 3 Element 2

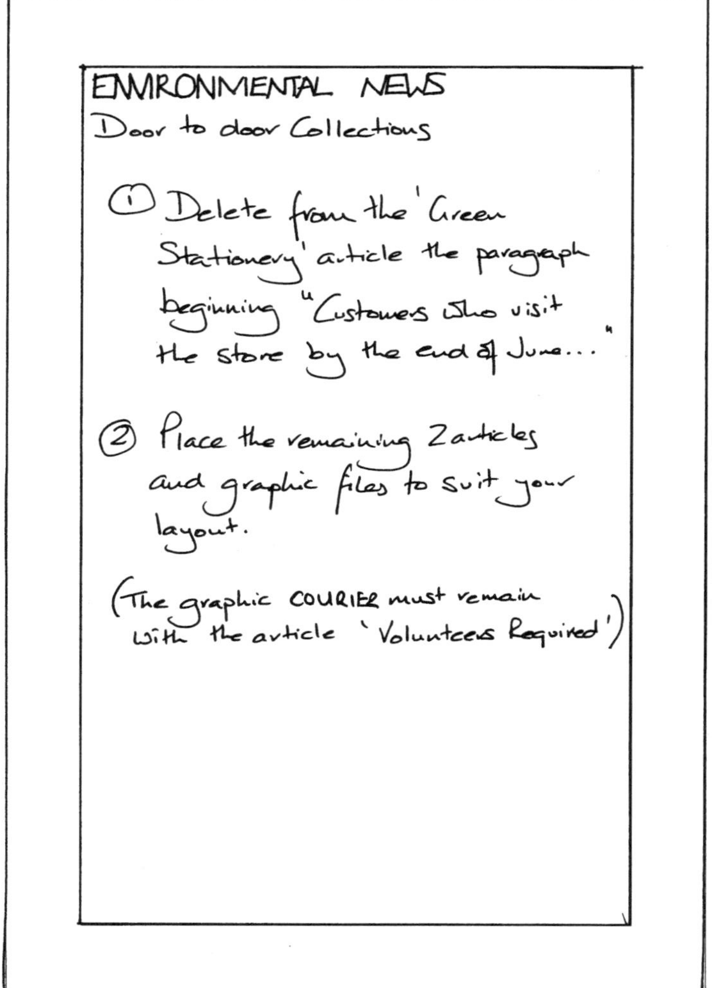

Element 3 – Prepare a publication for colour production

For this task you are required to produce a newsletter consisting of two pages. The publication should be designed and set up to produce a two-colour leaflet in green and black. However, you do not need a colour printer.

Text files: **CHESTER**; **HOTEL**; **CONF**

Image files: **SWAN**; **GOLF**

Assessment Objectives	
3.1a, 3.1b	Produce the publication from the page layout sketches on page 131. Follow the orientation and measurements given.
3.2a	Design the layout of the pages from the page layout sketches on page 131. Use 25mm margins.
3.6a	You will need to key in the text which appears on the page layout sketches, as this text is not included in your text files.
3.3a, 3.3b, 3.3c, 3.4a, 3.5a	Ensure that you follow all the instructions on the page layout sketches. The Assessment Objectives are identified alongside each relevant part of the sketch (eg 3.4a), these are for your reference and are not to be keyed in.
3.7a	Save the document as: **HOTEL1**.
	You must produce two printouts of each page, one for each colour. You may choose which images/parts of text are to be green, and which black. Be careful to ensure that each item of the publication appears on either the green or the black printout.
	Ensure that crop marks are included on the colour separated pages and indicate which page and colour is which (ie Page 1 – Black, Page 1 – Green, etc).

Page Layout for Exam Practice 3 Element 3 – Page 1

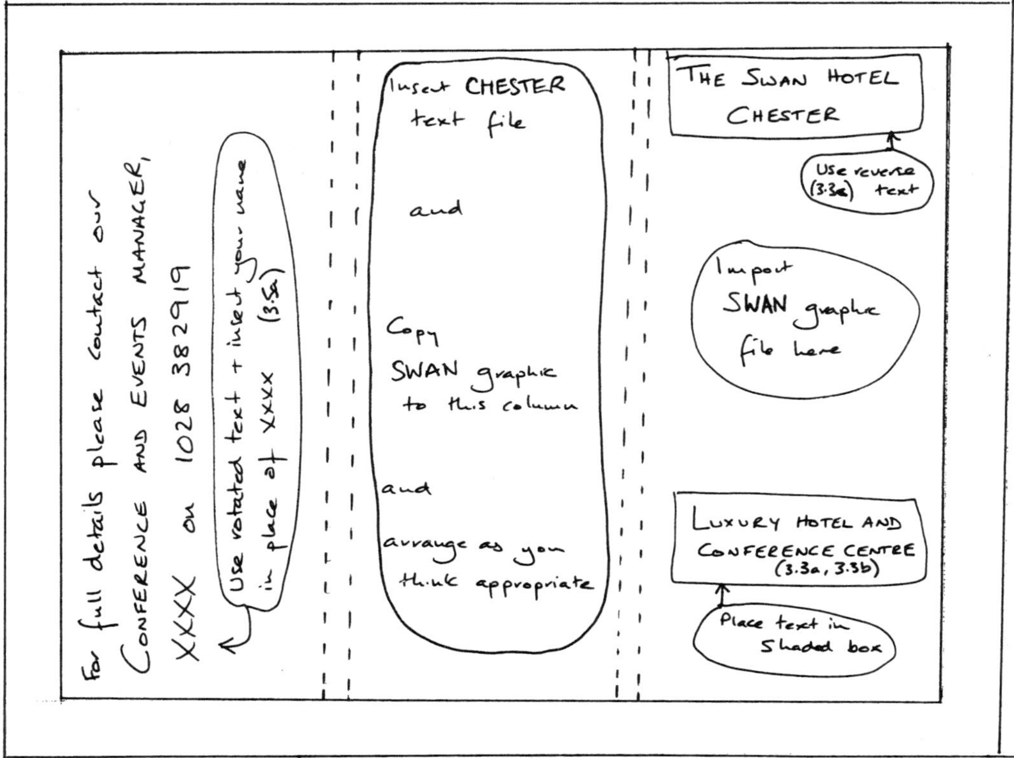

Page Layout for Exam Practice 3 Element 3 – Page 2

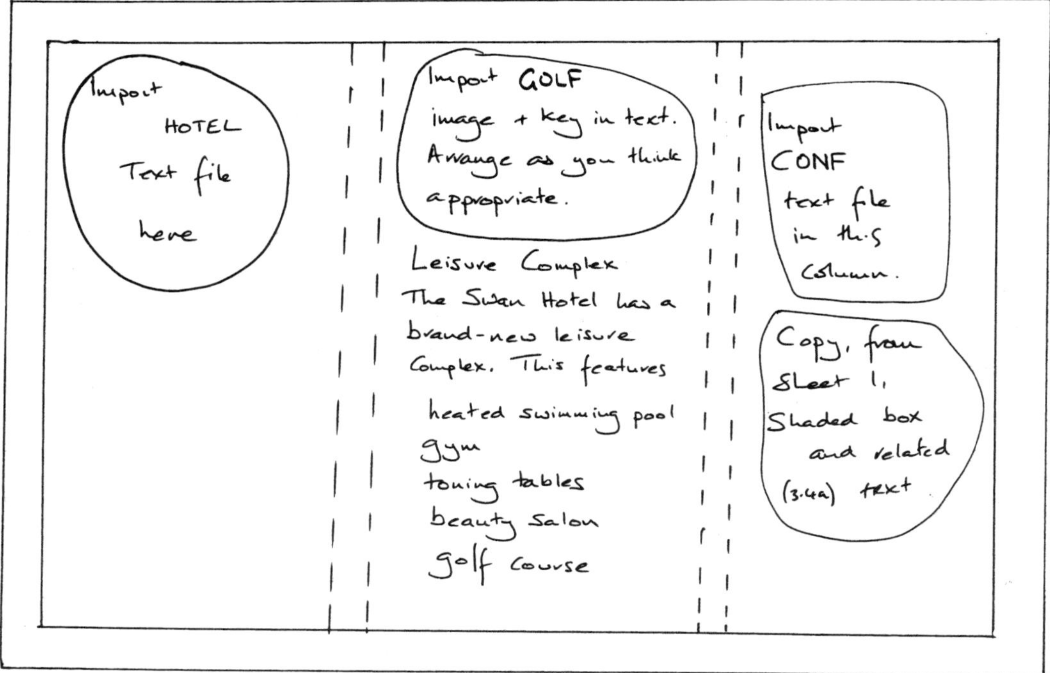

3

Stage III Checklist

Did you remember to …	Assessment Objective	Consolidation 3 Part 1	Consolidation 3 Part 3	Consolidation 3 Part 2	Exam Practice 3 Task 1	Exam Practice 3 Task 2	Exam Practice 3 Task 3
design a page layout displaying the text, graphics and lines as specified?	1.1a						
create a style sheet and apply the text styles correctly?	1.2a						
set up a table, aligning the columns consistently?	1.3a						
create dropped capitals for the first letter of each article, ensuring that the text flow around the capitals remained consistent?	1.4a						
key in all the required text without error?	1.5a 3.6a						
copyfit the document in accordance with instructions?	1.6a, 2.6a, 1.6b, 2.6b, 1.6c, 2.6c, 1.6d, 2.6d, 1.6e, 2.6e, 1.6f, 2.6f, 1.6g, 2.6g, 1.6h, 2.6h						
save and print your document correctly?	1.7a, 2.7a, 3.7a						
design an alternative layout as specified?	2.2a						
crop the graphic as specified?	2.3a, 2.3b						
create irregular text wrap around the graphic without hyphenation?	2.4a						
amend the kerning as specified?	2,4a						
amend the leading as specified?	2.5a						

Did you remember to …	Assessment Objective	Consolidation 3 Part 1	Part 3	Part 2	Exam Practice 3 Task 1	Task 2	Task 3
create a non-standard page size, with orientation and page measurements as specified and showing crop marks?	3.1a, 3.1b, 3.1c						
design a page layout within the given specifications?	3.2a						
produce multi-layer items and use shading and reverse text as specified?	3.3a, 3.3b, 3.3c						
copy the text and images as specified?	3.4a						
rotate text as specified?	3.5a						

3

Exercise 1.1

Parker Primary School Newsletter

Book Week

This year's Book Week was an enormous success. The children enjoyed the various activities and over £2000 was earned from the book sales.

Each day throughout the week, had a different theme, chosen from a popular children's story. The children discussed the story, drew pictures, made bookmarks and wrote and told stories of their own.

A local author of children's books came to visit the school on Wednesday afternoon. Harry Gloss read extracts from his latest book and presented the school with copies of all his novels. Great thanks must go to Harry for giving so generously.

The Book at Bedtime was, as usual, attended by a great many of the children. Stories started at 7.00 pm and hot chocolate was served at 7.30 pm. The PTA served tea and coffee to parents and there was an opportunity for parents to visit the book shop. Grateful thanks go to Mrs Gregory for her hard work and enthusiasm in arranging this event.

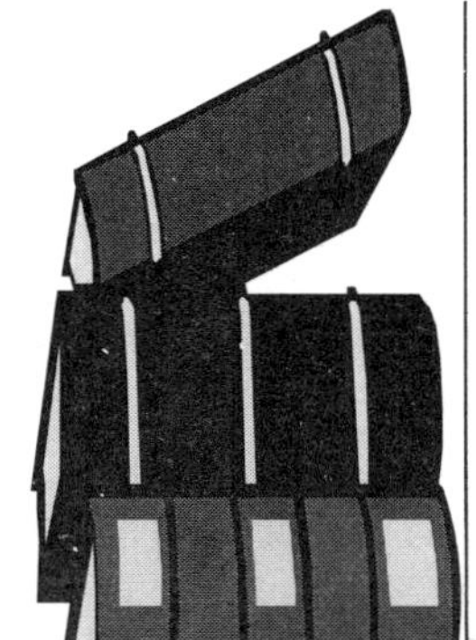

Competition Winners

Our annual painting competition results were announced last week. A large number of children entered this year and the theme was A Wild Animal. It was good to see the effort the children put into their pictures and, as usual, a very high standard of work was produced.

A display of these pictures is in the main hall and will be there until the end of term. Parents are welcome to visit the display after school each day.

The booksellers Gordons kindly agreed to sponsor this competition by giving book tokens for prizes.

The results are as follows:

Place	Name	Class
1st	Susan Handy	3
2nd	Michael Norman	5
3rd	Sam Jardine	3

Homework Policy

The school has recently revised its homework policy as part of our annual school review. The following guidelines have been drawn up to assist parents and teachers.

Homework will be given on at least a weekly basis for the lower juniors. This will comprise of a spelling test and mathematical tables. Homework will be set on a Monday, with tests taking place on Friday. Children may also be asked to complete work at home if the teacher considers it necessary.

Upper juniors will also be given weekly spelling and tables homework. In addition, they will also be asked to complete various pieces of topic work. These may take the form of completing worksheets or illustrating their written work. A clear timescale for completion will be given, as will deadlines for the return of their work.

We do hope that you will encourage your child to complete their homework. We feel that it teaches children to work to deadlines, encourages time management skills and provides a gentle lead in to the level of homework given at secondary school.

If you have any concerns, or would like further clarification of the homework policy, please discuss with the headteacher.

Exercise 1.2

HOME SAFETY

Safety in the Home

Many people require hospital treatment each year because of accidents in the home. A large number of the injuries suffered could have been avoided with a little care and forethought.

Those most at risk of accidents in the home are the elderly and children under five. Young children need to be constantly supervised as they have a natural curiosity, which often leads them into danger. Over half a million children receive hospital treatment each year due to accidents at home.

Children, especially babies and toddlers love to put things in their mouths. Toddlers can be very unsteady and have poor balance when they are learning to walk. Sharp objects such as table edges can be potentially dangerous. Older children are often tempted by matches and may inadvertently start a fire.

Elderly people may, because of arthritis or other diseases, suffer from reduced mobility and slower reflexes. They may also be more prone to accidents as their eyesight fails or they become more forgetful.

In order to prevent accidents, a careful look around your home should alert you to any hazards.

Potential Hazards

For the young almost everything in the home can be a potential danger. Sharp objects, such as kitchen knives left on the edges of worktops can easily be pulled off by inquisitive children. For toddlers, sharp furniture edges, exposed electrical sockets and trailing cables all cause accidents.

The kitchen holds many dangers. Sharp knives, boiling water, hot objects and household chemicals are all causes of major accidents.

The staircase is probably one of the most dangerous areas of the home. Badly-fitting carpets, loose edges or objects left lying on the stairs can cause people to trip. The staircase should be well lit and a handrail provided in order to minimise the risks.

Surprisingly, many accidents happen in the garden. Many plants are toxic and can be harmful if eaten. Some plants can cause a rash or allergic reaction if touched with the bare hand. Your local garden centre or nursery will be able to advise you on plants that are dangerous.

Trailing flexes from electric lawnmowers and barbecues that are not properly supervised are all potential areas of danger.

Children are fascinated by water and if you have a garden pond, ensure that small children are not left in the garden unsupervised.

Cigarettes that have not been properly extinguished and thrown into wastepaper baskets or left lying in an ashtray can cause a fire in a short space of time. Fires can spread rapidly throughout the house.

One potential hazard we may not be aware of is a faulty gas cooker, fire or boiler. These can emit poisonous carbon monoxide fumes, as can partially blocked chimneys.

How to Prevent Accidents

Most accidents could easily be avoided with a little thought and planning. Take a look at each room in your home and check the following.

Are there any sharp objects that a child could fall onto? Are the electrical sockets, including light switches in good order? Ensure that carpets are securely fitted and free from signs of wear and tear, especially stair carpets.

Ensure that all household chemicals and medicines are correctly labelled and kept out of the reach of children. Do not allow children to play with matches or cigarette lighters.

In the kitchen, ensure cables from electrical appliances are not hanging over the worktops. If you have small children, a cooker guard may be a worthwhile investment.

Smoke alarms are an absolute must. They are inexpensive and easy to fit. An average sized home should install two; one upstairs and one in the kitchen.

In the garden, ensure ponds and pools are fenced if young children regularly play near them. Make sure your plants and shrubs are harmless if eaten by animals or children. Empty paddling pools when not in use.

Ensure children are properly supervised, particularly when in the bath. Never leave a child alone in the bath as they can easily slip under the water. Fit a non-slip mat to your bath and ensure a handrail is available.

If you are unsure as to whether your gas appliance is safely installed, ask your local CORGI registered plumber to check it over. Gas boilers and fires should be serviced regularly, ideally once a year.

Most do-it-yourself stores will be able to advise you on suitable products that will assist you in making your home as accident free as possible.

Room	Hazard
Bathroom	Slippery surfaces
Bathroom	Electrical points
Kitchen	Sharp objects
Kitchen	Boiling water
Kitchen	Hot surfaces
Living room	Worn carpets
Stairs	Worn carpets
Stairs	Poor lighting
Garden	Poisonous plants

Exercise 1.4

BUYING A HOME

Finding a Property

Before you commit yourself to purchasing a property, you need to do some research. Take your time and view as many properties as possible in order to get a feel for what is on offer in your price range.
Make sure that you register with a number of estate agents in the area in which you wish to purchase. You will soon have an idea of the type of properties they sell. If you have specific requirements, for example you need to have an office in which to work from home, then make sure that the estate agent notes this on your file. Tell the estate agent how much you are prepared to pay for a property. If you are willing to undertake repairs and redecoration then this should also be noted. This information will help the estate agent arrange for you to view only suitable properties.
If you are moving to a different town then check out the facilities available such as local schools, shops, transport and amenities. Popular residential areas can command greater property prices than other similar properties in a less sought after district.

The Process

Once you have found your dream home you will need to have a valuation undertaken. Your mortgage lender may arrange this, however you can choose one of several different types of report.
A full structural survey will cost several hundred pounds but will provide a thorough report on the property. it will cover the plumbing, electrical wiring, plaster work and will check for problems such as damp, dry rot, the roof and structure of the building.
A homebuyer's report and valuation is much less expensive but will give only a basic report and valuation of the property. This is used by the mortgage lender to assess whether the property you wish to purchase will prove to be a sound investment.
At the time the valuation is being carried out, you will need to appoint a solicitor. The solicitor will deal with the legal process of conveyancing the property into your name. This means the transfer of title deeds from one party to another.
The solicitor will carry out a number of searches on your behalf. These many include local land searches and duties attached to the property you wish to buy. The land searches will show if the property and land are subject to any rights of way, if there are any relevant planning regulations affecting the property or if there are any covenants on the property.
Provided the searches are satisfactory, and that the contract of purchase is agreed, an exchange of contracts can take place. At this point a deposit is paid, contracts and exchanged and the contract becomes legally binding. A date for completion of the purchase is then set. During this time the solicitor will check the ownership of the property. This is to ensure the property is in fact, free to be sold.
Completion is when the deeds are signed and the balance of the purchase money is paid and the keys are handed over.
The solicitor should now register your ownership with the Land Registry and alter the Title of the Deeds of the property. The payment of stamp duty, which is a purchase tax payable to the government on all properties over a specified purchase price, if necessary, is due at this point.

Finance

Buying a home is a major investment and probably the most significant financial move in most people's lives.
The first step towards purchasing a property is to find out how much you can afford to spend. Most people will need to take out a mortgage. This is a loan given by a bank or building society specifically for the purchase of a property. Shop around the various mortgage lenders and find out how much they are prepared to lend you. As a general rule, most lenders will give you a loan of up to three times the principal earner's salary, plus the amount of the second income. Alternatively, they may lend up to two and a half times the joint income of both parties, whichever is the higher.
Make sure that you can easily meet the monthly repayments before entering into a loan. Keep in mind that if interest rates rise, the monthly repayments on the mortgage will also increase.

Income	Amount of Loan
£20,000	£60,000
£25,000	£75,000
£30,000	£90,000
£40,000	£120,000

Exercise 1.3

Life Style Sports and Social Club

Annual Day Out

This year we have decided to visit the City of Bath. This takes approximately 2½ hours by coach from London.
Bath is a wonderful City, full of interesting buildings, shops, art galleries, museums and restaurants. The streets full of Georgian buildings must be seen to be appreciated. Bath was recently made a World Heritage City. A trip around the Roman Baths and museum is a must for everyone. The Pump Room is a great place for morning coffee and to listen to the Pump Room Trio play. It is all very elegant. We have booked to have coffee here at 11.00 am.
The Museum of Costume, which is located within the Assembly Rooms, is also worth visiting. Fashion through the ages, in period settings, can be seen with many outfits belonging to celebrities and royalty. Other museums include American Museum, No1 Royal Crescent and the Holbourne Museum.
There are many excellent restaurants and cafes for you to choose from. Within walking distance of the City centre is the Royal Victoria Park, which has a boating lake, botanical gardens, acres of greenery and a large children's play area. We are sure we shall enjoy a great day out.
Bath is also home of course, to the Bath Rugby Club. It may be possible for us to arrange tickets to the afternoon match, if there is enough interest. Please let Mike Sims know if you would like tickets, by the end of this week as it may take some time to arrange.
We hope to start off at 8.00 am to arrive in Bath around 11.00 am. As usual, we would be grateful if you could arrive promptly. Last year, so many of you were late we were delayed by 25 minutes. This cuts down on the time you have at the venue. We hope to leave Bath at 6.00 pm to arrive back at the social club at approximately 8.30 pm.
The cost of the trip will be £8 per adult, £4 per child. The date will be confirmed later. If you are interested, contact Roy Jones on extension 650.

Forthcoming Events

We have booked some great entertainment at the social club. The cost of booking these acts has had to come from our rather small resources. Please attend these evenings if you can, otherwise we shall be forced to stop holding them.
As usual the entertainment will start at 7.30 pm and finish at 10.30 pm. The bar will be open normal hours. Remember, all drink prices are less than at your local pub. This means you can have a great night out for much less than usual. There will be bar snacks and meals available at these events, and Sarah is promising to come up with some super meals at reasonable prices.
The events booked for May are as follows.

Date	Act
7 May	The Saxophones
14 May	Sally Niles
21 May	Mike Young
28 May	The Sharks

As well as entertainment we are hoping to run a regular skittles night. This would be held on a Tuesday or Wednesday, starting at 8.00 pm and finishing around 10.30 pm. These promise to be great fun. Oliver is putting together teams. Contact him on extension 677 if you would like to play.
We also need to do some fundraising for the club. Ideas for this include a jumble sale and raffle. However we are sure you can come up with some more exciting ideas.
A meeting to discuss fund raising will be held on Thursday 17 April at 7.00 pm. Please come along and give your suggestions. If you cannot attend, let Peter have your ideas. he can be contacted on extension 642.

It's a Knockout Tournament

Those of you who enjoy a game of squash might be interested in our Knockout Tournament. Starting on the 7 May we will be holding games from 6 pm – 7.30 pm each evening. Players will be drawn according to age. There are four age groups: under 25; 26 – 35; 36 – 50; and 50 plus. There will be a separate tournament for ladies.
The matches will consist of three games. The winner will go on to the next round and so on. The tournament winners will receive a £50 sports voucher.
There is a small charge of £3 for entering the competition. If you are interested, please contact Steven Lunt on 684. The closing date for entries is 17 April.

Exercise 2.2

HOME SAFETY

Safety in the Home

Many people require hospital treatment each year because of accidents in the home. A large number of the injuries suffered could have been avoided with a little care and forethought.

Those most at risk of accidents in the home are the elderly and children under five. Young children need to be constantly supervised as they have a natural curiosity, which often leads them into danger. Over half a million children receive hospital treatment each year due to accidents at home.

Children, especially babies and toddlers love to put things in their mouths. Toddlers can be very unsteady and have poor balance when they are learning to walk. Sharp objects such as table edges can be potentially dangerous. Older children are often tempted by matches and may inadvertently start a fire.

Elderly people may, because of arthritis or other diseases, suffer from reduced mobility and slower reflexes. They may also be more prone to accidents as their eyesight fails or they become more forgetful.

In order to prevent accidents, a careful look around your home should alert you to any hazards.

Potential Hazards

For the young almost everything in the home can be a potential danger. Sharp objects, such as kitchen knives left on the edges of worktops can easily be pulled off by inquisitive children. For toddlers, sharp furniture edges, exposed electrical sockets and trailing cables all cause accidents.

The kitchen holds many dangers. Sharp knives, boiling water, hot objects and household chemicals are all causes of major accidents.

The staircase is probably one of the most dangerous areas of the home. Badly-fitting carpets, loose edges or objects left lying on the stairs can cause people to trip. The staircase should be well lit and a handrail provided in order to minimise the risks.

Surprisingly, many accidents happen in the garden. Many plants are toxic and can be harmful if eaten. Some plants can cause a rash or allergic reaction if touched with the bare hand. Your local garden centre or nursery will be able to advise you on plants that are dangerous.

Trailing flexes from electric lawnmowers and barbecues that are not properly supervised are all potential areas of danger.

Children are fascinated by water and if you have a garden pond, ensure that small children are not left in the garden unsupervised.

Cigarettes that have not been properly extinguished and thrown into wastepaper baskets or left lying in an ashtray can cause a fire in a short space of time. Fires can spread rapidly throughout the house.

One potential hazard we may not be aware of is a faulty gas cooker, fire or boiler. These can emit poisonous carbon monoxide fumes, as can partially blocked chimneys.

How to Prevent Accidents

Most accidents could easily be avoided with a little thought and planning. Take a look at each room in your home and check the following.

Are there any sharp objects that a child could fall onto? Are the electrical sockets, including light switches in good order? Ensure that carpets are securely fitted and free from signs of wear and tear, especially stair carpets.

Ensure that all household chemicals and medicines are correctly labelled and kept out of the reach of children. Do not allow children to play with matches or cigarette lighters.

In the kitchen, ensure cables from electrical appliances are not hanging over the worktops. If you have small children, a cooker guard may be a worthwhile investment.

Smoke alarms are an absolute must. They are inexpensive and easy to fit. An average sized home should install two; one upstairs and one in the kitchen.

In the garden, ensure ponds and pools are fenced if young children regularly play near them. Make sure your plants and shrubs are harmless if eaten by animals or children. Empty paddling pools when not in use.

Ensure children are properly supervised, particularly when in the bath. Never leave a child alone in the bath as they can easily slip under the water. Fit a non-slip mat to your bath and ensure a handrail is available.

If you are unsure as to whether your gas appliance is safely installed, ask your local CORGI registered plumber to check it over. Gas boilers and fires should be serviced regularly, ideally once a year.

Most do-it-yourself stores will be able to advise you on suitable products that will assist you in making your home as accident free as possible.

Exercise 2.1

Parker Primary School Newsletter

Homework Policy

The school has recently revised its homework policy as part of our annual school review. The following guidelines have been drawn up to assist parents and teachers.

Homework will be given on at least a weekly basis for the lower juniors. This will comprise of a spelling test and mathematical tables. Homework will be set on a Monday, with tests taking place on Friday. Children may also be asked to complete work at home if the teacher considers it necessary.

Upper juniors will also be given weekly spelling and tables homework. In addition, they will also be asked to complete various pieces of topic work. These may take the form of completing worksheets or illustrating their written work. A clear timescale for completion will be given, as will deadlines for the return of their work.

We do hope that you will encourage your child to complete their homework. We feel that it teaches children to work to deadlines, encourages time management skills and provides a gentle lead in to the level of homework given at secondary school.

If you have any concerns, or would like further clarification of the homework policy, please discuss with the headteacher.

Book Week

This year's Book Week was an enormous success. The children enjoyed the various activities and over £2000 was earned from the book sales.

Each day throughout the week, had a different theme, chosen from a popular children's story. The children discussed the story, drew pictures, made bookmarks and wrote and told stories of their own.

The Book at Bedtime was, as usual, attended by a great many of the children. Stories started at 7.00 pm and hot chocolate was served at 7.30 pm. The PTA served tea and coffee to parents and there was an opportunity for parents to visit the book shop. Grateful thanks go to Mrs Gregory for her hard work and enthusiasm in arranging this event.

Competition Winners

Our annual painting competition results were announced last week. A large number of children entered this year and the theme was A Wild Animal. It was good to see the effort the children put into their pictures and, as usual, a very high standard of work was produced.

A display of these pictures is in the main hall and will be there until the end of term. Parents are welcome to visit the display after school each day.

The booksellers Gordons kindly agreed to sponsor this competition by giving book tokens for prizes.

The results are as follows:

Place	Name	Class
1st	Susan Handy	3
2nd	Michael Norman	5
3rd	Sam Jardine	3
4th	Lisa Randle	2

Exercise 2.4

BUYING A HOME

Finance

Buying a home is a major investment and probably the most significant financial move in most people's lives.

The first step towards purchasing a property is to find out how much you can afford to spend. Most people will need to take out a mortgage. This is a loan given by a bank or building society specifically for the purchase of a property. Shop around the various mortgage lenders and find out how much they are prepared to lend you. As a general rule, most lenders will give you a loan of up to three times the principal earner's salary, plus the amount of the second income. Alternatively, they may lend up to two and a half times the joint income of both parties, whichever is the higher.

Make sure that you can easily meet the monthly repayments before entering into a loan. Keep in mind that if interest rates rise, the monthly repayments on the mortgage will also increase.

Finding a Property

Before you commit yourself to purchasing a property, you need to do some research. Take your time and view as many properties as possible in order to get a feel for what is on offer in your price range.

Make sure that you register with a number of estate agents in the area in which you wish to purchase. You will soon have an idea of the type of properties they sell. If you have specific requirements, for example you need to have an office in which to work from home, then make sure that the estate agent notes this on your file. Tell the estate agent how much you are prepared to pay for a property. If you are willing to undertake repairs and redecoration then this should also be noted. This information will help the estate agent arrange for you to view only suitable properties.

If you are moving to a different town then check out the facilities available such as local schools, shops, transport and amenities. Popular residential areas can command greater property prices than other similar properties in a less sought after district.

The Process

Once you have found your dream home you will need to have a valuation undertaken. Your mortgage lender may arrange this, however you can choose one of several different types of report.

A full structural survey will cost several hundred pounds but will provide a thorough report on the property. it will cover the plumbing, electrical wiring, plaster work and will check for problems such as damp, dry rot, the roof and structure of the building.

A homebuyer's report and valuation is much less expensive but will give only a basic report and valuation of the property. This is used by the mortgage lender to assess whether the property you wish to purchase will prove to be a sound investment.

At the time the valuation is being carried out, you will need to appoint a solicitor. The solicitor will deal with the legal process of conveyancing the property into your name. This means the transfer of title deeds from one party to another.

The solicitor will carry out a number of searches on your behalf. These many include local land searches and duties attached to the property you wish to buy.

The land searches will show if the property and land are subject to any rights of way, if there are any relevant planning regulations affecting the property or if there are any covenants on the property.

Provided the searches are satisfactory, and that the contract of purchase is agreed, an exchange of contracts can take place. At this point a deposit is paid, contracts and exchanged and the contract becomes legally binding. A date for completion of the purchase is then set. During this time the solicitor will check the ownership of the property. This is to ensure the property is in fact, free to be sold.

Completion is when the deeds are signed and the balance of the purchase money is paid and the keys are handed over.

The solicitor should now register your ownership with the Land Registry and alter the Title of the Deeds of the property. The payment of stamp duty, which is a purchase tax payable to the government on all properties over a specified purchase price, if necessary, is due at this point.

Exercise 2.3

Life Style Sports and Social Club

Forthcoming Events

We have booked some great entertainment at the social club. The cost of booking these acts has had to come from our rather small resources. Please attend these evenings if you can, otherwise we shall be forced to stop holding them.

As usual the entertainment will start at 7.30 pm and finish at 10.30 pm. The bar will be open normal hours. Remember, all drink prices are less than at your local pub. This means you can have a great night out for much less than usual. There will be bar snacks and meals available at these events, and Sarah is promising to come up with some super meals at reasonable prices.

The events booked for May are as follows.

Date	Act
7 May	The Saxophones
14 May	Sally Niles
21 May	Mike Young
28 May	The Sharks

As well as entertainment we are hoping to run a regular skittles night. This would be held on a Tuesday or Wednesday, starting at 8.00 pm and finishing around 10.30 pm. These promise to be great fun. Oliver is putting together teams. Contact him on extension 677 if you would like to play.

We also need to do some fundraising for the club. Ideas for this include a jumble sale and raffle. However we are sure you can come up with some more exciting ideas.

A meeting to discuss fund raising will be held on Thursday 17 April at 7.00 pm. Please come along and give your suggestions. If you cannot attend, let Peter have your ideas. he can be contacted on extension 642.

It's a Knockout Tournament

Those of you who enjoy a game of squash might be interested in our Knockout Tournament. Starting on the 7 May we will be holding games from 6 pm – 7.30 pm each evening. Players will be drawn according to age. There are four age groups: under 25; 26 – 35; 36 – 50; and 50 plus. There will be a separate tournament for ladies.

The matches will consist of three games. The winner will go on to the next round and so on. The tournament winners will receive a £50 sports voucher.

There is a small charge of £3 for entering the competition. If you are interested, please contact Steven Lunt on 684. The closing date for entries is 17

Annual Day Out

This year we have decided to visit the City of Bath. This takes approximately 2½ hours by coach from London.

Bath is a wonderful City, full of interesting buildings, shops, art galleries, museums and restaurants. The streets full of Georgian buildings must be seen to be appreciated. Bath was recently made a World Heritage City. A trip around the Roman Baths and museum is a must for everyone. The Pump Room is a great place for morning coffee and to listen to the Pump Room Trio play. It is all very elegant. We have booked to have coffee here at 11.00 am.

The Museum of Costume, which is located within the Assembly Rooms, is also worth visiting. Fashion through the ages, in period settings, can be seen with many outfits belonging to celebrities and royalty. Other museums include American Museum, No1 Royal Crescent and the Holbourne Museum.

There are many excellent restaurants and cafes for you to choose from. Within walking distance of the City centre is the Royal Victoria Park, which has a boating lake, botanical gardens, acres of greenery and a large children's play area. We are sure we shall enjoy a great day out.

We hope to start off at 8.00 am to arrive in Bath around 11.00 am. As usual, we would be grateful if you could arrive promptly. Last year, so many of you were late we were delayed by 25 minutes. This cuts down on the time you have at the venue. We hope to leave Bath at 6.00 pm to arrive back at the social club at approximately 8.30 pm.

The cost of the trip will be £8 per adult, £4 per child. The date will be confirmed later. If you are interested, contact Roy Jones on extension 650.

Exercise 3.1 – page 1

Exercise 3.1 – page 2

Exercise 3.2 – page 1

Tour America
with USA TODAY

We offer fly-drive or coach tours around the USA. Our unique service allows you to decide when, where and for how long.
Call XXXX now for a free colour brochure on 01736 289787.

Visit New England in the fall, ask for our New England brochure. It features over 20 different holidays.

Visit us on the Web on http:/www/tours.co.uk

St3p3ex3
page 1

21 March 1998 13:12
Composite

Exercise 3.2 – page 2

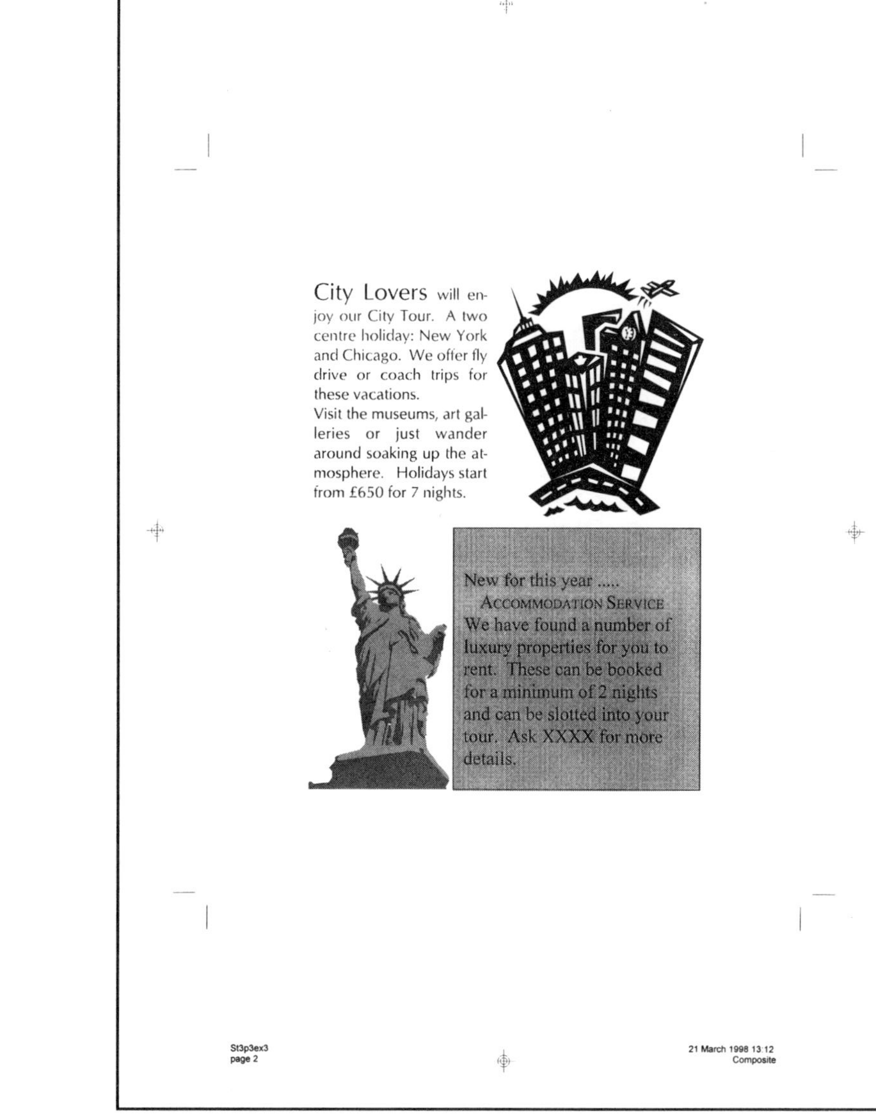

Exercise 3.3 – page 1

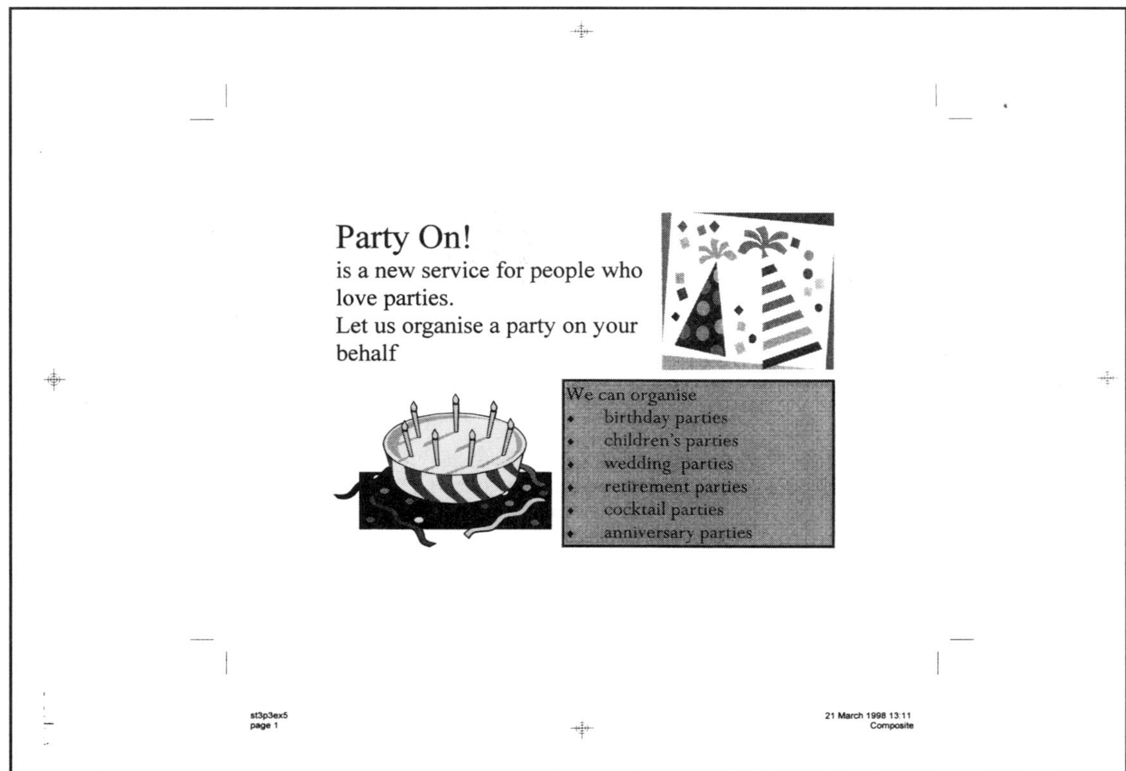

Exercise 3.3 – page 2

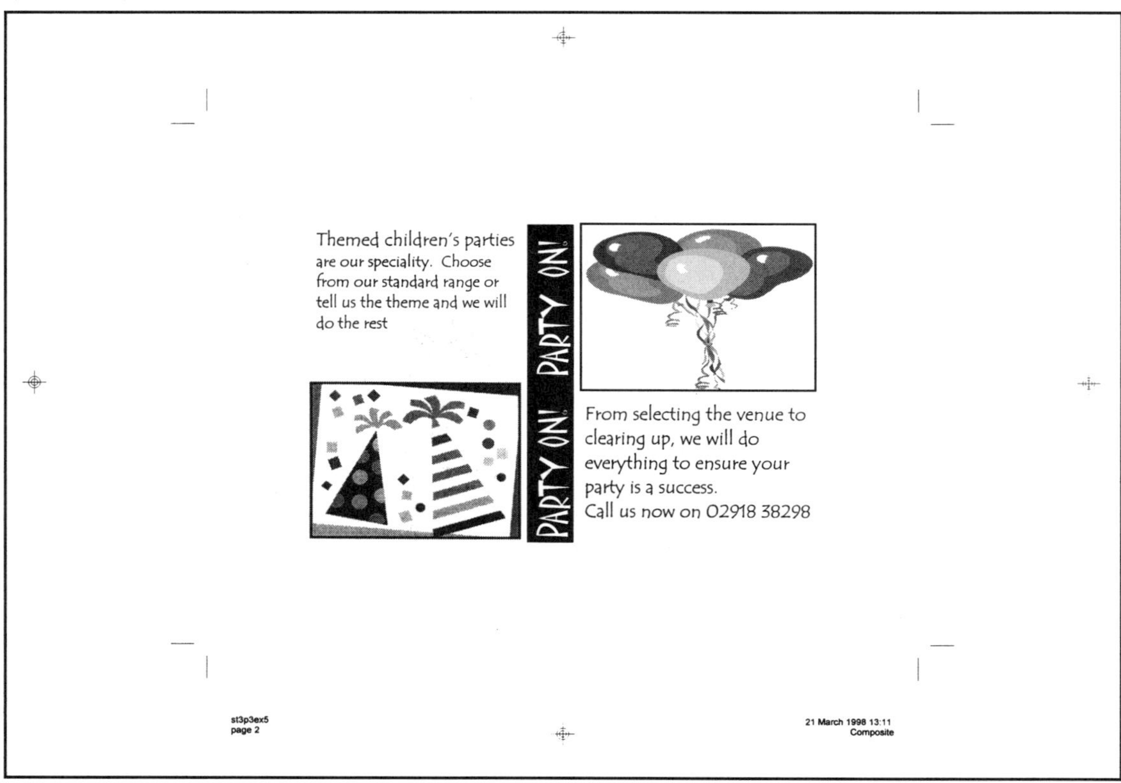

Exercise 3.4 – page 1

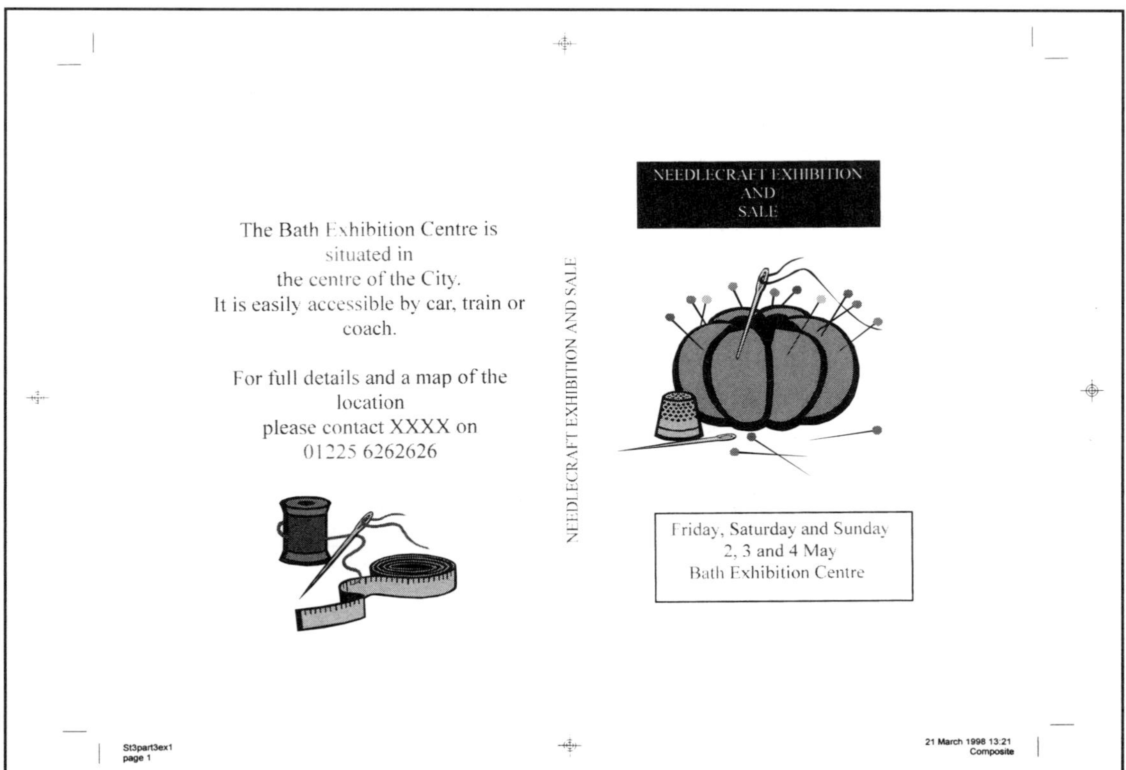

Exercise 3.3 – page 2

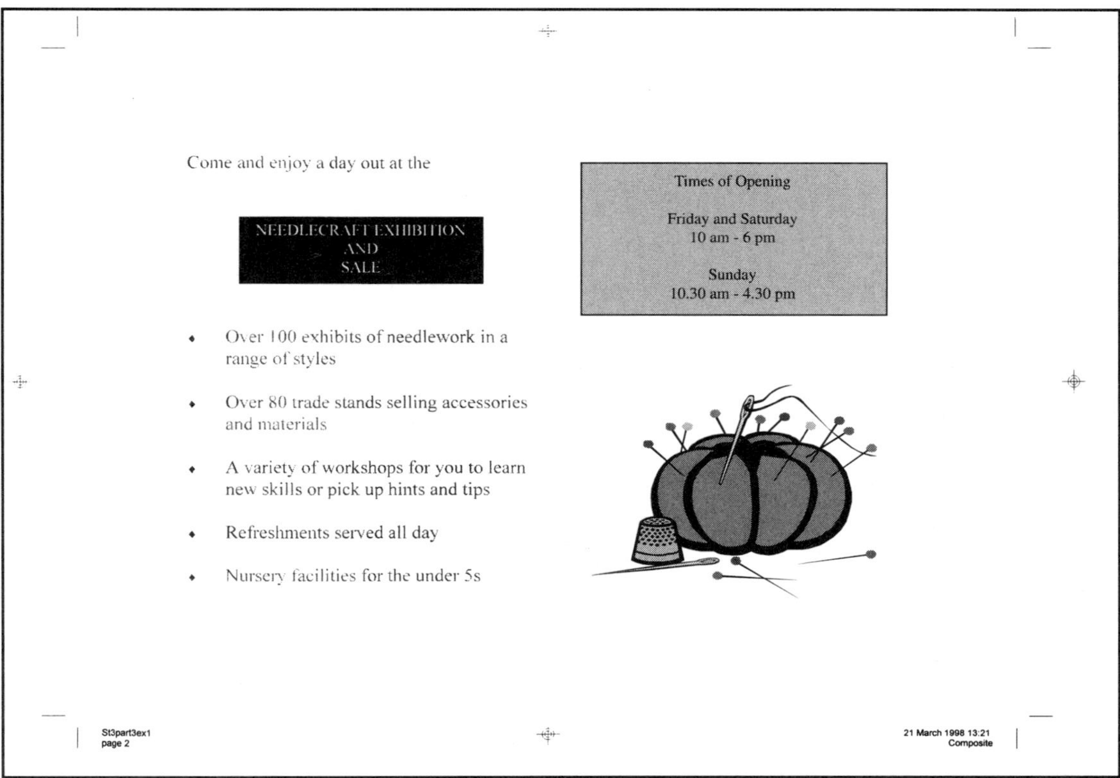

Consolidation 3 Part 1 – MYPL1

MAYPOLE BOOK CLUB

Membership Details

The Maypole Book Club allows you to enjoy selecting competitively priced, educational books for your children in the comfort of your own home.

Each month you will receive a magazine packed full of books at discount prices. Many of these have up to 50% off the publisher's recommended price. We do not sell remaindered titles and a large number of our books are hot off the press.

Each month our Editor selects a brand new title for her choice of the month. This title is automatically sent to you. We guarantee this title will be offered to you at a minimum of 15% less than the published price. However, you do have the option to return this book should you decide, after examination, that you do not wish to keep it. Twice a year we clear our warehouse by holding a huge book sale. Prices tumble to less than half the recommended price on these specially selected titles. Quality is never compromised even at these exceptionally low costs.

The minimum period of membership is one year. During this time you are asked to purchase at least six books. This means you are only obliged to purchase one book every two months. Books from our sale leaflet do not count towards the minimum purchase requirement. We are convinced you will wish to purchase many more.

After the initial membership period you will still receive our magazine, together with our sale leaflets and any other offers. You are not obliged to purchase any books, and you may cancel your membership at any time. All we ask is that you give us one month's notice.

Range of Goods

Maypole Book Club specialises in educational books for children. Each book has been carefully examined before it is selected for inclusion in our magazine. A book may be included because of the quality of illustrations, the suitability of content and/or its educational value. Although our books are educational, they are also enjoyable and suitable for the age of child for whom they are recommended. You will find many books by well-known children's authors in our selection, together with classic titles that have been popular for many years.

In addition to books we also sell, interactive CD-ROMS, story audio cassettes, videos, puzzles and stationery. These are also specially selected for their educational value.

Each magazine is divided into age groups so that you can easily see the books that are on offer for your children. The categories are as follows:

Age of Child	Category
0-3	Pre-school
4-6	Infants
7-8	Lower junior
9-11	Upper junior
11-13	Pre-teen
13+	Teenager

The age recommendations are quoted from the publisher. However it may be that depending on your child's reading ability, that they will find the category above or below their actual age more suitable.

Ordering Details

Ordering from Maypole Book Club could not be easier. Just fill in the order form ensuring you have the correct catalogue code for each item. Then either fax, e-mail, or post your order to us in the envelope provided. You can also telephone our helpful sales assistants.

Payment can be made by cheque payable to Maypole Book Club, or by credit or debit cards. Payment must be made at the time of ordering. If ordering by telephone please ensure you have your card number and expiry date to hand. In order to speed up the ordering process, please quote your membership number.

All our goods should reach you in perfect condition within 28 days of ordering. If you decide, after examination, that you do not wish to keep the goods, you may return them for a full refund.

If you are a playgroup, nursery or school we offer an extra five per cent discount on all our titles for orders over £60. Please order from us using your official order form and note the form supplied with the magazine. Please note that this offer does not apply to our twice-yearly sale leaflet.

Consolidation 3 Part 2 – MYPL2

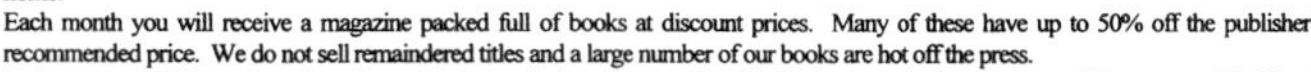

MAYPOLE BOOK CLUB

Membership Details

The Maypole Book Club allows you to enjoy selecting competitively priced, educational books for your children in the comfort of your own home.

Each month you will receive a magazine packed full of books at discount prices. Many of these have up to 50% off the publisher's recommended price. We do not sell remaindered titles and a large number of our books are hot off the press.

Each month our Editor selects a brand new title for her choice of the month. This title is automatically sent to you. We guarantee this title will be offered to you at a minimum of 15% less than the published price. However, you do have the option to return this book should you decide, after examination, that you do not wish to keep it. Twice a year we clear our warehouse by holding a huge book sale. Prices tumble to less than half the recommended price on these specially selected titles. Quality is never compromised even at these exceptionally low costs.

The minimum period of membership is one year. During this time you are asked to purchase at least six books. This means you are only obliged to purchase one book every two months. Books from our sale leaflet do not count towards the minimum purchase requirement. We are convinced you will wish to purchase many more.

After the initial membership period you will still receive our magazine, together with our sale leaflets and any other offers. You are not obliged to purchase any books, and you may cancel your membership at any time. All we ask is that you give us one month's notice.

Range of Goods

Maypole Book Club specialises in educational books for children. Each book has been carefully examined before it is selected for inclusion in our magazine. A book may be included because of the quality of illustrations, the suitability of content and/or its educational value. Although our books are educational, they are also enjoyable and suitable for the age of child for whom they are recommended. You will find many books by well-known children's authors in our selection, together with classic titles that have been popular for many years.

In addition to books we also sell, interactive CD-ROMS, story audio cassettes, videos, puzzles and stationery. These are also specially selected for their educational value.

Each magazine is divided into age groups so that you can easily see the books that are on offer for your children.

The age recommendations are quoted from the publisher. However it may be that depending on your child's reading ability, that they will find the category above or below their actual age more suitable.

Ordering Details

Ordering from Maypole Book Club could not be easier. Just fill in the order form ensuring you have the correct catalogue code for each item. Then either fax, e-mail, or post your order to us in the envelope provided.

You can also telephone our helpful sales assistants.

Payment can be made by cheque payable to Maypole Book Club, or by credit or debit cards. Payment must be made at the time of ordering. If ordering by telephone please ensure you have your card number and expiry date to hand. In order to speed up the ordering process, please quote your membership number.

All our goods should reach you in perfect condition within 28 days of ordering. If you decide, after examination, that you do not wish to keep the goods, you may return them for a full refund.

If you are a playgroup, nursery or school we offer an extra five per cent discount on all our titles for orders over £60. Please order from us using your official order form and note the form supplied with the magazine. Please note that this offer does not apply to our twice-yearly sale leaflet.

Consolidation 3 Part 3 – TOY1 – page 1

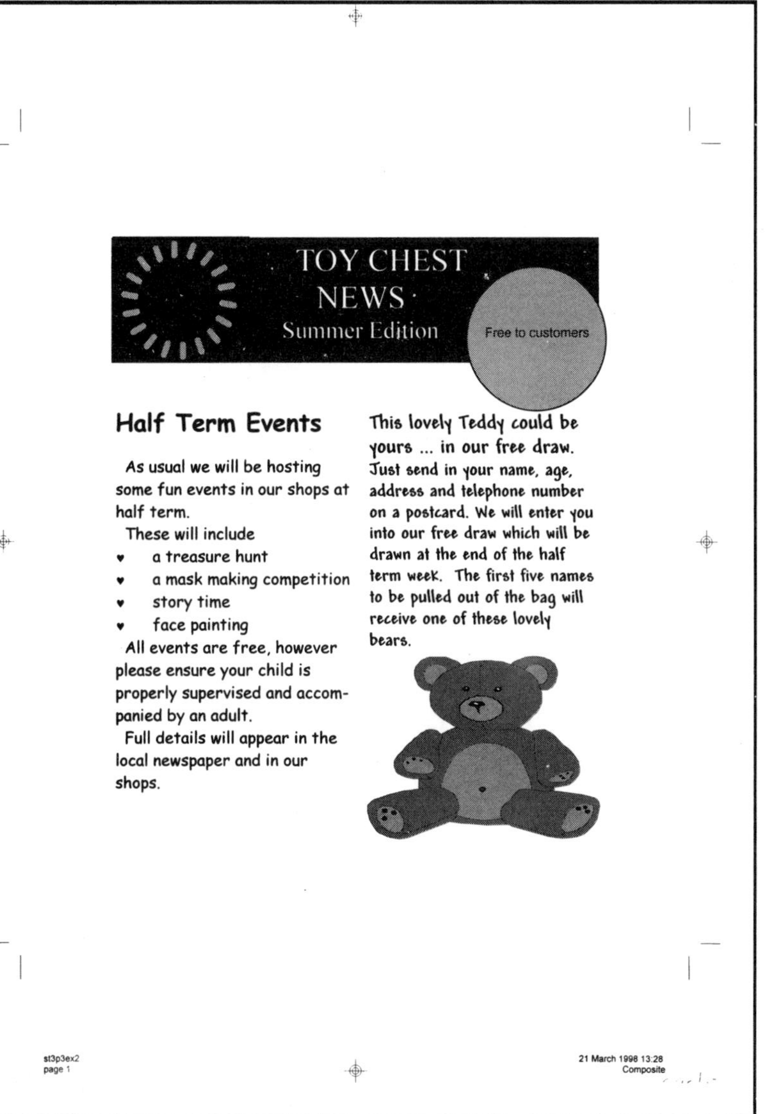

TOY CHEST NEWS
Summer Edition

Free to customers

Half Term Events

As usual we will be hosting some fun events in our shops at half term.

These will include
- a treasure hunt
- a mask making competition
- story time
- face painting

All events are free, however please ensure your child is properly supervised and accompanied by an adult.

Full details will appear in the local newspaper and in our shops.

This lovely Teddy could be yours ... in our free draw. Just send in your name, age, address and telephone number on a postcard. We will enter you into our free draw which will be drawn at the end of the half term week. The first five names to be pulled out of the bag will receive one of these lovely bears.

st3p3ex2
page 1

21 March 1998 13:28
Composite

Consolidation 3 Part 3 – TOY1 – page 2

Sand Castles

Having a beach holiday? Stock up on all the equipment you will need at Toy Chest shops. We have a large range of buckets and spades, paper flags and sand moulds. Prices start from only £1.50. Also new in stock is a super range of boats and yachts. Prices from £3.99.

JUST IN

A brand new range of quality wooden toys. See the new range in selected shops.

Call 0182 388299 for a mail order catalogue

COMING SOON ....

Watch out for the Autumn issue of Toy Chest News. We will be featuring some great new toys for the Christmas market.

Free to customers

st3p3ex2
page 2

21 March 1998 13:28
Composite

Exam Practice 3 – ENV2

ENVIRONMENTAL NEWS

Door to door collections

After many months of organisation, we are delighted to announce the door to door collection of recycling materials will commence on 20 April. The weekly collection will be on a different day from your usual refuse collection.
All you need to do is place your recycling material out for collection. The local authority green vans will do the rest. We can accept the following materials for recycling: clean rags, shoes, newspapers and magazines, aluminium foil, tins, plastic bottles, car batteries, glass jars and bottles.
Newspapers and magazines should be kept separate and tied together securely. Unfortunately, telephone directories and cardboard should not be included in the green boxes. There are facilities for recycli ng these items at the local authorit y waste disposal s i t e . Please ensure that articles left for recycling are clean. Obviousl y we cannot accept broken glass or tins that have r o u g h e d g e s . Please be aware of the safety of o u r collectors. If you have an old car battery for recycling, please ensure that this is placed outside on the day of collection only. Please remember that car batteries contain acid and this can be harmful if spilt.
We are providing strong plastic green boxes for your recycling materials. These will be delivered to you within the next week or two. If you do not intend to recycle any materials, please contact us and we will arrange to collect your box. If you do not receive your box within two weeks please let us know.
The provision of these boxes has been sponsored by Green Living, a local recycling company. The local authority is grateful for their help and assistance in setting up this marvellous new initiative. The local authority estimates that over £250,000 per year can be saved by the sale of these waste materials. By participating in the scheme you will be helping to conserve natural resources and reducing the energy used in manufacturing these materials. The whole community will benefit.
We urge you to support our recycling initiative.

Green Stationery

A new business has opened in the centre of the town selling recycled stationery. The days of thick, off-white sheets of paper have long gone and you will find it difficult to tell the difference between recycled and non-recycled materials.
All the stationery stocked in this new shop is made from recycled materials or has been produced from renewable sources. You will be impressed with the quality of our materials. The prices are also very competitive. A list of some of the current prices is given below.
We can provide you with recycled toner cartridges for your laser printers. We will also give a discount if you return the empty toner cartridge when you purchase your replacement.

Item	Quantity	Price
A4 paper	ream	1.95
C5 envelopes	ten	2.50
A3 paper	ream	4.50
A5 paper	ream	2.30
C4 evelopes	ten	2.00

Volunteers Required

The Environmental Watch desperately requires volunteers to help clear the local canal. An intensive programme of cleaning and renovation was started 18 months ago and several sections of the canal and bank have been transformed.
Volunteers are now required to join in our working parties. This can be during the week, or at weekends. If you can spare a few hours and would like to meet new people, keep fit and work for a deserving cause, then please contact us.
Volunteers are also required for a number of projects throughout the town. In particular we need people to assist with delivering leaflets around the area. If you can help with door to door deliveries of this and subsequent newsletters, then please let us know. We would be grateful for your help even if for just an hour or two per week.

Exam Practice 3 – ENV1

ENVIRONMENTAL NEWS

Door to door collections

After many months of organisation, we are delighted to announce the door to door collection of recycling materials will commence on 20 April. The weekly collection will be on a different day from your usual refuse collection.
All you need to do is place your recycling material out for collection. The local authority green vans will do the rest. We can accept the following materials for recycling: clean rags, shoes, newspapers and magazines, aluminium foil, tins, plastic bottles, car batteries, glass jars and bottles. Newspapers and magazines should be kept separate and tied together securely. Unfortunately, telephone directories and cardboard should not be included in the green boxes. There are facilities for recycling these items at the local authority waste disposal site.
Please ensure that articles left for recycling are clean. Obviously we cannot accept broken glass or tins that have rough edges. Please be aware of the safety of our collectors. If you have an old car battery for recycling, please ensure that this is placed outside on the day of collection only. Please remember that car batteries contain acid and this can be harmful if spilt.
We are providing strong plastic green boxes for your recycling materials. These will be delivered to you within the next week or two. If you do not intend to recycle any materials, please contact us and we will arrange to collect your box. If you do not receive your box within two weeks please let us know.
The provision of these boxes has been sponsored by Green Living, a local recycling company. The local authority is grateful for their help and assistance in setting up this marvellous new initiative. The local authority estimates that over £250,000 per year can be saved by the sale of these waste materials. By participating in the scheme you will be helping to conserve natural resources and reducing the energy used in manufacturing these materials. The whole community will benefit.
We urge you to support our recycling initiative.

Volunteers Required

The Environmental Watch desperately requires volunteers to help clear the local canal. An intensive programme of cleaning and renovation was started 18 months ago and several sections of the canal and bank have been transformed.
Volunteers are now required to join in our working parties. This can be during the week, or at weekends. If you can spare a few hours and would like to meet new people, keep fit and work for a deserving cause, then please contact us.
Volunteers are also required for a number of projects throughout the town. In particular we need people to assist with delivering leaflets around the area. If you can help with door to door deliveries of this and subsequent newsletters, then please let us know. We would be grateful for your help even if for just an hour or two per week.

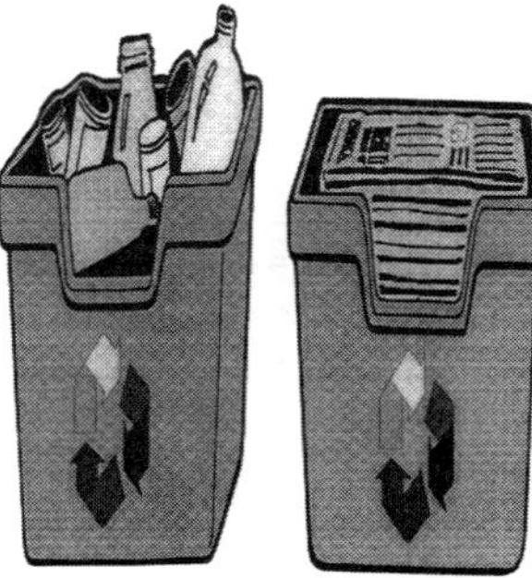

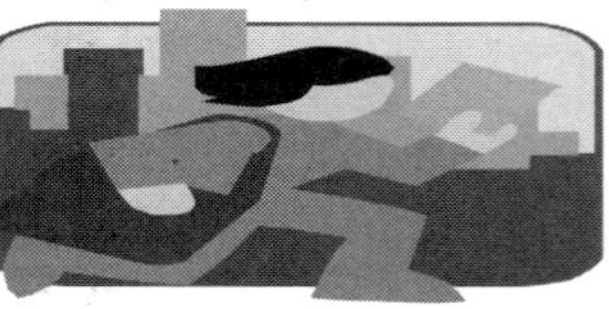

Green Stationery

A new business has opened in the centre of the town selling recycled stationery. The days of thick, off-white sheets of paper have long gone and you will find it difficult to tell the difference between recycled and non-recycled materials.
All the stationery stocked in this new shop is made from recycled materials or has been produced from renewable sources. You will be impressed with the quality of our materials. The prices are also very competitive. A list of some of the current prices is given below.
We can provide you with recycled toner cartridges for your laser printers. We will also give a discount if you return the empty toner cartridge when you purchase your replacement. Customers who visit the store by the end of June and bring along this newsletter, will receive a 5% discount on all purchases.

Item	Quantity	Price
A4 paper	ream	1.95
C5 envelopes	ten	2.50
A3 paper	ream	4.50
A5 paper	ream	2.30
C4 evelopes	ten	2.00

Exam Practice 3 – HOTEL1 – page 1

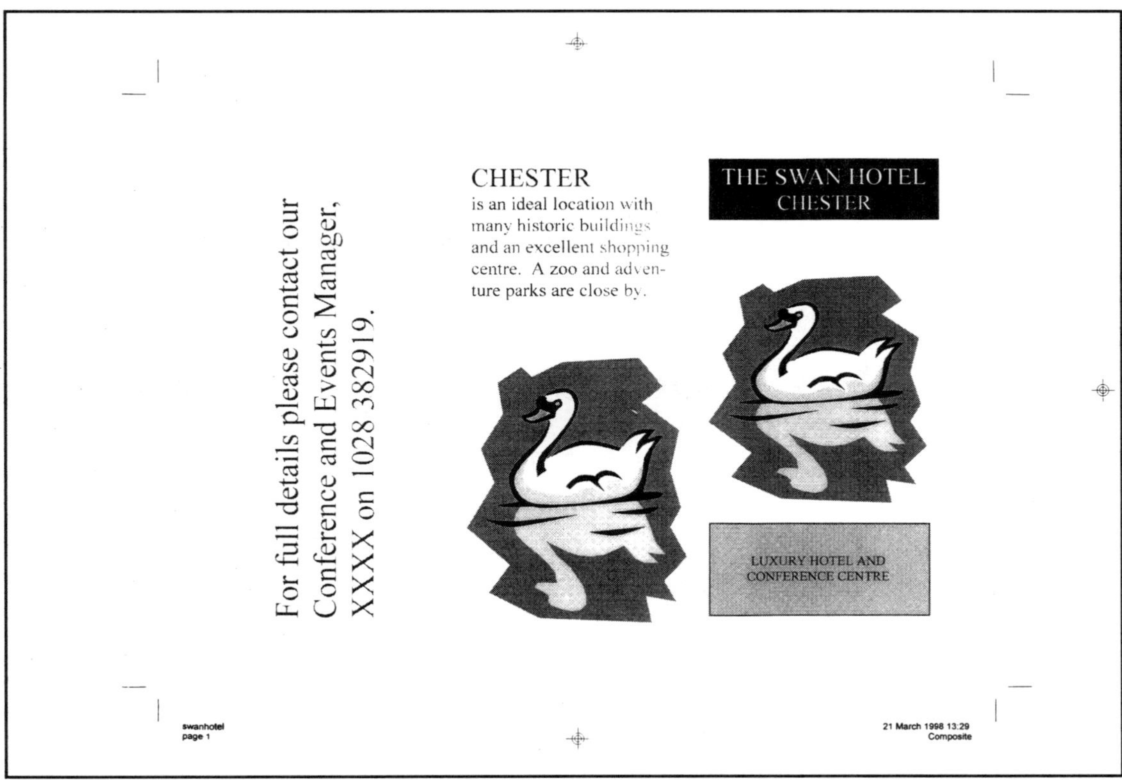

Exam Practice 3 – HOTEL1 – page 2

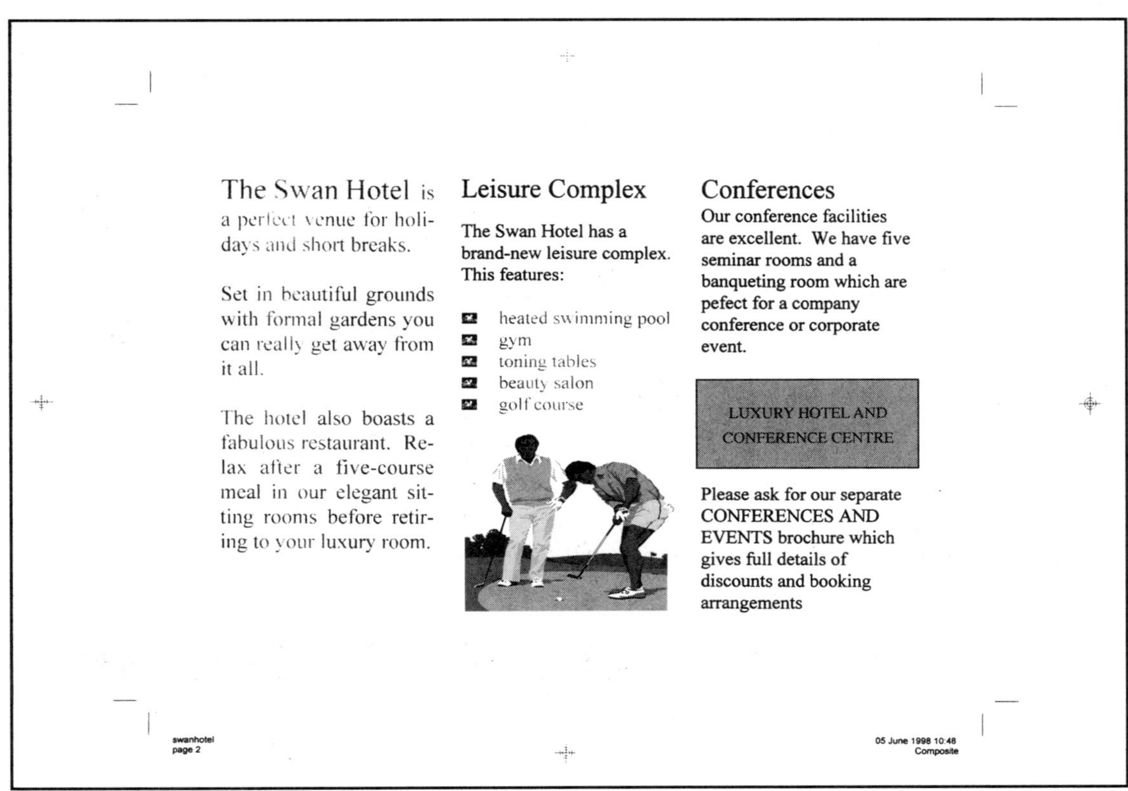

Glossary

Bold
A darker, thicker version of a font or typeface.

Bullet
A symbol that is used to highlight points instead of numbers. Often takes the form of a full stop that sits in the middle of the typing line.

Character
Letter, numbers or other symbols.

Clip art
Graphic images that are non-copyright.

Crop
To cut the edges of a graphic image.

Font
Typeface.

Footer
Text that is printed outside of the bottom margin.

Graphic
Picture, line or drawing.

Guide
Non-printing lines that allow you to place text and images accurately.

Gutter
Space between columns on a page.

Handle
A symbol shown when clicking the edge of a box to show that it can be moved or stretched.

Header
Text that is printed outside of the top margin.

Importing
Loading a text or graphic file into a desktop publishing document.

Indent
Text that is moved in from the left margin.

Italic
A sloping version of a typeface.

Justification
Alignment of text is flush to both margins.

Kerning
Altering the space between letters.

Landscape
Page orientation with the longer edge at the top.

Leading
The spacing between the lines of text.

Lower case
Small letters.

Master pages
Templates that are set for each page in a document or publication. Items that are placed on master pages will print on each page of the document.

Monospaced type
Each character takes up the same amount of space on the page regardless of its size.

Orphan

A line of text that appears on its own at the top of a page.

Point

A unit of measurement for type sizes and lines.

Portrait

Page orientation with the shorter edge at the top.

Proofreading

Checking a document for errors.

Proportional spacing

Each character uses only the amount of space it needs on the page.

Sans serif

A typeface that does not have strokes on the bottom of letters such as m, n and k.

Serif

A typeface that does have strokes on the bottom of letters such as m, n and k.

Style sheet

A set of formatting details that are set to be applied to sections of text in a document.

Text wrap

An invisible border of space around a graphic image that acts as a barrier between text and graphics.

Typeface

A family of type characters, for example, Times New Roman or Gill Sans.

Upper case

Capital letters.

Widow

A line of text that appears on its own at the bottom of a page or column.

Images	Page No.	Text	Page No.
Section 1			
CKBLN	10	FIFTIES	10
GLOBE	10	ICING	9
JUKEBOX	10	NAPOLEON	19
NB	19	TECH	10
SHIP	10	TRAINING	10
TEACHER	10	TRAVEL	18
TOWER	18	TUDOR	10
Section 2			
BASKET	41	1920S	50
BIDS	40	1930S	50
BRIEF	69	ACUP	72
CASH	39	BANK	39
COMP	39	CONGAR	65
COTT	63	EMP	69
DESK	39	EQUIP	49
DNK	50	FENG	51
FISH	51	HISTORY	49
FRUIT	41	HOLS	63
GLASS	49	HOM	72
HANDS	69	HOW	51
HOUSE	63	JANE	51
MAN	40	LOYALTY	41
MONEY	39	MKCON	65
PILLS	72	OFFICE	39
POT	65	SALE	40
SHAKE	51	WILL	51
Section 3			
BK	122	ACC	101
BLN	119	BATH	119
BOOKS	100	BOOK	100
BOXES	127	CHESTER	130
CAKE	119	CITY	116
COURIER	127	COMP	100
FLAG	116	CONF	130
GOLF	130	DAYOUT	103
HATS	119	DETAILS	119
HMWRK	100	DOOR	127
HSE	103	EVENTS	103
JACK	125	FIN	103
JAZZ	103	GOODS	122
LAWN	101	GREEN	127
MATCH	101	HAZ	101
PIN	119	HLFTRM	125
SAN	116	HOME	100
SEWING	119	HOTEL	130
SKY	116	KNOCK	103
SNOWMAN	116	MEMB	122
STATUE	116	NEWENG	116

Images	Page No.	Text	Page No.
Section 3 continued			
STEREO	122	ORDER	122
SUN	125	OUTING	119
SWAN	130	PARTY	119
TED	125	PROC	103
TREE	116	PROP	103
TROPHY	103	SAFE	101
YATCHT	125	SAND	125
		SANTA	116
		SNOW	116
		STALLS	116
		TEDDY	125
		THEME	119
		TIMES	119
		TOURS	116
		VOL	127

Index of Exercises

	Page	Design Brief	Print	Save as	Worked Example
Section 1					
1.1	7			ICING1	
1.2	7			TRAIN1	
1.3	7			COM1	
1.4	7			19501	
1.5	8			TUDOR1	
2.1	9–10			ICING2	
2.2	10			TRAIN2	
2.3	10			COM2	
2.4	10			19502	
2.5	10			TUDOR2	
3.1	15		✔	ICING3	22
3.2	15		✔	TRAIN3	22
3.3	15		✔	COM3	23
3.4	15		✔	19503	23
3.5	16		✔	TUDOR3	24
4.1	16		✔	ICING4	24
4.2	17		✔	TRAIN4	25
4.3	17		✔	COM4	25
4.4	17		✔	19504	26
4.5	17		✔	TUDOR4	26
Consol. 1	18		✔	PARIS1	27
	19		✔	PARIS2	27
Ex Pr 1			✔	NAP1	28
			✔	NAP2	28
Section 2					
1.1	35–6			DES1	
1.2	36			BANKS1	
1.3	36			AUC1	
1.4	37			SHOP1	
2.1	39	39	✔	DES2	77
2.2	39–40	40	✔	BANK2	78
2.3	40	40	✔	AUC2	79
2.4	41	41	✔	SHOP2	80
3.1	44	44	✔	DES3	81
3.2	44–5	45	✔	BANKS3	82
3.3	45	45	✔	AUC3	83
3.4	45–6	46	✔	SHOP3	84
4.1	48–9	49		DRINKS	
4.2	49–50	50		FASH	
4.3	50–51	51		INTER	
4.4	51–52	52		WRITE	
5.1	52	55	✔	DRINKS1	85
5.2	53	56	✔	FASH1	85
5.3	53	57	✔	INTER1	86
5.4	54	58	✔	WRITE1	86
6.1	61		✔	DRINKS2	87
6.2	61		✔	FASH2	87
6.3	62		✔	INTER2	88
6.4	62		✔	WRITE2	88

	Page	Design Brief	Print	Save as	Worked Example
Cons2 P1	63–4	64		HOLS1	
			✔	HOLS2	89
			✔	HOLS3	90
P2	65–6	65		GARD	
P3	66–8	67–8	✔	GARD1	91
ExPr2/El1	69–71	70–1		EMP1	
			✔	EMP2	91–2
			✔	EMP3	92–3
EPr2/EL2	71	72/73/74		MED	
			✔	MED1	93
Section 3					
1.1	100	102	✔	SCHOOL1	134
1.2	101	102	✔	SAFETY1	134
1.3	103	104	✔	CLUB1	135
1.4	103	104	✔	BUYHM1	135
2.1	107–8	109	✔	SCHOOL2	136
2.2	108	109	✔	SAFETY2	136
2.3	110	111	✔	CLUB2	137
2.4	110	111	✔	BUYHM2	137
3.1	116	117	✔	XMAS1	138
3.2	116	118	✔	USA1	139
3.3	119	120	✔	PARTY1	140
3.4	119	121	✔	SEW1	141
Con3/P1	122	123	✔	MYPL1	142
Con 3/P2	123–4	124	✔	MYPL2	142
Con 3/P3	125	126	✔	TOY1	143
ExPr3/EL1	127	128	✔	ENV1	144
ExPr3/EL2	128–9	129	✔	ENV2	144
ExPr3/EL3	130	131	✔	HOTEL1	145